Name	Type	Name	
Enabled	Property	End	
EndDoc	Method	Environ$	
EOF	Function	Erase	Statement
Erl	Function	Err	Function
Err	Statement	Error	Statement
Error$	Function	Exit	Statement
Exp	Function	File List Box	Control
FileAttr	Function	FileName	Property
FillColor	Property	FillStyle	Property
Fix	Function	FontBold	Property
FontCount	Property	FontItalic	Property
FontName	Property	Fonts	Property
FontSize	Property	FontStrikethru	Property
FontTransparent	Property	FontUnderline	Property
For...Next	Statement	ForeColor	Property
Form	Control	Format$	Function
FormName	Property	Frame	Control
FreeFile	Function	Function	Statement
Get	Statement	GetData	Method
GetFormat	Method	GetText	Method
Global	Statement	GoSub...Return	Statements
GotFocus	Event	GoTo	Statement
hDC	Property	Height	Property
Hex$	Function	Hidden	Property
Hide	Method	Horizontal Scroll Bar	Control
Hour	Function	hWnd	Property
Icon	Property	If...Then...Else	Statement
Image	Property	Index	Property
Input #	Statement	Input$	Function
InputBox$	Function	InStr	Function
Int	Function	Interval	Property
KeyDown	Event	KeyPress	Event
KeyUp	Event	Kill	Statement
Label	Control	LargeChange	Property
LBound	Function	LCase$	Function
Left	Property	Left$	Function
Len	Function	Let	Statement
Line Input #	Statement	Line	Method
LinkClose	Event	LinkError	Event

(continued on inside back cover)

Computer users are not all alike.
Neither are SYBEX books.

We know our customers have a variety of needs. They've told us so. And because we've listened, we've developed several distinct types of books to meet the needs of each of our customers. What are you looking for in computer help?

If you're looking for the basics, try the **ABC's** series. You'll find short, unintimidating tutorials and helpful illustrations. For a more visual approach, select **Teach Yourself,** featuring screen-by-screen illustrations of how to use your latest software purchase.

Learn Fast! books are really two books in one—a tutorial to get you off to a fast start and a reference to answer your questions when you're ready to tackle advanced tasks.

Mastering and **Understanding** titles offer you a step-by-step introduction, plus an in-depth examination of intermediate-level features, to use as you progress.

Our **Up & Running** series is designed for computer-literate consumers who want a no-nonsense overview of new programs. Just 20 basic lessons, and you're on your way.

We also publish two types of reference books. Our **Instant References** provide quick access to each of a program's commands and functions. SYBEX **Encyclopedias** and **Desktop References** provide a *comprehensive reference* and explanation of all of the commands, features, and functions of the subject software.

Our **programming** books are specifically written for a technically sophisticated audience and provide a no-nonsense value-added approach to each topic covered, with plenty of tips, tricks, and time-saving hints.

Sometimes a subject requires a special treatment that our standard series don't provide. So you'll find we have titles like **Advanced Techniques, Handbooks, Tips & Tricks,** and others that are specifically tailored to satisfy a unique need.

We carefully select our authors for their in-depth understanding of the software they're writing about, as well as their ability to write clearly and communicate effectively. Each manuscript is thoroughly reviewed by our technical staff to ensure its complete accuracy. Our production department makes sure it's easy to use. All of this adds up to the highest quality books available, consistently appearing on best-seller charts worldwide.

You'll find SYBEX publishes a variety of books on every popular software package. Looking for computer help? Help Yourself to SYBEX.

For a brochure of our best-selling publications:

SYBEX Inc. 2021 Challenger Drive, Alameda, CA 94501
Tel: (510) 523-8823 / (800) 227-2346 Telex: 336311
SYBEX   Fax: (510) 523-2373

PROGRAMMER'S INTRODUCTION

TO VISUAL

BASIC

PROGRAMMER'S INTRODUCTION

TO VISUAL BASIC™

Kenyon Brown

SYBEX®

SAN FRANCISCO ■ PARIS ■ DÜSSELDORF ■ SOEST

Acquisitions Editor: David Clark
Developmental Editor: Gary Masters
Editor: Stefan Grünwedel
Technical Editor: Nick Dargahi
Word Processors: Ann Dunn and Susan Trybull
Book Series Designer: Suzanne Albertson
Screen Graphics: Cuong Le and Richard Green
Desktop Publishing Production: Len Gilbert
Proofreader: Elizabeth G. Chuan
Indexer: Ted Laux
Cover Designer: Ingalls + Associates
Cover Photographer: David Bishop

Visual Basic is a trademark of Microsoft Coporation

SYBEX is a registered trademark of SYBEX Inc.

TRADEMARKS: SYBEX has attempted throughout this book to distinguish proprietary trademarks from descriptive terms by following the capitalization style used by the manufacturer.

SYBEX is not affiliated with any manufacturer.

Every effort has been made to supply complete and accurate information. However, SYBEX assumes no responsibility for its use, nor for any infringement of the intellectual property rights of third parties which would result from such use.

Library of Congress Card Number: 91-67906
ISBN: 0-7821-1015-0

Manufactured in the United States of America
10 9 8 7 6 5 4 3 2 1

ACKNOWLEDGMENTS

I want to thank those people who contributed so much of their time and talent to this book (and helped to make the project truly memorable):

- Stefan Grünwedel for his diligence and patience during the editing of the manuscript. Most memorable post-it note: "Please make sure the Reader understands what you are trying to do here."

- Gary Masters for his sense of humor, helpful suggestions, and keen vision during the development of the manuscript. Most memorable post-it note: "This is how you should do it."

- Nick Dargahi for his excellent technical review of the manuscript. Most memorable post-it note: "Are you sure you can do this?"

- Suzanne Albertson for creating a superb new design that served the book beautifully. Most memorable post-it note: "That's nice to hear."

- Elizabeth Chuan for guiding the manuscript through Production. Most memorable post-it note: "Hey, when are you going to start reading the galleys?"

- Ann Dunn and Susan Trybull in Word Processing for putting up with all the inserts and revisions. Most memorable post-it note: "Au: I've never seen something coded like this before."

- Len Gilbert in Typesetting for putting up with all the long program lines. Fortunately, he had the good sense not to write me any post-it notes.

I would also like to thank the following people:

- David Clark for taking a chance by signing me to write the book

- Barbara Gordon for her support and guidance

- James Gaston for his technical expertise, insight, and good spirit

CONTENTS AT A GLANCE

TABLE OF CONTENTS

PART IV

A Reference Guide to Visual Basic
Functions, Methods, Events, Objects, and Properties   337

INTRODUCTION

The *Programmer's Introduction to Visual Basic* is a hands-on introduction to using the Visual Basic environment to create real Windows applications with BASIC code. This book shows programmers how to create graphical applications that feature controls such as objects, menus, resizable windows, mouse support, and icons—all the elements that can be found in most Window applications.

The book guides you through the steps of building a Visual Basic application called *Window$ to Wealth,* a financial planning program. Before starting to create the program, you will learn about programming in a much different way than you're accustomed to. For instance, instead of creating a traditional flow chart that shows how program control moves from one procedure to another, you will learn to program "visually"; that is, you will learn how to plan the ways in which controls can work together to give any Windows application its functionality.

As you create Window$ to Wealth, you will be introduced to all of Visual Basic's powerful design and programming tools. The book also includes the functional code that gives the application its power. You can choose to enter the code or read the accompanying text to understand how it works. You should note, however, that the book presents the rudiments of each of the programs that comprise Window$ to Wealth. If you enter all of the code the way it is written, you will create a functional Windows application. However, you might discover ways to refine or modify the code for your own purposes.

Who Should Use This Book

This book is for programmers who want to create Windows applications in a relatively short period of time. The focus of the book is on showing programmers how to use Visual Basic, not on teaching users how to program in BASIC. Going from the "down-and-dirty" approach of writing an algorithm and coding it in BASIC to programming in the rich, object-oriented environment of Visual Basic can be disconcerting to anyone new to this type of programming. However, the modular approach introduces a wholly new and effective style of Windows programming that can save you time. This book demonstrates that Visual Basic is an extraordinarily powerful and flexible Windows development tool that allows programmers (and nonprogrammers) to create dynamic applications quickly.

Programming Windows the Visual Basic Way

Programming Windows has never been for the faint-hearted. The traditional approach to Windows application development has been to program with Microsoft C and to use the Windows Software Development Kit. Believe me, you wouldn't have a good time.

The development cycle would go something like this: You would build a Windows program by sketching out all the main modules and the logic that would link them together. You would then continue writing the program by repeatedly compiling, linking, and debugging the code. Icons, menus, dialog boxes, and all the other controls in the user interface would have to be designed and compiled separately. All these components would be controlled by the main program through a maze of functions and messages. If you wanted to modify the interface, you would have to search through the source code to make the change.

The Visual Basic philosophy of programming is much more simple: first you create controls such as windows, icons, and menus; then you write the procedures that invoke each of the controls. This is different from the traditional method of writing a program, in which structures exist for controlling program-flow from one procedure to another in a logical manner until the program ends.

Any experienced programmer will be amazed at how easy it is to write Windows applications *visually*—that is, to create objects and then to write the procedures in BASIC that activate them. Programming objects is a flexible and convenient method of writing Windows programs. You can write the code for an object you've created and then make multiple copies of the same object with the code still attached. You don't have to write the same code again.

This book demonstrates through sample applications that Visual Basic is an event-oriented development system. A programmer doesn't have to write code to create the objects that make up an interface; he or she only has to write code to make something happen when users interact with those objects.

How This Book Is Organized

Part I: Using the Visual Basic Environment

Chapter 1: *Introducing Visual Basic* guides you through the steps of installing Visual Basic on your system and explains Visual Basic's event-driven approach to writing code. Windows terminology is defined to help you understand Visual Basic's functionality. To illustrate how easy it is to build an application, you create your first Visual Basic program.

Chapter 2: *Interacting with Visual Basic* introduces you to the Visual Basic interface. All menus, dialog boxes, and windows are described and explained.

Chapter 3: *Creating Controls with the Toolbox* describes each of the 16 tools that are included on the Visual Basic Toolbox. These tools draw, move, and resize the controls on your form to which you later attach the functional BASIC code.

Chapter 4: *Adapting Code Written in Other Versions of BASIC* shows you how easy it is to import programs written in BASIC or QuickBasic to Visual Basic. The chapter discusses the modifications you usually have to make when you want to import programs.

Chapter 5: *Building an Effective Graphical User Interface* discusses issues you need to consider when creating a graphical user interface. The Calculator and Cardfile applications that are provided with Visual Basic are dissected to show you the code that was written for each of the forms and controls that comprise the application.

Part II: Programming in Visual Basic

Chapter 6: *Creating Controls and Setting Their Properties* shows you how to create all of the controls for a sample application called *Window$ to Wealth*. The chapter shows you how to set the properties for each of the controls through the Properties bar.

Chapter 7: *Attaching Code and Designating Events* guides you through writing all the code for each of the forms that comprise the Window$ to Wealth application. The chapter describes the differences between setting properties through the Properties bar at design time and setting properties at runtime.

Chapter 8: *Getting Keyboard and Mouse Input* discusses the importance of providing the user with different ways to set a control's focus, either through the keyboard or with the mouse, in order to input data.

Chapter 9: *Displaying Screen Output* shows you how to format data on the screen so that they are legible for the user to read.

Chapter 10: *Creating Menus for Forms* guides you through learning to use the Menu Design window that is provided with Visual Basic. The chapter shows you how to create the sample application's menu system and to designate access and shortcut keys for menu commands.

Part III: Using Advanced Visual Basic Features

Chapter 11: *Tapping the Power of Windows' Dynamic Data Exchange* shows you how to create data links between a Visual Basic application and other applications that support Windows DDE. The chapter discusses how to establish a client and server relationship between two applications in order to update them automatically and continuously.

Chapter 12: *Formatting Output to a Printer* shows you how to format data that you want to direct for output to a printer. The chapter shows you how you can take advantage of different Visual Basic functions to format data that are aligned in columns.

Chapter 13: *Debugging an Application* introduces you to Visual Basic's powerful debugging capabilities. By leaving the syntax-checking feature on, you'll make sure that Visual Basic catches most syntax errors as you write statements during design time. The chapter shows you how to debug code during runtime by setting breakpoints in the code where you know that errors exist. You are shown how you can also write your own error handlers that will trap specific errors in code.

Chapter 14: *Drawing Bitmaps and Adding Dynamic Graphical Effects* introduces you to the Windows Application Programming Interface (API) and how you can take advantage of the hundreds of Dynamic Link Library functions that are included with the API. The chapter takes you through the steps of using one API function to create a dynamic graphical effect for one form.

Part IV: A Reference Guide to Visual Basic Statements, Functions, Methods, Events, Objects, and Properties

This is an alphabetical listing of all the controls, statements, functions, methods, properties, and events that comprise the Visual Basic programming language.

P A R T I

Using the Visual Basic Environment

Part I introduces you to programming in Visual Basic, a powerful graphical programming system that enables you to create real Windows applications with BASIC code. The Visual Basic programming system allows you to create objects, called *controls,* set and change their properties, and then attach the functional BASIC code to them. Visual Basic requires that you program in an entirely different way when writing code for applications. Visual Basic uses an *event procedure* to structure code, where the procedure establishes a relationship between a control and an event. It is this relationship that enables you to invoke code and tell the application to perform a specific task.

Your first impression of Visual Basic may lead you to believe that you can simply import programs you've written in other versions of BASIC and run them as they are. Most BASIC programs will have to be adapted and modified, however, before you can use the code in Visual Basic applications, especially if direct input or output is involved. If your BASIC programs use procedures (and more than likely they will), you will have to look at them closely to see how they perform certain operations.

Visual Basic enables you to design an application's interface, using the Windows interface in order to give users a consistent method of interacting with the computer. Consistency is probably an interface's greatest advantage. All applications use similar commands and controls. When you learn one Visual Basic application you already know a lot about other Visual Basic applications.

Ultimately, a person will run the application that you have created *outside* of Visual Basic just like any other Windows application. Therefore, creating an effective program starts with having a good design and a broad overview of the application's contents and purpose. The way you organize an application depends on what information it contains and how you expect people to use it. Remember that you create applications for people to *use*, not simply to look at. By going through the process of clarifying the needs of the users of your application, you will create an application that anybody can work with.

CHAPTER
ONE

Introducing Visual Basic

- An Overview of Event-Driven Programming

- Installing Visual Basic

- Creating a Control

- Setting Properties

- Writing Functional BASIC Code

Visual Basic is a powerful graphical programming system that enables you to create real Windows applications with BASIC code. This system is a tremendous breakthrough for developers, as it combines the simplified syntax of BASICA and GWBASIC with the programming structure of QBASIC and QuickBasic. If you are an experienced programmer but unfamiliar with programming in Windows, Visual Basic provides you with the necessary tools to easily create the same graphical elements that are common to most Windows applications. Figure 1.1 shows an example of a Windows application that was created with Visual Basic.

The Visual Basic programming system allows you to create *objects,* set and change their properties, and then attach the functional BASIC code to them. The Visual Basic philosophy of programming is first to create objects such as windows, icons, and menus, and then to write the procedures that invoke each of these objects. This is different from the traditional method of writing a program, in which structures exist for controlling program flow from one to procedure to another in a logical manner until the program ends.

Any experienced programmer will be amazed at how easy it is to write Windows applications *visually*—that is, to create objects and then write the procedures in

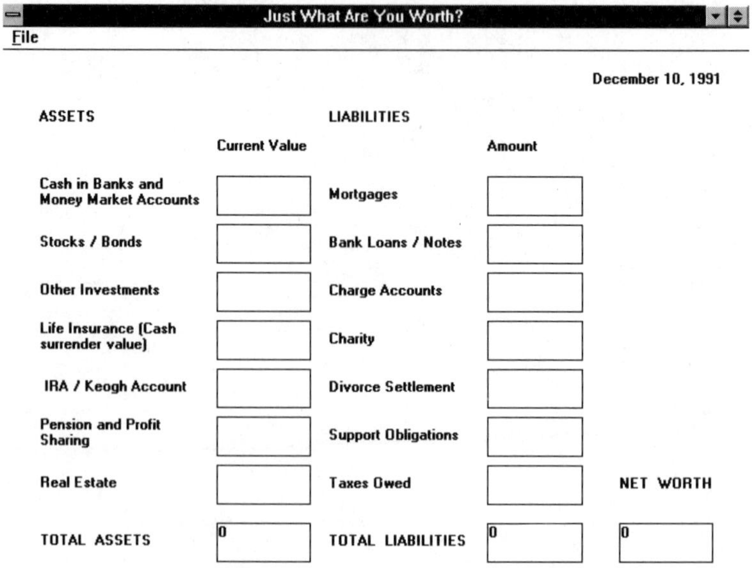

FIGURE 1.1:

This Windows application was created in Visual Basic. As you can see, the application resembles a spreadsheet

BASIC that activate them. Programming objects is a flexible and convenient method of writing Windows programs. For instance, you can write the code for an object you've created and then make multiple copies of the same object with the code still attached; you don't have to write the same code again.

I'm tempted to call Visual Basic an *object-oriented programming system,* although I'd be wrong. You *do* create objects, called *forms* and *controls,* that make your applications work. However, without going too deeply into the subject, these objects lack the properties of inheritance and polymorphism, which have to be present in a true object-oriented environment. Furthermore, you're creating applications that will run in Windows, which is a *visually-oriented* environment that provides libraries of tools and objects for programming applications.

For those of you who are new to the Windows interface, I'll describe Windows as the visually-oriented, graphical operating environment for DOS that allows you to display and share data between several applications at the same time. One of the advantages of using Visual Basic is that you can develop powerful and complex applications that users can run as stand-alone programs in Windows. To run any application in Windows outside of Visual Basic, you must create an executable file. If you distribute the file, you have to install the VBRUN100.DLL—Dynamic Link Library—runtime file in the Windows directory. (The file can be found in the Visual Basic directory.) Microsoft allows you to distribute this DLL with every application at no extra cost.

The major advantage of using Windows is that it provides a consistent and manageable interface for displaying information in many different applications that share similar controls. The Windows interface philosophy is based on using visual metaphors for performing actions and tasks. The paradigm is simple: After you've used one Windows application, you can easily learn to use another because you're familiar with the interface. Macintosh users have benefitted from this "ease of use" interface philosophy for years. By utilizing Windows controls such as menus, icons, scroll bars, and dialog boxes, information is presented to users in a visually interesting and dynamic format. Moreover, many people have argued that manipulating information in a graphical format is better than entering information at the DOS command line, where you have to memorize commands.

Programming Graphical User Interfaces the Visual Basic Way

The Visual Basic programming system opens a world of possibilities for designing effective graphical user interfaces in Windows that weren't available to you before, unless you programmed in C and used the Windows Software Development Kit (SDK). A *graphical user interface* (GUI) is what a user sees when a Windows application is opened. Using a GUI (pronounced "gooey") enables a person to interact with a program and manipulate its features and functions. The controls that comprise a program's interface are provided to help guide the user through the application in order to perform tasks.

Visual Basic is unique because it allows you to design the interface, write code in BASIC, and then attach the code to the application's controls quickly and easily. This process is very different from the often painstaking task of writing a program in C with the SDK.

Visual Basic drastically reduces the difficulty and amount of time involved in programming in Windows. Creating a Windows application in C could take you months in development time; with Visual Basic, you can build a dynamic Windows application in a few days. Since this language is *interpreted*, rather than compiled, applications are ready to run as soon as you finish writing the code. In a compiled language, by contrast, a program must be compiled before it can be executed. This means that a compiler converts programs into machine language, which consists of the binary numbers that your computer understands. The conversion is done only once. Whenever the program is run, the machine language is already available and can be directly executed by the computer.

In an interpreted language like Visual Basic, the procedure statements can be executed as soon as they are typed. The interpreter reads one line from a procedure and sends the appropriate instructions to the computer for execution. When the line is complete, the interpreter moves to the next line and interprets and executes it. Having an application immediately ready to run makes program development much faster. This is why Visual Basic is a tremendous advancement in Windows programming tools. Even casual programmers (and nonprogrammers) can take advantage of Visual Basic's powerful features to become effective Windows developers.

Writing Event-Driven Programs

A large amount of your time will be spent creating an application's interface at design time. This is the time when you're building an application by creating forms, drawing controls, and writing code modules. When you start an application at runtime, only the forms that you created and programmed will be visible.

A *form* is a window that you create and customize for every application. It is the foundation of any Visual Basic application that will eventually run as a stand-alone program in Windows. A *control* is the precise name for any object that you draw on a form, but it also refers to the form itself. Examples of controls are command buttons, menus, dialog boxes, and scroll bars. When a user activates a control by, say, clicking on it, BASIC code that is attached to the control is invoked and performs a specific task. A *module* is a structure for writing the code that you attach to a form and its controls. After drawing the controls you want to appear on a form, you write the functional code for each control that users can invoke.

Visual Basic uses the metaphor of the "event" to describe its programming paradigm. You will always use this event-driven approach when creating an application. *Event-driven* means that all controls you draw on a form specify how the interface will behave. In other words, Visual Basic's controls wait for particular events to happen before they respond. An *event* is an action that is recognized by a control. You write the code for each control in order to make something happen when users interact with the form.

You need to understand, however, that the code isn't stored in a single place where you can open it, look at it, make changes to it, or print it out. In fact, there is no single program that you edit and debug. Using Visual Basic is different from the linear approach of writing, running, and debugging a program, in which the process starts at the top, passes control from one procedure to the next, and then proceeds downward until it stops.

While you're in Visual Basic and you run an application, every line of code is separately interpreted and executed every time it's encountered. It is this individual execution of every line that can make an interpreted program run more slowly than a compiled program. The finished program file is usually larger, too. Of course, after the program is compiled into an executable file, the program is no longer interpreted. The absence of a separate compilation step before a program can be run makes application development faster with an interpreted language. Unless your application is unusually large or complex, you will probably never notice the loss in execution speed.

Installing and Starting Windows

Before you can run the setup program that installs Visual Basic, you must have Windows on your computer. In case you are new to Windows and haven't installed it yet, you should make sure that your system has the minimum requirements to run Windows before you begin the installation. Please read the documentation that is included with your Windows package. To proceed, follow these steps:

1. Insert Disk 1 in drive A.

2. Make the floppy drive the default drive.

3. Type `setup`.

4. Press Enter to start the installation.

5. Follow the instructions that appear on the screen.

To start Windows from the DOS prompt, follow these steps:

1. Type

   `win [/S][/3]`

   (switch options are in brackets).

2. Press Enter.

The Program Manager window appears automatically on your monitor screen, similar to Figure 1.2, unless you've modified the Windows Setup so that the Program Manager icon or another application appears instead.

To reduce screen clutter, you may want to set the Windows option so that the Program Manager is minimized when you start Visual Basic. To set that option now:

1. Click on the Options menu.

2. Select the Minimize on Use command.

FIGURE 1.2:

The Program Manager appears automatically each time you start Windows, unless you change your Windows setup

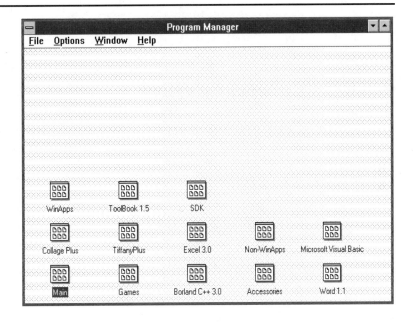

Now when you start Visual Basic, the Program Manager will appear as an icon.

Reviewing Windows Terminology

Here I review some of the Windows terminology that you'll need to know in order to use Visual Basic.

The Desktop

The entire area of your screen where you use the mouse to do your work is called the *Desktop*. It is the primary metaphor for the Windows environment. Windows uses the Desktop metaphor to organize the whole screen as a work area in the same way that you organize the surface of your desk to do your work.

No matter how cluttered the surface of your desk may get, you know that somewhere underneath the stacks of books and papers is the desktop. You might also have a container to hold your pencils and pens (I use an old coffee mug), stacked plastic trays to keep empty file folders and pads of paper within reach, an old address book for telephone numbers that you've been intending to update since last January, and a clock that stopped working about the same time.

Similarly, the Desktop is always underneath, in the background, with other windows programs layered on top of it. Furthermore, instead of using real tools to help organize your Desktop, you manipulate graphical representations—*objects*—of tools, applications, files, and other programs. When you want to use a program, you point the mouse to click on the object associated with it, thereby activating it and opening the particular window. You launch Visual Basic programs in the same way.

The Program Manager

The Program Manager is usually what you first see when you start Windows. It is a Windows program that organizes and runs other Windows programs. When you start the Program Manager, you will see that it, like all Windows programs, appears in a window on top of the Desktop.

As you can see by the way I've organized the Program Manager on my computer in Figure 1.2, it looks like a series of iconized windows. No matter how you organize the Desktop and arrange your other applications into smaller group windows, the Program Manager organizes everything neatly for you in its own window.

Windows Elements

When you look more closely at the *structure* of the Program Manager window, you'll discover that the overall design is typical of all Windows applications. Most of the elements are also found in Visual Basic. Furthermore, all of the applications you create will include these elements.

As illustrated by the example in Figure 1.3, the standard layout of a window contains the following elements:

- Frame
- Title bar

- Menu bar
- Control box
- File menu
- Minimize button
- Maximize button
- Vertical scroll bar
- Horizontal scroll bar
- Scroll boxes

Reviewing the structure of a window may seem too basic at first. However, a Visual Basic application is a Windows application and uses the same elements. You need to become familiar with these elements because you will be incorporating them in your applications.

The *frame* is the outside edge of the window, which controls the size of the window. The *control box* is located in the upper-left corner of the window. When you click on the box, you open a menu which allows you to choose from several different commands in order to manipulate the window.

FIGURE 1.3:
The Write program window is comprised of elements that are common to most Windows programs

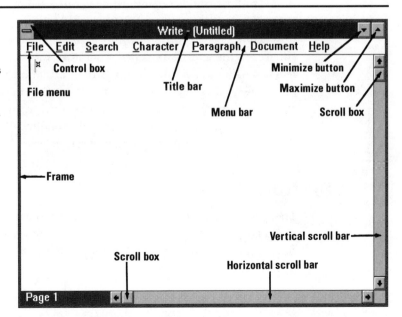

The *title bar* presents the name of the active application. If you're working with a particular document in a window, the name of the file will also appear. If you have a color monitor, you can tell when a window is active by the color of the title bar. For example, on my VGA color monitor, the default color for an active window is blue; an inactive window is white (or gray).

The horizontal *menu bar,* which appears below the title bar, contains a row of menus listed by name. When you click on a menu name, a menu drops down to let you make command choices. The *File menu* is a fairly standard menu that appears in most program windows. It contains options such as New, Open, Save, and Exit, which allow you to perform various operations on your files. Menu options vary from program to program.

The *maximize button,* the up-arrow box in the upper-right corner of a window, enlarges the window so it fills the entire Desktop. (This button becomes the restore button once the window is maximized.) The *minimize button,* the down-arrow box, reduces a window to either a group or program icon without ending the particular application. The *restore button,* the box with two arrows, reduces a maximized window to the size it was before it was maximized.

Often, information will extend horizontally and vertically beyond the work area of a window because only a limited portion of the total information can appear at one time. The horizontal and vertical *scroll bars* allow you to reposition this information in the window. Using the scroll bars lets you move around, or scroll, within a window to locate the portion of information that you want to see. The highlighted squares on the scroll bars, called *scroll boxes,* move along the bars and show the *position* in the file of your current screen of information. Clicking above or below a scroll box takes you from one section of information in a window to the next. The box moves within the scroll bar to indicate which relative portion of the window you are viewing at any given moment. By dragging the box up and down with the mouse, you cause the information to scroll.

The Mouse

There are two methods you can use to execute commands in Windows: typing commands on the keyboard or selecting commands with the *mouse.* Usually, the only time you type commands in Windows is to use a shortcut key. Otherwise, you use a mouse or trackball.

A mouse is a pointing device that provides a way for a user to manipulate controls. In a Visual Basic application, you can change the shape of a mouse without changing its functionality. You roll the mouse across a pad or table top—any flat surface will do—to move the pointer anywhere on your monitor. By using the mouse, you can select commands from menus and click on icons to execute commands; you don't have to use the keyboard to type them.

For all the tutorials in this book, you will use the mouse to make menu selections, execute commands, and activate icons and buttons. However, I will also include equivalent keyboard commands that you can use in Visual Basic as shortcuts.

If you're an experienced Windows user, then you already know how important the mouse is when performing operations and navigating through applications. Likewise, the mouse is one of the most important tools you use in Visual Basic. Your mouse may have one, two, or three buttons, but most often it will have two.

Here are a few mouse terms that are used throughout the book:

Mouse Term	Meaning
Point	Move the tip of the mouse cursor to something on the screen
Drag	Move the mouse while holding down a mouse button
Click	Quickly press and release a mouse button (in this book, *click* always refers to the left button)
Double-click	Quickly press and release the left mouse button *twice*
Select	Point to a menu command or object with the mouse pointer and click to activate that command or object
Press	Hold down a mouse button until some other action is completed, instead of releasing the button as you do when you click

Pressing the left button on the mouse is equivalent to pressing the Enter key on the keyboard. In the beginning, if you don't have a lot of experience using the mouse, clicking it may feel awkward because you haven't developed finger control. Practice pressing and releasing the mouse button until this feels comfortable.

Installing Visual Basic

Visual Basic runs in either *standard* or *enhanced* mode of Microsoft Windows 3.0 or higher. The Visual Basic package includes:

- a set of two high-density 1.44MB 5¼-inch disks
- a set of three low-density 720K 3½-inch disks

Before you can install and run Visual Basic, you need to make sure that you have the basic system requirements:

- a DOS-based machine with a 80286 processor or higher
- MS-DOS version 3.1 or higher
- Windows version 3.0 or higher in standard or enhanced mode
- 1MB of memory
- a hard disk with at least 2MB available
- a mouse
- a CGA, EGA, VGA, SVGA, XGA, 8514/A, Hercules, or compatible display (although EGA or higher resolution is recommended)

You start the Setup program from Windows. When you run the Setup program to install Visual Basic on your computer, you will perform two tasks: you'll set a path for Visual Basic and select which of the Visual Basic files you want to install on your system. *You should make sure that you have 4095K of hard disk space available to install all the selected Visual Basic files on your system. Otherwise, you will have to cancel Setup, delete files until you have enough disk space, and then start the Setup program again.*

You can select the following groups of files to install on your hard disk:

Icon Library offers an extensive library of graphical icons (about 400) that you can use in your applications. These can be found in the ICON subdirectory under the following categories:

- Arrows
- Communication
- Computers
- Flags

- Mail
- Miscellaneous
- Office
- Traffic
- Writing

Samples are good examples of Windows applications created in Visual Basic, which provide you with the functional code as well. The Samples directory also supplies an interesting application called IconWorks, which enables you to create your own icons. Although the Icon Library is extensive, it obviously can't supply every possible graphical icon. IconWorks provides a set of drawing tools and a color palette to create icons quickly and easily.

Tutorial provides a good introduction to learning the Visual Basic programming system and guides the user through the steps of building a sample application. It is accessed through the Visual Basic Help menu.

Visual Basic automatically creates separate directories in which to store these files, except for the tutorial, which becomes part of the Visual Basic Help system when you install it.

To start the Setup program from Windows, follow these steps:

1. Insert Visual Basic Disk 1 in drive A (or B).

2. Click on the File menu and select Run.

3. Type a:setup (or b:setup) in the Run dialog box and press Enter. The Visual Basic Setup screen will appear, as shown in Figure 1.4.

4. Select the default Visual Basic directory (VB on the C drive) or specify the name of another directory or drive where you want the Visual Basic files copied by modifying the highlighted path. Click on Continue.

5. Select the parts of the Visual Basic package that you want installed on your system. As you can see in Figure 1.5, you must have a minimum of 4095K of hard disk space available to install all the directories.

6. Follow the Setup instructions that appear on the screen. Figure 1.6 shows the percentage bar that is displayed to indicate the progress of the installation, which lasts a few minutes. Remove/insert the other Setup disk(s) as needed.

7. When Setup is complete, read the last dialog box, click on Exit, and remove the disk from the floppy drive.

8. Start Visual Basic from Windows. The Visual Basic programming environment will appear, as shown in Figure 1.7.

FIGURE 1.4:

The Visual Basic Setup screen appears when you run Setup from Windows

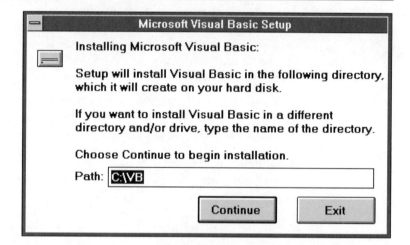

FIGURE 1.5:

The Setup program displays the amount of hard disk space required to install the various parts of the Visual Basic package and the amount available on your system

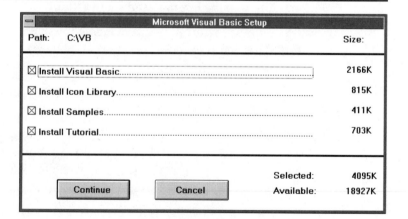

FIGURE 1.6:

The Setup program displays a
percentage bar to indicate the
progress of the installation

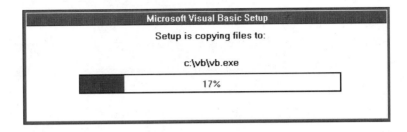

FIGURE 1.7:

The Visual Basic programming
environment appears after you
launch the program

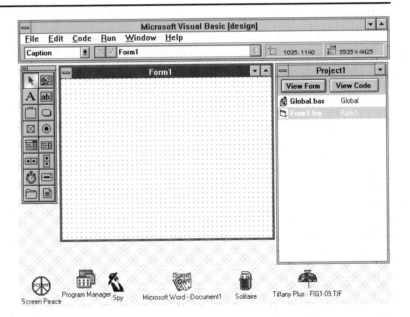

Understanding
Visual Basic Terminology

You need to become familiar with Visual Basic terminology because of the
software's unique event-driven approach to programming applications. The following terms are used to describe the elements of a Visual Basic application:

- *Control:* a general term used to describe any form or graphical element that
  you draw on a form, including text boxes, list boxes, command buttons,

picture boxes, scroll bars, and icons. A more precise definition of a control is data coupled with a set of routines, known as *methods* (defined below). These methods are used exclusively to access and manipulate the control. The only operations that can be performed on a control are those defined as methods for it. In Visual Basic, the terms *control* and *object* are used interchangeably (although *control* is preferable).

- *Event:* an action recognized by a Visual Basic control.

- *Form:* a window that you create and customize for your application.

- *Method:* a Visual Basic keyword that is similar to a function or statement, but which always acts on a particular control. For each control, Visual Basic predefines a set of methods you can use.

- *Procedure:* a term that refers to both Sub and Function procedures. A procedure is simply a sequence of Visual Basic statements that are executed as a group at run time. There are two types of procedures: *event procedures* and *general procedures.* Event procedures are restricted to forms and controls, whereas general procedures are used throughout an application and can be called by event procedures.

- *Project:* a collection of all the files that make up your application.

- *Property:* a characteristic or attribute of a control. For each type of control, Visual Basic defines a set of properties that apply to that control only.

- *Setting:* a property's value. You can change the settings of most properties while you are building an application. The code of a running application can also change settings.

Building Your First Visual Basic Application

The best way to learn about Visual Basic is to build an application. To show you how easy it is to create a Windows application in Visual Basic, I am going to create a program that displays the phrase "Welcome to Visual Basic!" when you run it. I will explain the process after I finish. (Bear with me as you follow along...)

Creating a Control

As mentioned above, a control is any graphical element that you draw on a form, which makes up your user interface. You use controls to perform tasks and navigate in an application. In this example, you will create a text box. Follow these steps:

1. Click the Text Box tool to select it. When you select any tool, the pointer changes to a crosshair.

2. Position the crosshair somewhere in the form.

3. Hold the left mouse button down and drag the crosshair to create a text box about three inches long and one inch wide.

4. Release the mouse button. The caption Text1 appears inside the text box, and *selection handles* appear around the text box to indicate that it is selected.

5. Center the text box on the form, as shown in Figure 1.8, by dragging the text box.

6. You may also drag the selection handles to increase or decrease the size of the text box.

SHORTCUT Double-clicking on the Text Box tool will create a default-size text box automatically in the center of the form.

Changing a Control's Properties

Now that you have created a text box control, you can set the properties for both the form and the text box so they appear the way you want them.

Change the caption that appears in the form's title bar:

1. Select the form by clicking on it (unless it's already selected). The name Form1 appears in the Settings list box for the Caption property. (The Settings list box is in the middle of the Properties bar, below the Visual Basic menu bar.)

2. Move the mouse pointer to the Settings list box. It will change to an I-shaped cursor, called an I-beam.

FIGURE 1.8:
Your first control, a text box centered
on the form

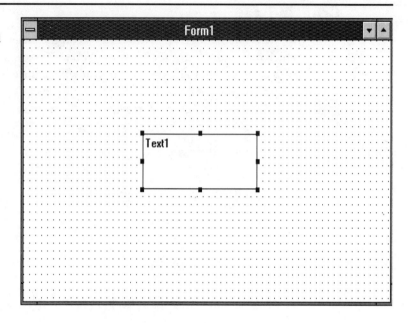

3. Highlight the caption by double-clicking on it or by positioning the I-beam at the beginning of the word and dragging it to the right.

4. Press the Delete key to remove the caption.

5. Type Welcome and press Enter to confirm the new setting, or click the Enter button (the one with a check mark).

SHORTCUT   After you select a control's property, simply enter the new text. The old text will be replaced automatically as you type.

Now change the text box's CtlName property so that you can refer to it in a procedure:

1. With the text box on the form selected, click on the Properties list box (to the left of the Settings list box).

2. Select the CtlName property, if it is not already selected. The name Text1 appears in the Settings list box.

3. Type Display in the Settings list box and press Enter to confirm the change.

Next, change the control's Text property:

1. Select the Text property in the Properties list box. The name Text1 appears in the Settings list box.

2. Double-click inside the Settings list box to highlight the text.

3. Press the Delete key to remove the text.

4. Press Enter to confirm the change.

Finally, change the control's BorderStyle property:

1. Click the Properties list box open, scroll the list up, and select the BorderStyle property. The 1 default setting appears in the Settings box, which is the default value for a fixed single line.

2. Click on the arrow at the right of the Settings list box (the arrow indicates there are more settings for the property). A list appears.

3. Select the 0 setting, which is the value for no border.

4. Click the Enter button to confirm the change. The text box should look like the one in Figure 1.9.

Writing the Program's Functional Code

Now that you've created and modified the interface for the "Welcome" application, you need to write the BASIC code that tells the form how to respond when the program is started at runtime—otherwise, the application will do nothing. Remember, you have to write the code for each control in order to make something happen. It's a lot like taking control of your own life—if you don't, nothing interesting will happen.

When you want a control to respond to an event, you have to write instructions in the form of code called an *event procedure*. To make the application display a "Welcome to Visual Basic!" message, you have to write code for the Load event procedure. *Click* is the default event for a form. You have to change the event to *Load* so that when the program is run, a procedure is invoked that "loads" the application automatically—the user won't have to perform any action. You can always change the event if you want the user to perform a different action that invokes a procedure.

FIGURE 1.9:

The label's appearance has been changed by modifying its properties

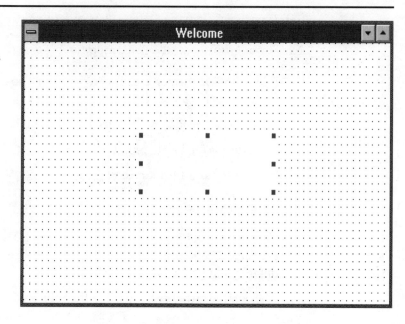

To write the code for the Load event, follow these steps:

1. Double-click anywhere on the form. The code window will appear, as shown in Figure 1.10. A *code template* automatically appears, displaying the first and last lines of the event procedure. In this example, the event procedure is identified by the name Form_Click ().

TIP

To display the code window for any control, double-click on it. When the code window appears, you can write the procedure statements for the control inside the code template.

2. Click on the down arrow to the right of the Procedures list box.

3. Choose Load. The new event will appear in the code template automatically.

4. Position the blinking insertion bar between the Sub and End Sub statements.

FIGURE 1.10:

The code window with the Click event procedure displayed for the form

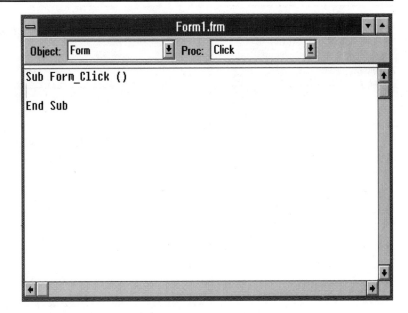

5. Press the Tab key to indent this line. (It's good programming style to indent statements.)

6. Type

   ```
   Display.Text = "Welcome to Visual Basic!"
   ```

7. Double-click on the control box to close the code window.

8. Open the Run menu and select the Start command to run the program. The application will display the message Welcome to Visual Basic!, as shown in Figure 1.11.

9. Open the Run menu again the select the End command to stop program execution.

SHORTCUT   You can also press F5 to run an application.

FIGURE 1.11:
The form displays the message "Welcome to Visual Basic!" when the application is run

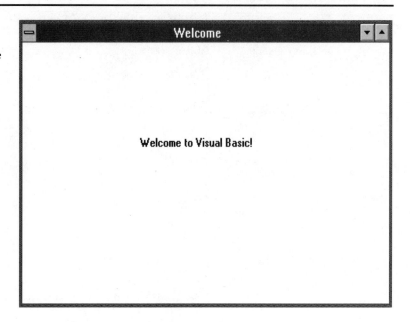

Saving the Application

When you finish writing your application, you need to save it. You should also get into the habit of saving an application periodically, in case something happens to the file that prevents you from opening it. If you've had the experience of working days and nights on a program, and then mysteriously lost it in the black hole of your computer, you know what I mean.

When you save a file the first time, you are actually performing a two-step process. The first step saves the project file that holds all the source files for your application. The second step saves each form that makes up your application.

To save the application, follow these steps:

1. Open the File menu and select the Save Project command. A dialog box will appear, as shown in Figure 1.12, prompting you to save the file.

2. To give the file a name, type Welcome in the text box. The file name will appear automatically in the Project window.

3. Click on the OK button. Another dialog will appear, as shown in Figure 1.13, prompting you to save the project.

4. To give the project a name, type Example (or another descriptive name) in the text box. The new project name will replace the default name.

FIGURE 1.12:
This dialog box appears first when you select the Save Project command from the File menu

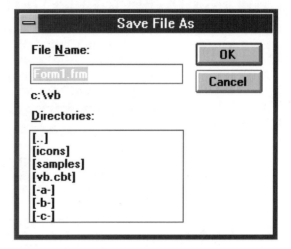

FIGURE 1.13:
Another dialog box appears, prompting you to save the project

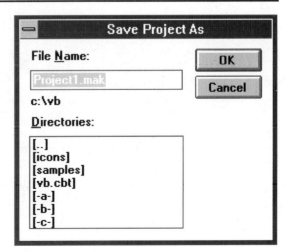

5. Click on the OK button.

Voilà! You've just created your first Windows application—a boring one, but nevertheless a Windows application.

Stepping through the Program

You may be asking yourself what actually happens when you run the program. It's really quite simple. After you start the program, an event procedure is invoked. In this case, the form recognizes the Load event and responds to it by displaying a window with the message "Welcome to Visual Basic!" You programmed this response by writing the procedure statement

```
Display.Text = "Welcome to Visual Basic!"
```

In this statement, the property setting for the control is changed at runtime when the event procedure is invoked. The line uses this syntax:

```
controlname.propertyname = new setting
```

Every control (except for a form) has a CtlName property that you can refer to in code. The name before the period determines what control to act on and the name after the period determines the property to change.

As you learned earlier, you can use the Properties bar to change initial settings for properties. For example, you changed the BorderStyle property for the text box. The default CtlName property for the text box was Text1. You changed the text box's CtlName property to Display so you could refer to it in the event procedure's statement. You also deleted the default setting for the Text property so that nothing was initially displayed inside the text box.

When you ran the application, the event procedure was triggered by the system once the form was loaded. The user did nothing in this case. The form responded to the code that was attached to the event by displaying "Welcome to Visual Basic!" You should understand, however, that you don't *have* to write code for every control. If there isn't any code attached to a control, Visual Basic will simply ignore it.

Summary

In this chapter, you were introduced to the Visual Basic programming system. The chapter covered:

- Reviewing Windows fundamentals, such as navigating the Program Manager, using a mouse, and moving around the Desktop.
- Running the Visual Basic Setup program.
- Creating a simple Visual Basic application.
- Learning how to create a control.
- Setting a control's properties from the Properties bar.
- Writing the functional BASIC code for an event procedure that you attached to a control.

Visual Basic enables you to create fully functional Windows applications with BASIC code. This system combines the simplified syntax of BASIC and GWBASIC with the programming structure of QuickBasic and QBASIC. However, programming in Visual Basic is different from traditional programming. In a procedural language like QuickBasic, for example, you use a top-down approach to writing code. After you run a program, each statement is executed, and control flow is passed from one procedure to another until the program ends.

Visual Basic uses a *visual* approach to programming that is based on an *event-driven* philosophy. Every Windows application is comprised of graphical elements that the user manipulates to perform tasks. These graphical elements are called *forms* and *controls.* When an application is launched, the system responds to events and procedures associated with the controls in the application.

Every control (and form) has a series of predefined events that is associated with it. For example, when a user clicks on a command button control, the system responds to the particular Click event that has been associated with the control. If the system recognizes the event—that is, if the Click event is one of the predefined events associated with a command button control—an *event procedure* is invoked that is attached to the control. An event procedure is a small program comprised of a series of statements that is executed in the order they are written. When an event procedure is invoked, the application performs a task. Remember: A control will always remain idle until its event procedure has been invoked.

CHAPTER

TWO

2

Interacting with Visual Basic

- **Accessing the Menu Bar**

- **Examining the Properties Bar**

- **Creating Controls in the Form Window**

- **Opening the Code Window**

Y ou experienced firsthand in the previous chapter that it's easy to create a simple Windows application. As you begin to create user interfaces, it's important that you understand how other interfaces have been designed to enable people to do their work. A good way to begin is by looking at the Visual Basic interface and seeing how it has been designed. By understanding how you interact with various Visual Basic controls, you'll be in a better position to create and incorporate similar controls in your applications.

The Visual Basic programming environment is comprised of five elements that you access in order to create your applications:

- Menu bar
- Properties bar
- Toolbox
- Form window
- Project window

These windows are what you first see each time you start Visual Basic, as shown in Figure 2.1.

NOTE   To make a window active, you simply click on it.

The windows contain the menus and commands you use, and the tools, properties, and settings you select, when creating the controls that comprise your applications. Each window is described in the following sections.

Menu Bar

You use the menu bar to choose Visual Basic commands. The menu bar displays the names of the menus that are available for use in the active window. Above the menu bar is the title bar, the maximize and minimize buttons, and the control box, which are shown in Figure 2.2.

FIGURE 2.1:

The Visual Basic programming environment

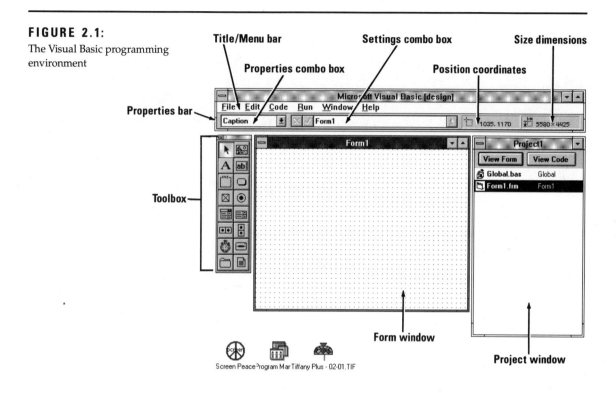

Title/Menu bar

Settings combo box

Size dimensions

Properties combo box

Position coordinates

Properties bar

Toolbox

Form window

Project window

Screen PeaceProgram MarTiffany Plus - 02-01.TIF

FIGURE 2.2:

The menu bar and title bar

You can access the menu bar in several ways: You can click on a menu name to open the menu and display its commands, or you can press a menu name's accelerator key (which is also called the access key) to open the menu. The accelerator key is the letter that is underlined in the menu name. For example, the accelerator key for the File menu is *F.*

To choose a command after you've opened a menu, do one of the following:

- Click on the command name.

- Press the command's accelerator key.

31

If there is a shortcut key for the command (which is displayed next to the command name on the menu), press the key or keystroke combination that is indicated. This shortcut is meant for you to access the command without having to open the command's menu.

If you select a command that is followed by an ellipsis (...), a dialog box will display more information for you to respond to before the command is executed.

Other elements of the menu bar are as follows:

Title Bar   Is located above the menu bar. Like any Windows program, the title bar will always display the name of the current application or document, which in this case is Microsoft Visual Basic. It will also display the word "design" in brackets to indicate that you are currently designing an application. At the ends of the title bar are three items: the control box and the minimize and maximize buttons.

Control Box   Is the box at the left side of the title bar. The control box has two functions. First, it can open a menu, called the Control menu. Most of the commands on this menu let you control the size of the window from the keyboard, so if you're using a mouse, you don't have to be concerned with them. Second, the control box will close the window (terminate the program or close the document) when you double-click on it.

Minimize Button   Is one of the two buttons at the right side of the title bar. It is the button with the arrow pointing downward. When you click on the minimize button, the window will be reduced to an icon at the bottom of the Desktop.

Maximize Button   Is the other button at the right of the title bar. It is the button with the arrow pointing upwards. When you click on the maximize button, the window will expand to fill the entire application window. This may or may not take up the entire screen, depending on whether the application has been maximized. After a window has been maximized, the maximize button changes to the restore button. The restore button displays arrows pointing upward and downward.

File Menu

```
File
New Project
Open Project...
Save Project
Save Project As...

New Form
New Module
Add File...          Ctrl+F12
Remove File
Save File            Shift+F12
Save File As...      F12

Print...

Make EXE File...

Exit
```

You use File menu commands to control Visual Basic projects and files. The menu options are described below (with keyboard shortcuts shown in parentheses):

New Project Allows you to begin a new project. When you start Visual Basic, the default is automatically set to open a new project and display the Project window. The application is the actual program that the user runs, while the project is the set of files the developer uses to build the application.

Open Project... Allows you to select projects that you want to modify or test. When you choose it, a dialog box appears, listing projects you can choose to open. After you double-click on a project name, the name will appear automatically in the Project window.

Save Project Saves all the files in the current project and the project file itself in binary format on disk. As you work on a project, it's a good idea to save your files regularly so that you have a copy of your most recent work. Visual Basic will prompt you to save the files in a project to disk whenever changes would otherwise be lost (for example, when quitting Visual Basic).

The first time you save a project a dialog box appears, prompting you to name the project. When you give a project a name, the default .MAK extension is automatically appended to the file name. The project file itself doesn't contain any files or code. It is simply a list of all the files associated with a particular project. This list is automatically updated every time you save the project.

Save Project As... Enables you to save the project file under a new name, while retaining the original file.

New Form Creates a new form to add to the current project.

New Module Allows you to create a module that contains a collection of procedures and data declarations, which are stored in a single file and not attached to a form. Procedures in a module are recognized throughout an application.

Add File... **(Ctrl-F2)** Adds a new or renamed form to a project.

Remove File Deletes a form or module from a project window without removing it from your hard disk. If you delete a file outside of Visual Basic using standard deletion procedures and then open the project, however, Visual Basic will display an error message to warn you that the file is missing.

Save File (Shift-F12) Saves the currently selected form or module in binary format on disk. When you save a form file, you also save any code that you've attached to both the form and controls. Visual Basic prompts you to name each of the forms in the project and gives them the default extension .FRM.

Save File As... **(F12)** Saves a file under a new name that you specify, while also retaining the name of the original file. The new file remains in the project, but the original file is closed and removed from it.

Print... You choose the Print command to print from Visual Basic. You can print the contents of a form, which includes the form itself and code. However, you must first set up your printer in Windows.

Make EXE File... Creates an executable file after you have finished designing and coding an application that will allow you to run the application under Windows, outside of Visual Basic. The command prompts you to name the file and then appends the file name with the default extension .EXE. You can distribute the file to others by also giving them a copy of the Visual Basic runtime file (VBRUN100.DLL) that is in the Visual Basic directory. The file must be installed in the Windows directory. Otherwise, you will be unable to run any Visual Basic stand-alone application. You can distribute copies of the runtime file free of charge; no additional license or payment to Microsoft Corporation is necessary.

Exit   Closes the current project and returns you to the Program Manager. If you haven't recently saved your work, Visual Basic will prompt you to save any current changes that you made to the project.

Edit Menu

You use Edit menu commands to alter form window and code window contents, to set up Dynamic Data Exchange (DDE) links, and to control the use of the drawing grid. The Edit menu options are listed below (with keyboard shortcuts in parentheses):

Undo (Alt-Backspace)   Reverses the last editing action. Be aware that this command is unavailable (dimmed) if there has been no editing action.

Cut (Shift-Del)   Removes the selected (or highlighted) control or text and places it on the Windows Clipboard.

Copy (Ctrl-Ins)   Copies the selected (or highlighted) control or text to the Clipboard.

Paste (Shift-Ins)   Inserts a control or text from the Clipboard. Text is placed at the current insertion point; a control is placed at the upper-left corner of the active form. When you paste any control, it keeps the same properties and control name as the original control you copied. For example, you can keep the same name and create a *control array,* or you can paste the control and give it a different control name.

Paste Link   Inserts the Clipboard contents copied from another Windows application. It also creates a link with that application to update the copied data automatically.

NOTE   The Paste Link command is unavailable unless Visual Basic determines that the Clipboard contents came from an application that can transfer data to Visual Basic.

Delete (Del)   Erases the currently selected control or text.

Grid Settings...   Turns the grid on and off. It also allows you to change the distance between grid points. After you select the command, a dialog box appears, from which you can change grid settings. This command is only available when the form window is active.

Align to Grid   Aligns selected controls to the current grid, which takes the guesswork out of positioning controls on a form. Be aware that this command is only available when a form window is active.

Code Menu

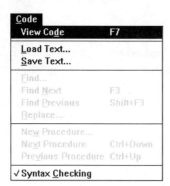

You use the Code menu to create, alter, or display code. You can also use commands to search for specific text. The Code menu options are shown below (with keyboard shortcuts in parentheses):

View Code (F7)   Displays the code for the active control or form. To see the code for a selected form, choose the form in the project window and click the View Code button. The code window will open and display the code.

Load Text...   Loads the code that was created in another application or with a text editor into a Visual Basic application code window. The code can either be loaded as a complete module or merged into an existing module. For example, you can import code written in other versions of BASIC by first saving it in ASCII text format and then loading it in a Visual Basic application. (More on this in Chapter 5.)

Save Text...   Saves the code in a Visual Basic application to disk in ASCII text format.

Find...   Searches code in the project for text that you specify.

Find Next (F3)   Searches code for the next occurrence of the specified text.

Find Previous (Shift-F3)   Searches code in the project for the previous occurrence of the specified text.

Replace...   Searches code for specified text and replaces it with new text.

New Procedure...   Creates a new Sub or Function procedure. However, you can also create a new procedure by typing `Sub ProcedureName` and `Function ProcedureName` in a module.

Next Procedure... (Ctrl-↓)   Displays the next procedure.

Previous Procedure (Ctrl-↑)   Displays the previous procedure.

Syntax Checking   Turns the Visual Basic syntax checker on or off. You can turn it on to check your code for syntax errors as you write it in the code window, or you can turn it off if you prefer to write all your code first and check for errors later. When Syntax Checking is turned on, a check mark appears next to the command in the Code menu. Because Visual Basic is an interpreted language, it checks each line of code for syntax errors as you write it. This process alerts you if there are errors such as misspelled keywords or missing separators. If the syntax is correct, Visual Basic translates the code into internal form that can be understood by the system in order to run the application.

Run Menu

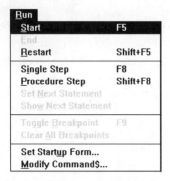

You use Run menu commands to control application execution and to provide debugging tools. The Run menu options are shown below (with keyboard shortcuts in parentheses):

Start (F5)   Runs the application from the beginning. The first form you create in an application is automatically designated as the default startup form, unless you designate another form with the Set Startup Form command. This command is available only at design time; to run an application in Windows outside of Visual Basic, you have to create an executable file.

Break (Ctrl-Break)   Stops the execution of a program while it's running. It is available only at runtime. If a statement is being executed when you choose this command, that statement will be displayed in the code window with a thin border around it. If the application is waiting for events in the idle loop (i.e., no statement is being executed), no statement will be highlighted.

Continue (F5)   Continues execution of your application after any kind of interruption. This includes runtime errors, a Stop statement, a breakpoint in your code, choosing the Break command, or pressing Ctrl-Break while your application is running.

End   Stops running the application and returns to design time.

Restart (Shift-F5)   Sets application variables to their initial value and starts running the application from the beginning. You can use this command to reset the variables before running an application that has been interrupted or halted.

Single Step (F8)   Executes one executable statement, advances to the next executable statement, and then halts. This command is available only while in break mode. Use this command to run your code one line at a time when you want to see the effects of each statement on the variables. Be aware that single stepping traces through every line of a Sub or Function procedure as it is invoked in your application. If the next executable statement is outside of the current module in an application that shares code, Visual Basic will automatically open the appropriate code window.

Procedure Step (Shift-F8)   Executes one executable statement at a time. It treats a Sub or Function procedure as one step, advances to the next executable statement, and then halts. This command is available only while in break mode.

Set Next Statement   Changes the execution sequence of your code so that the next statement executed is the one currently selected. Any intervening code is not executed. This command is available only while in break mode by displaying the Immediate window. With the window displayed, you can use the command to rerun a statement or skip over statements you don't want to execute. You can't use this command to jump from the middle of one procedure to the middle of another, however.

Show Next Statement   Shows the next statement to be executed. The command is available only while in break mode with the Immediate window displayed.

Toggle Breakpoint (F9)   Sets or removes a breakpoint at the current line. After you select this command, a line of code in which a breakpoint has been set appears in bold. The command is not available during runtime.

Clear All Breakpoints   Removes all breakpoints set in your code. By turning off all breakpoints, your application can run in its entirety. This command is not available during runtime.

Set Startup Form…   Enables you to specify the form that you want your application to start with. After you select this command, a dialog box appears, from which you select the startup form.

**Modify Command$**…   Enables you to test your application's response to new command lines. The command is not available during runtime. You can use this command to debug an application that uses the Command$ function to access information from the command line.

Window Menu

You use the Window menu to open or close Visual Basic windows: the Color Palette, the Immediate window, the Menu Design window, the project window, and the Toolbox. The Window menu options are shown below:

Color Palette   Opens the Color Palette. You can also activate the Color Palette when you select the BackColor and ForeColor properties from the Properties bar.

Immediate Window   Opens the Immediate window. After you select this command, you can use this window to execute individual lines of code or test your code. The Immediate window is only available during runtime.

Menu Design Window   Opens the Menu Design window. One of Visual Basic's best features is that it enables you to create menus easily. Like the menus that you access through the Visual Basic menu bar, you can add customized menu bars to all your applications. With this capability, you can design menus and commands that can be accessed with accelerator keys, and you can create commands that will display dialog boxes.

Project Window   Opens or activates the project window.

Toolbox   Activates the Toolbox, which is covered in Chapter 3.

Help Menu

You use the Help menu to display Help topics, to start the Visual Basic Tutorial, and to display the current version information for Visual Basic. The Help menu options are shown below:

Index   Opens Visual Basic's Help system, in which information is displayed in categories. You can browse through the Help screen or search for specific information. You have the option of installing Help during the Setup procedure.

Keyboard   Displays a table of key combinations that let you bypass some menus and dialog boxes.

Tutorial   Starts Visual Basic's Tutorial. Be aware that you must have installed the Tutorial during Setup or it won't be available.

Using Help   Displays information on how to access the Help application.

About...   Displays the version number for Visual Basic, copyright notice, and amount of available memory.

Properties Bar

You use the Properties bar to view and alter characteristics of a form or control. The information displayed in the Properties bar reflects the specific characteristics of forms and controls. The Properties bar is shown in Figure 2.3. Its elements are as follows:

Properties List Box   Is at the left of the bar. It lists all the properties that apply to the selected form or control.

Settings List Box   Is in the middle of the bar. It displays property settings and values of settings that you can edit. When you click inside this box, two buttons appear to the left: you click on the × button to cancel the changes you've made or click on the ✓ button to enter or confirm the changes you've made.

Sometimes after you select a property from the Properties list box, a ↓ button will appear to the right. Click on this button to display settings for *enumerated* or *Boolean values.* Enumerated values indicate more than one setting for a particular property. Boolean values indicate that a particular property can be set to True or False.

Selecting other properties (such as BackColor or ForeColor) will display an ellipsis on this button. Click on this button now to display a dialog box (such as the Color Palette) from which you can select a desired property setting.

Position Box   Is at the right of the Settings list box. This shows the current x and y coordinate position of the upper-left corner of a selected form or control. Choose the Left and Top properties in the Properties list box to reposition the form or control, then simply enter new values in the Settings list box. You can also reposition a form or control directly with the mouse. Click and drag the control; its new position will appear in the Position box.

Size Box Is at the right of the Position box. This indicates the current size of a selected form or control in *twips*. (A twip is $1/20$ of a point; there are 1,440 twips in an inch.) To resize a form or control, choose the Height and Width properties from the Properties list box and enter new values in the Settings list box. You can also resize a form or control directly with the mouse. Just click and drag one of the control's sizing handles or drag one of the four corners.

Form Window

The form is the heart of the Visual Basic interface. You use a form window to create the windows and dialog boxes in your applications. You can draw up to 255 controls on a form. A form has a set of predefined properties that defines how it looks and works. A form also can respond to a set of predefined events for which procedures have been written. A sample form window is shown in Figure 2.4.

Project Window

You use a project window to organize, display, and open all forms and modules in your application. A project window is shown in Figure 2.5.

FIGURE 2.4:
A sample form window

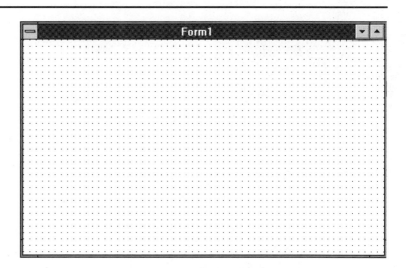

FIGURE 2.5:

A project window

Global Module

A global module contains all the global variable, constant, and type declarations that are recognized by an entire application. It is automatically created for each project. It cannot contain any procedures. A global module is shown in Figure 2.6.

Toolbox

The Toolbox is the set of 16 tools you use to create all the graphical controls for your applications. This is discussed in detail in Chapter 3.

Color Palette

You use the Color Palette to change the colors of a form or control and set up a custom color scheme for your applications. You can change the ForeColor and BackColor properties of a form with it as well. The Color Palette is shown in Figure 2.7.

FIGURE 2.6:
A global module

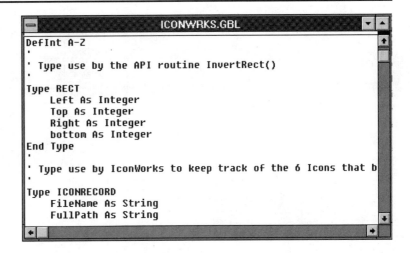

```
DefInt A-Z
'
' Type use by the API routine InvertRect()
'
Type RECT
    Left As Integer
    Top As Integer
    Right As Integer
    bottom As Integer
End Type
'
' Type use by IconWorks to keep track of the 6 Icons that b
'
Type ICONRECORD
    FileName As String
    FullPath As String
```

FIGURE 2.7:
The Color Palette

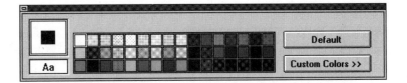

Menu Design Window

You use the Menu Design window to create custom menus for your applications. The Menu Design window is shown in Figure 2.8.

Code Window

You use a code window to write, display, and edit the code that you attach to controls. An example of a code window is shown in Figure 2.9. It doesn't function like a text editor in the traditional sense. The code window does allow you to edit, cut, paste, and copy text, but it does not have an automatic word-wrapping capability,

FIGURE 2.8:

The Menu Design window

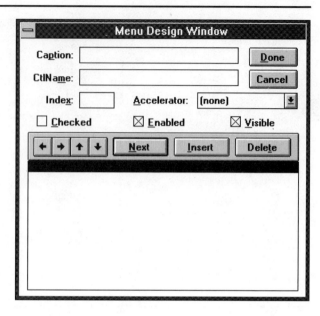

FIGURE 2.9:

A sample code window

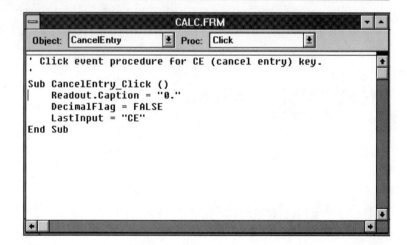

nor does it save the text in ASCII format unless you select the Save Text command from the Code menu. Each statement must be written on a single line and *cannot* be broken, although you can include multiple statements on one line by separating each with a colon. Otherwise, Visual Basic will respond with an error message. You can enter a maximum of 255 characters on a single line.

The elements of a code window are as follows:

Object List Box   Is located at the upper-left corner. It lists all the forms and controls currently in your project.

Procedure List Box   Is located to the right of the Object list box. If you are editing form code, it lists all the events that Visual Basic recognizes for the form or control displayed in the Object list box. When you select an event, the event procedure associated with it—or a code template—is displayed in the code window. If (general) is displayed in the Object list box, the Procedure list box lists all of the general procedures that have been created for the form. If you are editing module code, the Procedure list box will list all of the general procedures that are included in the module.

Finally, a *split bar* is located at the top of the vertical scroll bar. Dragging this bar down splits the code window into two horizontal panes, each of which scrolls separately. This enables you to view two different parts of your code at the same time. The information in the Object and Procedure list boxes applies to the code in the pane that is active, or has the *focus*. Dragging the bar to the top of the window closes the top pane. The split bar is also available in the module window.

Module Window

You use a module window in the same way you use a code window, except that you write, display, and edit general procedures and declarations instead. A module window is shown in Figure 2.10. The Object list box is located at the upper-left of the module window. It shows that you are working on general procedures for the project. The Procedures list box to the right lists all the general procedures that you have created for a form. The procedure you select in the Procedure list box is displayed below in the code window.

FIGURE 2.10:

A module window

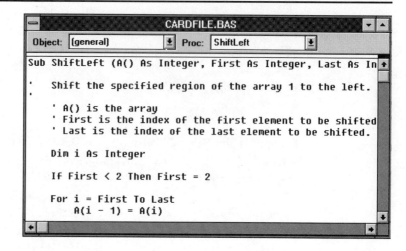

Immediate Window

You use the Immediate window to debug code in break mode or to quickly execute code at runtime. When you run a program, the Immediate window appears automatically. An example of the Immediate window is shown in Figure 2.11.

FIGURE 2.11:

The Immediate window

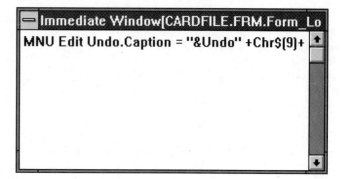

Summary

In this chapter, you have learned about the Visual Basic programming environment. The dynamic system of windows, menus, and tools enables you to create forms and controls, manage project files, manipulate text, run programs, and debug code. Several of Visual Basic's more interesting features include the following:

- When you start a program at runtime, you can select commands from the Code menu to set toggle breakpoints in the code and to "step through" a program in order to evaluate how statements are executed.

- The Immediate window lets you see how a particular statement is being executed as you run a program.

- The powerful Menu Design window is available for creating menus with accelerator keys.

- A complete Help system, Tutorial, and index can be accessed through the Help menu.

- The Properties bar provides you with a convenient way to select control properties and change settings at design time; you don't have to write code to change control properties.

- The Toolbox enables you to create 15 different types of controls on a form.

- A default form window appears automatically when you start Visual Basic. When you click on a form or control, a code window appears in which you write the functional code for an application.

- The code window displays list boxes from which you select the names of controls and events, and the names of general procedures.

- The project window organizes and displays the names of all the forms and modules that are part of a particular application. You can display the code for a form by highlighting the file name in the project window and clicking the View Code button; you don't have to display the actual form (or control) first in order to view the code.

Creating Controls
with the Toolbox

- **Examining the Visual Basic Toolbox**

- **Drawing a Control and Creating a Control Automatically**

The Visual Basic Toolbox contains a set of 16 tools—shown in Figure 3.1—that you can use to draw, move, or resize the controls on your form to which you later attach the functional BASIC code. Each one is described in the following sections.

Sometimes the Toolbox is in the way when you're modifying a form or control, or writing code in the code window. If you don't want the Toolbox displayed, you can close it by following these steps:

1. Click on the Toolbox control box and hold the mouse button down. Don't release the mouse button or the control box will close.

2. Move the highlight to select the Close command. The Toolbox will close.

If the Toolbox is closed, you can open the Toolbox from the menu bar by clicking on the Window menu and selecting the Toolbox command.

Creating a Control

To create any control, follow these steps:

1. Click on the tool. The mouse pointer will change to a crosshair.

FIGURE 3.1:

The Visual Basic Toolbox

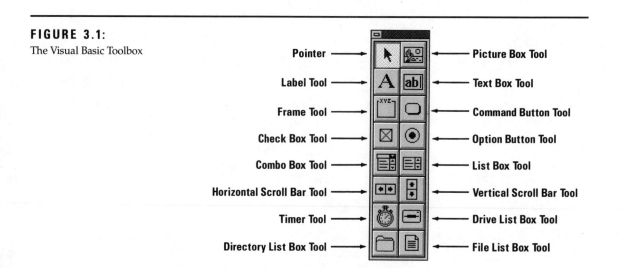

52

2. Position the crosshair on the form in the desired location.

3. Hold the left mouse button down and drag the crosshair downward diagonally to the right until the control is the desired size.

4. Release the mouse button. The control will appear on the form, with selection handles around it.

TIP As a shortcut, you can create any control by double-clicking the appropriate tool in the Toolbox. A default- sized control will appear in the center of the form. You can then resize and drag the control where you want it on the form. If you have many controls to draw, you may find it handy to create the controls all at once and then arrange them.

The Visual Basic Toolbox

The Pointer

 The Pointer is the only tool on the Toolbox that you *can't* use to draw a control. You use the Pointer to select a control when you want to change its properties and settings, and to resize or move a control after you've drawn it on the form.

The Picture Box Tool

 You use the Picture Box tool to display a graphical image from a bitmap, icon, or metafile on your form. For example, you can draw a bitmap in Microsoft Windows Paintbrush, copy it to the Clipboard, then paste it in a picture box that you've drawn. Images can be decorative or functional like an icon. Figure 3.2 illustrates a typical use for a picture box. The bitmap graphic of the eucalyptus tree was created in Paintbrush.

A form containing a picture box,
label, and text box

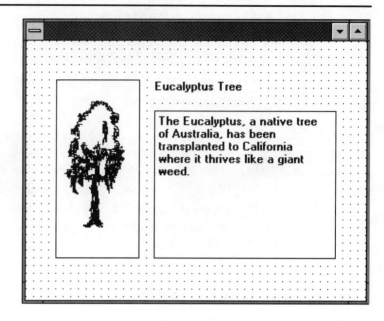

Eucalyptus Tree

The Eucalyptus, a native tree
of Australia, has been
transplanted to California
where it thrives like a giant
weed.

The Label Tool

You use the Label tool to draw a box for text that you don't want a user to change.
You typically use labels to create captions under graphics or identify the contents
of text boxes. Figure 3.2 also shows an example of a label. The label displays the caption Eucalyptus Tree.

The Text Box Tool

You use the Text Box tool to draw a box that holds text which the user can either
enter or change. A text box is one of the most important and convenient controls
that you can draw in your applications. It is an efficient way to accept user input
and to display output. Figure 3.2 also shows an example of a text box. When you
want to display more than one line of text in a text box, you have to set the control's
MultiLine property to True. A multiline text box wraps text automatically as you
type text that extends beyond the control's display area.

The Frame Tool

 You use the Frame tool to create a graphical or functional grouping for controls. Grouping controls this way makes it easier to change the properties and settings for several controls at the same time. Figure 3.3 also shows an example of a frame.

FIGURE 3.3:
A frame with controls inside it

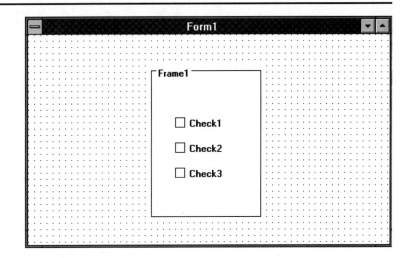

The Command Button Tool

 You use the Command Button tool to create a visible object that the user can choose to perform a task. An example is clicking a button to display another window or exit an application. Figure 3.4 shows an example of a command button. The control's caption reads Save.

The Check Box Tool

 You use the Check Box tool to create a check box that the user can easily choose to indicate if something is true or false, or to display multiple choices when the user can choose more than one. Figure 3.4 also shows an example of a check box.

FIGURE 3.4:

A command button and check box have been added to the form about the eucalyptus tree

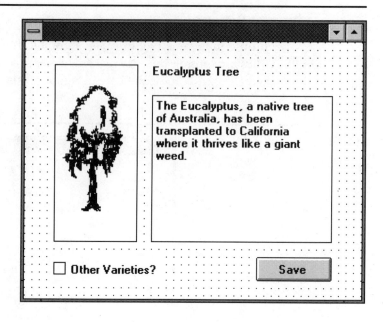

The Option Button Tool

You use the Option Button tool in a group to display multiple choices from which the user can choose only one. Figure 3.5 shows an example of two option buttons.

The Combo Box Tool

You use the Combo Box tool to draw a combination list box and text box. The user can either choose an item from the list or enter a value in the text box. Figure 3.6 shows an example of a combo box.

The List Box Tool

You use the List Box tool to display a list of items from which the user can choose only one. The list can be scrolled if it has more items than can be displayed at one time. Figure 3.6 also shows an example of a list box.

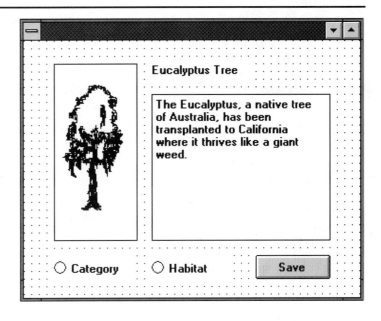

FIGURE 3.5:
Two option buttons in place of the check box on the form about the eucalyptus tree

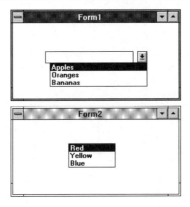

FIGURE 3.6:
A combo box (top) and list box (bottom)

The Horizontal Scroll Bar Tool

 You use the Horizontal Scroll Bar tool to create a graphical control for quickly navigating through a long list of items or a large amount of information, and for indicating the current, relative position. You can also use this control as an input device or indicator of speed or quantity. Figure 3.7 shows an example of a horizontal scroll bar.

The Vertical Scroll Bar Tool

 You use the Vertical Scroll Bar tool to create a graphical control for quickly navigating through a long list of items or a large amount of information, and for indicating the current, relative position. You can also use this control as an input device or indicator of speed or quantity. Figure 3.7 also shows an example of a vertical scroll bar.

The Timer Tool

 You use the Timer tool to indicate timer events at intervals that you set. This control is visible only at design time; it is invisible at runtime. Figure 3.8 illustrates how the Timer tool can be used. A 24-hour clock displays the time.

FIGURE 3.7:

A horizontal scroll bar and vertical scroll bar

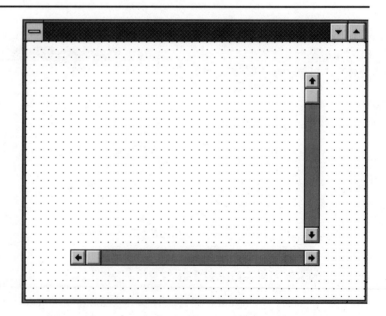

A timed event caused by the Timer tool

The Drive List Box Tool

You use the Drive List Box tool to display the valid drives in the user's system. Figure 3.9 shows an example of a drive list box.

The Directory List Box Tool

You use the Directory List Box tool to display a hierarchical list of directories in the user's system. Figure 3.10 shows an example of a directory list box.

The File List Box Tool

You use the File List Box tool to display a list of files that the user can open, save, or otherwise manipulate. Figure 3.11 shows an example of a file list box.

FIGURE 3.9:
A drive list box showing the C drive

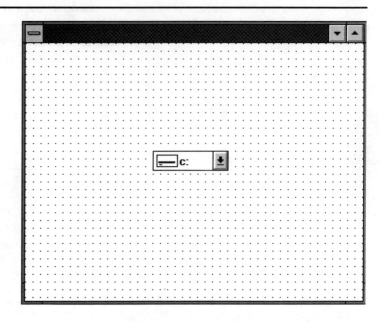

FIGURE 3.10:
A directory list box showing the VB
directory on drive C

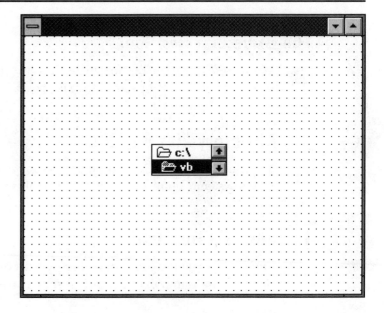

FIGURE 3.11:

A file list box showing two files,
A.FRM and B.FRM

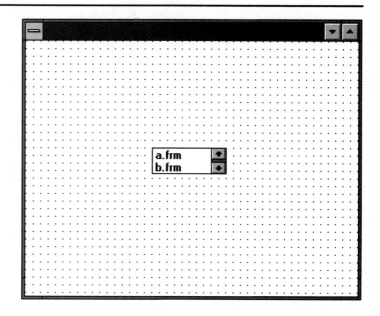

Summary

This chapter introduced you to the Visual Basic Toolbox. In addition to the Pointer, there are 15 tools available for creating a variety of decorative and functional controls.

To create any control automatically, you simply double-click on the particular tool. A default-size control will appear in the center of the form. To resize a control, you drag its selection handles. To reposition a control, just drag it to another location on the form.

CHAPTER

FOUR

Adapting Code Written in Other Versions of BASIC

4

- Modifying BASICA, GWBASIC, QBASIC, and QuickBasic Programs

- Identifying Unsupported Keywords

- Writing Procedures

Your first impression of Visual Basic may lead you to believe that you can simply import programs you've written in other versions of BASIC and run them as they are. It's understandable that you will probably want to take BASIC code you've written elsewhere and use it in a Visual Basic application. However, most BASIC programs will have to be adapted and modified before you can use the code in Visual Basic applications, especially if direct input or output is involved. If your BASIC programs use procedures (and more than likely they will), you will have to look at them closely to see how they perform certain operations.

Visual Basic requires that you program in an entirely new way. You can't just take a BASIC program that performs a simple calculation, plop it into a form, and expect it to run. Visual Basic uses an *event procedure* to structure code, where the procedure establishes a relationship between a control and an event. It is this relationship between a control and an event that enables you to invoke code and tell the application to perform a specific task.

Procedures in QBASIC and QuickBasic *do* correspond in some ways to event procedures and general procedures in Visual Basic. In fact, procedures that you write in QBASIC and QuickBasic can usually be translated into event procedures and general procedures in Visual Basic with slight modifications. However, you will have to look carefully at certain keywords to see whether they are supported in Visual Basic. Sometimes a keyword is not supported because Visual Basic uses a different approach to achieve the same result. In some cases, Visual Basic doesn't support a keyword because it tries to perform an operation that conflicts with Windows. Table 4.1 identifies keywords that are not supported in Visual Basic.

NOTE   You cannot import function libraries from QBASIC or QuickBasic, either.

Importing BASIC Programs

Suppose you wanted to create an application that calculates a person's weekly paycheck by multiplying the pay rate by the number of hours worked, and then displays the result. In a QuickBasic program, you could write a procedure that took the values of pay rate and hours and calculated the result. In a Visual Basic application,

TABLE 4.1: Unsupported BASICA, GWBASIC, QBASIC, and QuickBasic Keywords

BLOAD	BSAVE	CALL ABSOLUTE	CALLS
CHAIN	CLEAR	COLOR	COM
CSRLIN	CVD	CVDMBF	CVI
CVS	CVSMBF	DATA	DEF FN
DEF SEG	DRAW	ERDEV	ERDEV$
FIELD	FILES	FRE	INKEY$
INP	IOCTL	IOCTL$	KEY
LOCATE	LPOS	LPRINT	MKD$
MKI$	MKL$	MKS$	MKSMBF$
ON COM	ON KEY	ON PLAY	ON STRIG
ON TIMER	OUT	PAINT	PALETTE
PCOPY	PEEK	PEN	PLAY
PMAP	POKE	POS	PRESERVE
PRESET	RESTORE	RUN	SADD
SCREEN	SETMEM	SLEEP	SOUND
STICK	STRIG	SWAP	TROFF
TRON	USING$	VARPTR	VARPTR$
VARSEG	VIEW	WAIT	WIDTH LPRINT
WINDOW			

you could achieve the same result by writing an event procedure. You could create three text boxes on a form that would accept user input and display output: one text box would accept the input of pay rate, one text box would accept the input of hours, and one text box would output the result of the calculation.

How would the application do this? You could attach the event procedure to another control—say, a command button. After pay rate and hours were entered in the first two text boxes, the user could click the command button to invoke the procedure that outputs the result in the third text box. The process could be described in this way: The user clicks (*an event*) on the command button (*control*) to execute the code (*event procedure*) that calculates and displays the output (*result of the calculation*). In short, you must begin to think in terms of what result you want to achieve when an event occurs. You also have to consider how you want the result to appear on the screen to the user. Otherwise, you won't be able to make anything happen in Visual Basic.

When you import a DOS BASIC (BASICA or GWBASIC) or QuickBasic program into Visual Basic, you have to understand where to place the code in an application. This is the difficult part of planning an application. On the other hand, it's relatively easy to import a program file physically into Visual Basic. Suppose you wrote the following DOS BASIC program that calculates a person's weekly paycheck:

```
1    REM***PAY CALCULATION PROGRAM
10   REM PROGRAM TO COMPUTE PAYCHECK
100  LET R=4.95
110  LET H=40
120  LET P=R*H
130  PRINT P
140  STOP
150  END
```

Before you can import the program into Visual Basic, you must first save it as an ASCII file. (A QuickBasic program must be saved using the text format option that is specific to QuickBasic.) To save the file in ASCII format, follow these steps:

1. Start BASICA or GWBASIC.

2. Load the program.

3. Save the program as an ASCII file by using the **,A** switch:

   ```
   SAVE filename. BAS,A
   ```

4. Exit BASICA or GWBASIC.

After you've saved the program as an ASCII file, you can import it into Visual Basic. You load the program in the code window of a Visual Basic module or in the form code of an existing Visual Basic application.

To import a DOS BASIC or QuickBasic program into Visual Basic, follow these steps:

1. Open the Code menu and choose the Load Text command. A dialog box will appear.

2. Type the file's name and extension. (Include the directory where the file is located, if necessary.)

3. Click the New button. The program will be loaded in the default Module1.bas code window, as shown in Figure 4.1. (You can also replace the existing code in a module with this new code or merge the new code into an existing module.)

4. Double-click on the control box. The code window will close and the module name will appear in the project window. (If the project window is not open, select Project Window from the Window menu.) You can also save the module under a different name by choosing the Save File command.

5. To open the module again, double-click on its file name in the project window. The module's code window will open.

After you've imported the program, try running it in Visual Basic:

1. Press F5.

2. If an error message box appears, click on the OK button.

3. Double-click on the control box to close the code window.

If the program runs successfully, follow these steps when the program stops:

1. Open the Run menu.

2. Select the End command.

FIGURE 4.1:

A DOS BASIC program that has been imported into Visual Basic

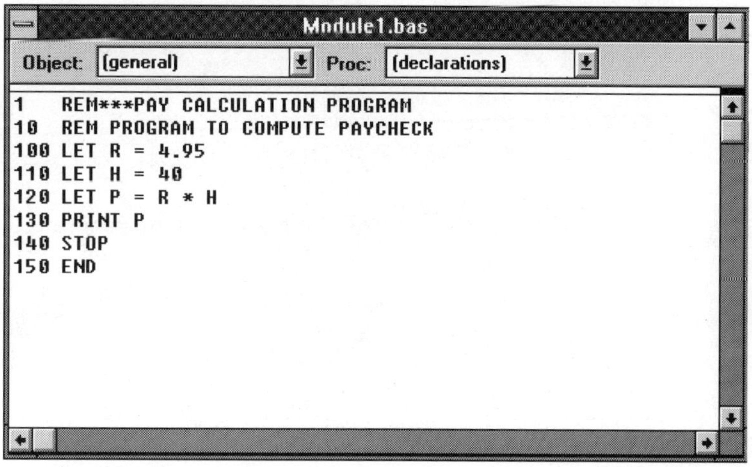

```
Module1.bas

Object: [general]        Proc: [declarations]

1    REM***PAY CALCULATION PROGRAM
10   REM PROGRAM TO COMPUTE PAYCHECK
100  LET R = 4.95
110  LET H = 40
120  LET P = R * H
130  PRINT P
140  STOP
150  END
```

When you run the program, probably nothing will happen, or a dialog box will appear displaying an error message. The reason is simple: the statements aren't written in code that the application can interpret. By looking more closely at the structure of a Visual Basic program, you will learn how to write code so that an application can execute the statements and perform a desired task.

Importing a DOS BASIC Program

Let's look at a simple BASIC program. The paycheck calculation program uses an algorithm that performs the following steps:

1. Assigns values to data fields.

2. Calculates the gross pay.

3. Outputs the gross pay amount.

4. Ends the program.

The program can be summarized as follows:

Input	Hourly rate: $4.95
	Number of hours worked: 40
Processing	Multiply hourly rate times hours worked, giving gross pay
Output	Gross pay

When you run the program, you get the output

```
RUN
      198
Break in 140
Ok
```

However, if you tried to run this same program in Visual Basic, you'd get an error message.

Importing a QuickBasic Program

Suppose you imported a QuickBasic program that performs the same calculation. The program might look like this:

```
REM PAY.BAS
'This program calculates pay
DECLARE SUB PrintPay (Rate!, Hours!)
CLS
CALL PrintPay(4.95, 40)          ' 4.95 and 40 are arguments
END
SUB PrintPay (Rate!, Hours!)  ' Rate! and Hours! are parameters
     Pay! = Rate! * Hours!
     PRINT Pay!
END SUB
```

The output would give you this result:

```
198
```

As you saw earlier, you will have problems if you try to run either of these programs in a Visual Basic application as they are written. You need to understand that in Visual Basic all executable code—the statements that perform some action at runtime—must be placed inside a Sub or Function procedure. In most applications, statements are usually executable except when they include variable declarations, Def*type* statements, and constant and Type definitions.

At this point, you are only *storing* the program in a module. The code isn't written in a form that a Visual Basic application can understand. If you wanted to use the program, the fundamental problem you'd face is where to place the code in the application. For this reason, it's *not* a good idea to import any DOS BASIC or QuickBasic program before you've decided how you want Visual Basic to use the code.

Neither of these programs is elegant, but they do serve a purpose: they both perform a simple calculation. Both of the programs are static, however, because they don't allow the user to input other values for rate and hours at runtime. Remember, a Visual Basic application uses controls that invoke event procedures that perform specific tasks. In the case of the paycheck calculation program, controls could be used to accept the input of data, calculate a value, and display the result of the calculation.

Since the program involves performing a calculation, you would need to decide which control to create and what event to use in order to execute the code statements. If you only wanted the program to perform the same calculation based on the same rate and same number of hours, you could place the code in a procedure that would be invoked when the application was *loaded* at runtime. The program wouldn't involve any user input.

When you ran the program, it would always display the same amount. The output would never change. But what would be the benefit of running a program like that? It would be as static as the program you created at the end of Chapter 1, and it certainly wouldn't be any better than either the DOS BASIC or QuickBasic program.

A better way to design the application would be to allow a user to input different values for *rate* and *hours,* and then calculate the *pay.* For example, you could modify the QuickBasic program by adding INPUT statements:

```
REM PAY.BAS
'This program calculates pay
DECLARE SUB PrintPay (Rate!, Hours!)
CLS
INPUT R!
INPUT H!
CALL PrintPay(R!, H!)          ' Pass two arguments
END
SUB PrintPay (Rate!, Hours!)   ' Two parameters
    Pay! = Rate! * Hours!
    PRINT Pay!
END SUB
```

This modification would allow a user to enter different values. The output would then look like this:

```
? 4.95
? 40
 198
```

If you tried to run this program in Visual Basic, however, you would still get an error message.

The program still doesn't look like much, but at least it allows the user to input different values for rate and hours. If you were to transform this program into a Windows application, you'd want to incorporate graphical elements in the application's design in order to make it as visually dynamic and aesthetically interesting as possible.

This is where Visual Basic excels: it provides you with a set of powerful tools to turn an ugly duckling of a program into a Windows application that's as perfect as any swan. Since this program involves input and output, your first task would be to design how the input and output should appear on a form to the user.

Developing Visual Basic Procedures

In general, you probably won't be able to run any program you import, especially if it is a QuickBasic program that uses procedures. If you are importing a DOS BASIC program, though, you probably will—as long as you place the statements in form code before you run it.

A Visual Basic application can include three kinds of files: forms, modules, and a global module. A *form* is a file that contains visual elements, or *controls*, such as icons, menus, and dialog boxes. Each control can have functional code attached to it in the form of an event procedure. You can only place event procedures in *form code*, which is any code that is attached to one form.

A *module* is a separate file that contains general procedures and declarations. After you define a general procedure, you can call it from anywhere in the application. You can place a general procedure in either form code or in a module. Because an application can be a single form or be comprised of several forms, different event procedures may need the same actions performed. For example, an event procedure in a form can call a general procedure that tells the application how to perform a specific task.

A *global module* is created automatically for each new project, although you don't have to use a global module in an application. The global module can only contain declarations such as variables, constants, and type information that is shared by the entire application. *A global module cannot store any procedures;* they must be placed in either form code or in a module.

BASICA and GWBASIC are not procedural languages; QuickBasic is a procedural language. This difference is significant because the structure of any imported program that uses procedures must be adapted. This usually involves placing the procedures in form code that is attached to specific controls or the form itself.

Defining an Event Procedure

An *event procedure* is the foundation for any Visual Basic application. It is code that is invoked when a form or control recognizes that a particular event has occurred. In other words, an event procedure tells the application to perform a task. For each type of control that you create, Visual Basic defines a set of events that you can respond to by writing code.

Each event procedure is associated with a particular Visual Basic control that you create and an event that can happen to that control. To create an event procedure, follow these steps:

1. Double-click on a form or control. A code window will open, displaying the code template for the event procedure. The default control name and event name are also shown.

2. Click on the arrow in the Procedure list box to see a list of other events that are recognized by the current form or control.

3. Select a different event name if you want to change the event. The new event will appear automatically in the code template.

NOTE   You can only attach *one* event procedure to a form or control.

4. Type the local variable and constant declarations, and the statements for the event procedure.

5. When you are finished writing the event procedure, double-click on the control box to close the code window.

The name of the event procedure always follows this Visual Basic convention:

```
controlname_eventname
```

The name itself always defines the association between the procedure and the event. When you run an application, Visual Basic automatically invokes the appropriate procedure each time an event occurs.

When you want to define an event procedure for a control, a code template is automatically created for the control when you open its code window. The code template always uses this syntax structure:

```
Sub controlname_event ()

End Sub
```

The Sub procedure is a sequence of statements in a Sub...End Sub structure. As you can see in the example, the Sub procedure appears with a unique name. All forms and controls have default names, which you can change. The name also includes the default event name associated with it, which you can also change.

Developing a General Procedure

A *general procedure* is code that is invoked when any part of an application calls it. General procedures and declarations don't have to be associated with a specific form; they can be recognized throughout an application. Therefore, a good programming strategy to follow is to place general procedures that will only be used by one form in form code; general procedures that will used by multiple forms should be placed in a module.

There are two types of general procedures you can create: Sub and Function procedures. A Function procedure returns a value, but a Sub procedure does not. Event procedures and general procedures can both use the Sub procedure. However, only general procedures can use the Function procedure.

To create a general procedure, follow these steps:

1. Open the code window for a form or module where you want to write the general procedure.

2. Select the New Procedure command from the Code menu. A dialog box will appear, as shown in Figure 4.2.

3. Type in the name for the general procedure.

4. Select either the Sub option button to create a Sub procedure or the Function option button to create a Function procedure.

5. Click on the OK button. The code window for the general procedure will appear, displaying a code template.

6. Type the local variable and constant declarations, and statements, using this syntax for Sub procedures:

```
Sub ProcedureName (arguments)
     local variable and constant declarations
     statements
End Sub
```

or using this syntax for Function procedures:

```
Function ProcedureName (arguments [as type])
     local variable and constant declarations
     statements
End Function
```

TIP

Writing general procedures allows you to reuse complex code in different applications. There's no law against copying a general procedure you've created in one application and using it in another application, especially if it performs a complicated task. Recycling code can save you a lot of programming time. Just make sure that you change the old procedure names to match the new ones used in the current application.

Writing general procedures for an application enables you to divide large programs with complex code into smaller, more manageable parts. This structure also makes it extremely easy to pinpoint programming errors and debug code. You should consider using general procedures

- when you want several controls on *one* form to share code. You can create an event procedure for each control and then write a general procedure in form code that is called by each event procedure.

- when you want *several* forms to share code. You can create a module and write a general procedure, then attach an event procedure to each form or control that you want to share the code where the event procedure calls the general procedure.

FIGURE 4.2:
The New Procedure dialog box

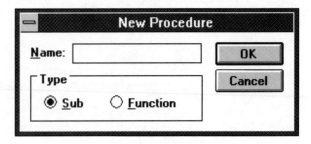

74

Modifying a BASIC Program to Use in Visual Basic

Figure 4.3 illustrates an example of how you might design a Visual Basic form using the previously described BASIC programs. As you can see, the application uses several controls to accept user input, execute the statements, and display the output.

Drawing the Controls

A closer look at the application's controls provides a better understanding of how it was built.

Form

The *form* is the window that you customize to display the controls for the paycheck calculator application.

Labels

The *labels* identify what will be displayed in the text boxes. To create the three labels, follow these steps:

1. Double-click on the Label tool. A label will appear automatically in the center of the form.

2. Drag the label to where you want it on the form, using Figure 4.4 as a guide.

3. Repeat steps 1–2 to create two more labels.

4. Align the labels.

5. Drag the selection handles on each label to increase its size, if you want.

> **TIP**
>
> You may wish to move several controls at a time, especially if they are aligned on a form. Click on one control, hold down the Ctrl Key and then click on another control. Repeat this step for every control you want to move. All the selected controls will display dimmed selection handles. Drag the group of controls to the desired location like you would drag a single control.

FIGURE 4.3:

An example of how the pay calculation program might appear as a Visual Basic application

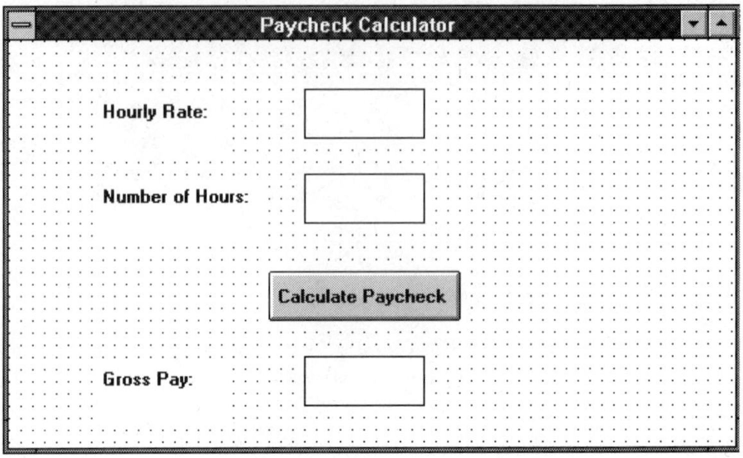

FIGURE 4.4:

The application appears this way after the controls have been created and positioned on the form

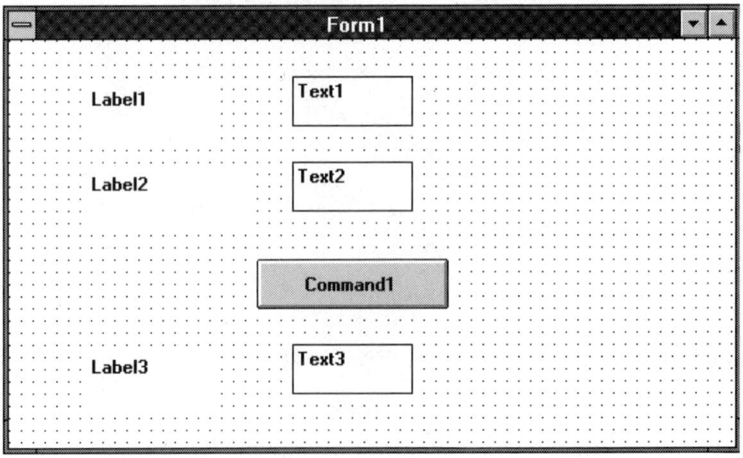

Text Boxes

The *text boxes* above the command button accept user input and the *text box* below the command button displays program output, which is the result of the calculation. To create the three text boxes, follow these steps:

1. Double-click on the Text Box tool. A text box will appear automatically in the center of the form.

2. Drag the text box next to the label at the top of the form.

3. Repeat step 1 to create two more text boxes.

4. Drag each text box next to a label and align them with each other.

5. Drag the selection handles on each text box to increase its size, if you wish.

Command Button

The *command button* is the control that you click to invoke the procedure that performs the calculation. To create the command button, follow these steps:

1. Double-click on the Command Button tool. A command button will appear in the center of the form.

2. Drag the command button to position it as shown in Figure 4.4.

3. Drag the command button's selection handles to increase its size. The form should look similar to Figure 4.4.

Setting the Properties for Each Control

Table 4.2 summarizes the property settings for the controls used in the Paycheck Calculator application. For each control on the form, refer to the table to specify the settings for the given properties. Be sure the correct property is shown in the Properties list box before changing the text in the Settings list box. (These are only suggested property settings; you may change the settings to anything you want.)

Attaching the Functional Code to a Control

When you click on the command button, the text box at the bottom of the form outputs the result of the calculation. For this to happen, you have to write the code for the button's event procedure. To write the code, follow these steps:

1. Double-click on the command button. A code window will open and display the editing area, as shown in Figure 4.5. As you can see, a code template is displayed for the Sub CalcPay_Click procedure. *Click* is the default event name attached to the command button.

TABLE 4.2: Property Settings for Each Control

Default Control Name	CtlName Setting	Caption Setting	Text Setting
Form1	(none)	Paycheck Calculator	
Label1	Label1	Hourly Rate:	
Label2	Label2	Number of Hours:	
Label3	Label3	Gross Pay:	
Text1	RateText		(blank)
Text2	HoursText		(blank)
Text3	PayText		(blank)
Command1	CalcPay	Calculate Paycheck	

> **NOTE**
>
> The code window is comprised of two drop-down list boxes and an editing area. The Object list box on the left displays "general," the names of all the controls on the form, and "Form." The Procedure list box on the right lists all of the events that are recognized by the control selected in the Object box. The Procedure box displays a default event for a form or control, which is usually the Click event.

2. Press the Tab key to indent the first line of code. The other statements will also be indented automatically.

3. Type the following text exactly as it appears. You don't have to worry about inserting spaces in the syntax, since Visual Basic automatically inserts spaces for you after you press the Enter key at the end of each line:

```
Rate = Val(RateText.Text)
Hours = Val(HoursText.Text)
Pay = Rate * Hours
PayText.Text = Format$(Pay, "$ #,###.00")
```

4. Double-click on the control box to close the code window.

5. Press F5 to run the application, or choose Start from the Run menu.

FIGURE 4.5:

The code window is where you write, edit, and display Visual Basic code

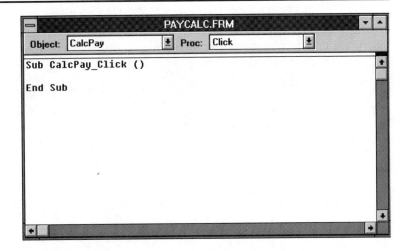

Understanding the Event Procedure's Code

You'll always follow the same general steps that you used in the previous example whenever you attach the code for an event procedure to a form or control. The four lines of code use names that you assigned to the controls when you set their properties. The statements also assign values to three variables and one property reference.

The variables *Rate* and *Hours* retrieve and store the values of the properties in their respective text boxes. This is done by placing a reference to the specific property on the right side of the assignment statement:

```
Rate = Val(RateText.Text)
Hours = Val(HoursText.Text)
```

When a user types data into the *RateText* and *HoursText* text boxes, those values are assigned to *Rate* and *Hours,* respectively.

The *Text* property is a string of characters that specifies the contents of a text box, list box, or combo box. However, the Val function has been used to convert the strings into numbers. Therefore, the strings of characters that were entered in the two text boxes are converted to numeric values.

The next statement performs the calculation:

```
Pay = Rate * Hours
```

The values of the variables *Rate* and *Hours* are multiplied, and then the value of the product is assigned to the variable *Pay*. In other words, the statement tells the application to copy the information on the right side of the assignment statement to the left side.

As you've already learned, you can set the properties of controls at design time by using the Properties bar. However, you can also set properties at runtime. In the event procedure, you set the value of the PayText.Text (*controlname.property*) text box by placing a reference to the property on the left side of the assignment statement:

```
PayText.Text = Format$(Pay, "$ #,###.00")
```

This statement uses the Format$ function to convert a number to a string and format it according to the instructions in the format expression, which details how the number is to be displayed. In this case, the value of the *Pay* variable is displayed in a dollar currency format. The # is used as a digit placeholder.

Rewriting an Event Procedure as a General Procedure

The application can be summarized in this way: First, the user enters values in the text boxes labeled *Hourly Rate* and *Number of Hours,* respectively. Next, the user clicks the *Calculate Paycheck* button. When this command button is clicked, the application recognizes that Click is the event attached to the control and invokes the code. (The form only uses one event procedure, which is attached to the command button.) Finally, the statements in the event procedure are executed: a value is calculated and displayed in the text box labeled *Gross Pay*.

The sample application performs a straightforward calculation. This action is caused by the Sub CalcPay_Click event procedure that is attached to the command button, which executes the code statements. This event procedure performs a single task: it calculates and displays a value based on the values you enter in the two text boxes. If other controls on the form needed to use the same code, writing a general procedure would be the most efficient way to enable these controls to share the code. Instead of placing all the statements in the event procedure, you could create a general procedure and have the event procedure call it.

Cutting Text

You don't have to completely rewrite the event procedure as a general procedure. You can take advantage of Visual Basic's "cut-and-paste" features that enable you to cut or copy selected text, place it in the Windows Clipboard, and paste it somewhere else (as long as it's another Windows application). To modify the event procedure as it is written, follow these steps:

1. Double-click on the command button. The code window opens, displaying the event procedure.

2. Highlight the code statements between the Sub...End Sub lines by holding down the left mouse button and dragging the text I-beam over the text.

3. Open the Edit menu and select the Cut command. The highlighted text will be "cut" from the event procedure and placed in the Clipboard. The event procedure should now look like this:

```
Sub CalcPay_Click

End Sub
```

SHORTCUT Press Shift-Del to cut highlighted text and place it in the Clipboard. The text will be erased from the window.

4. Press the mouse button to display the text insertion bar and place the bar between the two lines of code.

5. Press the Tab key to indent the text insertion bar.

6. Type `PayResult`.

The event procedure Sub CalcPay_Click now calls the general procedure Pay-Result.

Pasting Text

Now that you've created the call to the general procedure, you have to write the general procedure itself. By using the code statements that you cut from the event procedure and pasting them in the general procedure, you can save yourself a lot of time. To create the general procedure, follow these steps:

1. With the code window still open, click on the Code menu.

2. Select the New Procedure command. A dialog box will appear.

3. Type the procedure name PayResult.

4. Select the Sub option button (if it isn't already selected).

5. Click the OK button. The code window appears for the general procedure. The code template is displayed with the name of the general procedure.

6. Press the Tab key to indent the text insertion bar.

7. Open the Edit menu and select the Paste command. The text that you cut from the event procedure will appear. The general procedure should look like this:

```
Sub PayResult
    Rate = Val(RateText.Text)
    Hours = Val(HoursText.Text)
    Pay = Rate * Hours
    PayText.Text = Format$(Pay, "$ #,###.00")
End Sub
```

SHORTCUT   Press Shift-Ins to paste the text in the code window.

8. Double-click on the control box to close the code window.

9. Press F5 to run the application.

If there were other controls on the form that wanted to use this general procedure, each control would have to call it. Therefore, the statement PayResult would need to be included in the particular control's event procedure.

Summary

Input and output are the major functions of any program. Therefore, when you want to modify a DOS BASIC (BASICA and GWBASIC) or procedural BASIC (QBASIC and QuickBasic) program to use in a Visual Basic application, you have to make sure that all input and output are handled correctly by the appropriate controls. If you import a program into Visual Basic without making any modifications, it is more than likely that the program won't run.

A procedure that you write in QBASIC and QuickBasic can usually be translated into an event procedure or general procedure in Visual Basic. However, you will have to look closely at certain keywords to see whether they are supported in Visual Basic.

Building an Effective Graphical User Interface

5

- **Establishing Guidelines for Creating Single-Form and Multi-Form Applications**

- **Determining the Scope of Variables**

- **Examining the Windows Calculator Application**

- **Examining the Windows Cardfile Application**

The term *user interface* is notoriously difficult to define. If you ask several software developers how they would define a user interface, you'd probably get very different responses simply because there isn't a user interface standard for DOS-based applications. Although Windows applications may reflect Application Programming Interface (API) specifications that developers can follow in order to maintain functional consistency among applications, consistency isn't enforced. This is not to say that Windows applications don't conform to general designated conventions. However, a certain amount of latitude can be exercised, which often results in Windows applications that are as different as the developers who create them.

What Is an Interface?

A lot has been written about designing effective graphical user interfaces (GUIs). The area of graphical user interfaces encompasses everything from the philosophical to the psychological and has grown into an important discipline, attracting the attention of developers and researchers from the areas of computer science, engineering, and cognitive psychology. What has emerged is a view of the user—a person, perhaps like yourself, who uses a computer to perform many tasks and get his or her work done.

Usually, the interface between you and your computer consists of the monitor screen, keyboard, and mouse. It is what presents information to you and accepts information from you. You interact with your computer by responding to what you see on the screen, then typing commands on the keyboard or pointing and clicking with the mouse.

Through an application, you communicate with or, more accurately, *interface* with your computer. In fact, a Visual Basic application, like all Windows applications, is accessed through Microsoft's graphical-user interface. An interface is more than a visual display of objects, text, graphics, and patterns. A graphical-user interface—or human-computer interface—such as an application, is the "dialog" that occurs between a computer and its users. In this case, the user interacts with the computer by giving it commands; the computer, in turn, responds to the user by performing a task. In other words, the interface is that component of an application which translates a user's action into one or more requests for performing functions and provides feedback to the user about the consequences of his or her actions.

Visual Basic enables you to design an application's interface using the Windows interface in order to give users a consistent method of interacting with the computer. Consistency is probably an interface's greatest advantage. All applications use similar commands and controls. When you learn one Visual Basic application you already know a lot about other Visual Basic applications. One way that Visual Basic maintains consistency from one application to another is through its use of objects and real-life metaphors. The windows metaphor is used because it represents a real-life experience that most of us understand.

Creating an effective application starts with having a good design and a broad overview of the application's contents and purpose. The way you organize an application depends on what information it contains and how you expect users to use it. Remember that you create applications for people to *use*, not simply to look at.

Ultimately, a person will run the application that you have created *outside* of Visual Basic just like any other Windows application. Therefore, it's important that you stop and ask yourself several fundamental questions that will affect your design:

- What is the *purpose* of the application?
- What *reason(s)* does the user have for using the application?
- What *information* is presented in the application?
- How is information *conveyed* in the application?
- How does the user *find* the information in the application?
- What *directions* does the application give the user?

By answering these questions, you'll be in a much better position to begin building an effective application. If you give some consideration to the design of an application before you begin, you'll see better results and save yourself a lot of time—and headaches.

By going through the process of clarifying the needs of the users of your application, you will create an application that anybody can use. Users should be able to navigate through an application easily, following a logical, intuitive, nonlinear path marked by clear directions. One of the ways to give directions is to represent them by controls. A well-designed application should guide users from one point to another, allowing them to exit at any time. Therefore, the controls you place in your application become the road markers that users follow. In that way, they won't get lost.

Guidelines for Interface Design

There are many different ways to approach the task of designing an interface and building an application. However, you can follow these general steps:

1. Create a new project (or use the new project created when you start Visual Basic) to organize the parts of your application.

2. Create a form for each window in your application.

3. Draw the controls for each form.

4. Create a menu bar for the main form.

5. Set form and control properties.

6. Write event procedures and general procedures.

7. Save your work.

8. Debug your code.

9. Create an executable file to turn the project into an application.

10. Create an icon that you click to open the application from the Program Manager. (You can create your own icon with the Icon Works application that is included with Visual Basic, or you can use any of the hundreds of icons that are included in Visual Basic's icon library.)

In order to analyze the design of an interface, let's look at the Visual Basic environment again. When you open Visual Basic, what do you notice first? What do you think about the different windows as you explore them? Are the menus and commands easy to access? Are the Toolbox, Properties bar, default form, and project windows useful? Do all these elements enhance or detract from using Visual Basic? More importantly, do they help you?

Ideally, an application's content and design should complement each other, where one reflects the intent of the other. Any controls you create should serve an obvious function and help users navigate throughout an application.

Determining the Scope of Local and Global Variables

This is a good place to discuss the "scope of variables" in applications. All high-level programming languages work on the principle of establishing a scope of local and global variables. The *scope of variables* refers to how an application recognizes each of the variables that have been declared in an application. In Visual Basic, scope is determined on the basis of where you declare the variables: in the global module, in a module, or in the form itself.

Variables and constants are often declared in the application's global module. (You cannot place procedures or functions in the global module; you can only declare variables, constants, and types.) Placing declarations here gives variables their broadest scope, hence the name "global." Their placement also puts them at the farthest level of scope in an application. The advantage of declaring variables at the global level is that they always retain their value throughout an application at runtime; they don't change. In other words, global variables remain persistent.

Module-level variables are declared in the declarations section of a separate module, not the declarations section of a form. The advantage of declaring variables in a module is that all the procedures in the application can recognize and share the variables. This is important when you have more than one form in an application calling the same general procedures and functions. For example, you only have to declare the variables once in a module's general procedure. Any event procedure within the entire application can then call the general procedure.

Form-level variables are declared in the declarations section of a form's general procedure. You always declare form-level variables when you want several procedures within the form to share information; a form-level variable is recognized by all the procedures attached to the form. Both form-level and module-level are also considered persistent; they retain their values after a procedure has been executed—but only within the form.

Local variables are only recognized by the procedure in which they appear (hence the name "local"). They also have the nearest level of scope. Using a local variable is a good way to declare any variable that is temporary, since the value of the variable can often change in a procedure. Furthermore, each procedure can declare a variable by the same name; you can name as many local variables with the same name, as long as you place them in separate procedures. If you change one variable name, the other variables by the same name won't be affected.

You need to be aware that conflicts can occur when you declare a local variable with the same name that you have given a variable at another level. Since a local variable has the nearest level of scope, any reference to the variable will be addressed first. If a variable by the same name exists at a higher level, the statement in which the variable is found might not be executed properly—resulting in an error. When debugging a program, there is nothing more frustrating than discovering that the culprit is a variable-name conflict. When at all possible, declare a variable in only one location.

Sample Visual Basic Applications

When you installed Visual Basic on your system, you had the option of installing three sample Windows programs, called Calculator, Cardfile and Icon Works. (If you chose this option, the files can be found in the Visual Basic SAMPLES directory.) Each one of these programs is a fully functional Windows application that you can add to the Program Manager. The programs are also excellent examples of three different user interfaces. In this chapter, I'll discuss how the Calculator and Cardfile applications were created. I discuss the Icon Works application in Chapter 14.

> **NOTE** Microsoft gives you a "royalty-free right" to use and modify any of the Sample Application files for your own purposes. Therefore, I encourage you to use the code in your applications.

To get ideas for how applications are designed, I suggest that you look at the Calculator and Cardfile applications. If you didn't select the SAMPLES option during the Setup procedure, you can do so now by running Setup again, and then selecting SAMPLES. Otherwise, you should follow along. To open the Calculator application, follow the steps below (you can follow the same procedures to open the Cardfile application):

1. Select Open Project from the File menu.

2. Choose the SAMPLES directory and then choose the CALC subdirectory.

3. Double-click on CALC.MAK.

The Single-Form Calculator Application

The Calculator application is a simulation of a standard hand-held calculator. It consists of a single form, as shown in Figure 5.1. As you can see, I've indicated the seven event procedures that the application uses. The application is also comprised of 20 controls that give the Calculator its functionality. I will only discuss those

FIGURE 5.1:
The event procedures associated with the Calculator application

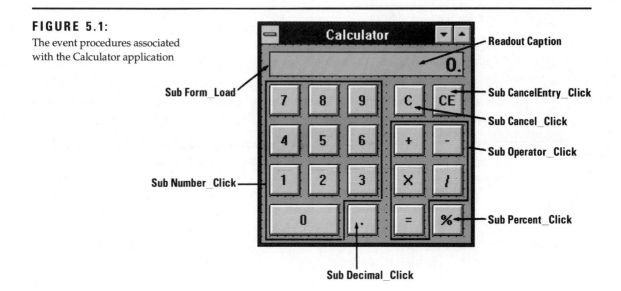

controls whose property settings aren't obvious from the figure.

The size of the Calculator is important; in this case, the developer wanted to create the appearance of simplicity and compactness. To achieve the current size, the Left, Top, Width, and Height properties have been set to 3075, 1665, 3360, and 3390, respectively.

All input and output are displayed in the one Label control, **Readout.** Its Caption property is set to 0 and its Alignment property is set to Right-Justify. If you have a color monitor, the label's BackColor property is set to Yellow.

The remaining 19 controls are all command buttons. The number keys comprise the control array, **Number.** The operator keys comprise the control array, **Operator.** Control arrays will be discussed in greater detail in another section.

All local variables and constants are defined in the declarations section of the application's general procedure, which is found in the Calculator code window and called up in the Object drop-down list box:

```
Dim Op1 As Double          ' Previously input operand.
Dim Op2 As Double          ' Second operand.
Dim DecimalFlag As Integer ' Decimal point present yet?
Dim NumOps As Integer      ' Number of operands.
Dim LastInput As String    ' Indicate type of last keypress.
Dim OpFlag As String       ' Indicate pending operation.

Const TRUE = -1
Const FALSE = 0
```

By declaring all the variables and constants in one central location, each event procedure can reference the variables and constants without having to declare them separately.

Next, all the variables are set to initial values through the initialization routine that occurs when the application executes the **Sub Form_Load** event procedure. This procedure is also found in the Calculator code window under the name "Form" in the Object list box:

```
Sub Form_Load ()
    DecimalFlag = FALSE
    NumOps = 0
    LastInput = "NONE"
    OpFlag = " "
End Sub
```

The **Sub Percent_Click** event procedure is attached to the percent key (%) command button. When the key is selected, the click event procedure computes and displays a percentage of the first operand:

```
Sub Percent_Click ()
    Readout.Caption = Format$(Op1 * Val(Readout.Caption) / 100)
End Sub
```

The **Sub Cancel_Click** event procedure is attached to the cancel (C) command button. When this key is selected, the click event procedure resets the display and initializes all of the variables by calling the Form_Load procedure:

```
Sub Cancel_Click ()
    Readout.Caption = "0."
    Form_Load
End Sub
```

The **Sub Decimal_Click** event procedure is attached to the decimal point (.) command button. When this key is selected, the click event initializes the display readout to 0 if the last keypress was an operator. Otherwise, the click event appends a decimal point to the display:

```
Sub Decimal_Click ()
    If LastInput <> "NUMS" Then
        Readout.Caption = "0."
    ElseIf DecimalFlag = FALSE Then
        Readout.Caption = Readout.Caption + "."
    End If
    DecimalFlag = TRUE
    LastInput = "NUMS"
End Sub
```

The **Sub CancelEntry_Click** event procedure is attached to the cancel entry (CE) command button. When this key is selected, the display readout is reinitialized to 0:

```
Sub CancelEntry_Click ()
    Readout.Caption = "0."
    DecimalFlag = FALSE
    LastInput = "CE"
End Sub
```

The **Sub Number_Click** event procedure is attached to the ten command buttons 0–9, which comprise a control array. A *control array* is a group of controls which have a common function and are identified by the same name. Individual controls are given a common name and Visual Basic automatically gives them separate *index numbers* to distinguish among them. It's efficient to use a control array to work with a group of controls which perform essentially the same action, such as the number keys. Otherwise, a separate event procedure would have to be written for each number key.

The CtlName property for the array of number keys is Number and the Index property value for each one is set to 0, 1, 2, 3, 4, 5, 6, 7, 8, and 9, respectively, as part of the array's index. When a number is selected, the click event automatically passes the index value corresponding to the key that is selected, which is specified by the argument Index As Integer, and appends a new number to the number in the display:

```
Sub Number_Click (Index As Integer)
        If LastInput <> "NUMS" Then
                Readout.Caption = ""
                DecimalFlag = FALSE
        End If
        Readout.Caption = Readout.Caption + Number(Index).Caption
        LastInput = "NUMS"
End Sub
```

The **Sub Operator_Click** event procedure also uses a control array, which in this case is an array of operator keys (+, −, ×, /, =). The click event increments NumOps if the immediately preceeding keypress was part of a number. If one operand is present, the event procedure sets Op1. If two operands are present, the event procedure sets Op1 equal to the result of the operation on Op1 and the current input string, and displays the result:

```
Sub Operator_Click (Index As Integer)
    If LastInput = "NUMS" Then
        NumOps = NumOps + 1
    End If
    If NumOps = 1 Then
        Op1 = Val(Readout.Caption)
    ElseIf NumOps = 2 Then
        Op2 = Val(Readout.Caption)
        Select Case OpFlag
            Case "+"
                Op1 = Op1 + Op2
            Case "-"
                Op1 = Op1 - Op2
            Case "X"
                Op1 = Op1 * Op2
            Case "/"
                If Op2 = 0 Then
```

```
                            MsgBox "Can't divide by zero", 48, "Calculator"
                    Else
                            Op1 = Op1 / Op2
                    End If
                Case "="
                        Op1 = Op2
            End Select
            Readout.Caption = Format$(Op1)
            NumOps = 1
        End If
        LastInput = "OPS"
        OpFlag = Operator(Index).Caption
End Sub
```

The Multi-Form Cardfile Application

The Cardfile application is a standard Windows program that consists of seven forms. The main form, from which all the other forms are accessed, is shown in Figure 5.2. As you can see, it is similar to the Cardfile application found in the Program Manager. Here I indicate where the other forms (dialog boxes) are called from the main form. Each of these forms will be described in the rest of the chapter.

Global Module Declarations

The constants and variables that are declared in the application's global module (CARDFILE.GBL) define the main Cardfile data structure, such as the headings of all the cards, the contents of the cards, the indexes for Headers() and Cards(), and the lengths of the index arrays:

```
Global Headers(1 To 200) As String
Global Cards(1 To 200) As String
Global CardIndex(1 To 200) As Integer

'Dim Length As Integer
'
' Explanation:
'CardIndex(n) is an index to the nth
'card alphabetically.
'
```

FIGURE 5.2:

The main Cardfile form calls the seven other forms: File Form, Page Setup, Index, Add, Go To, Find, and About Cardfile

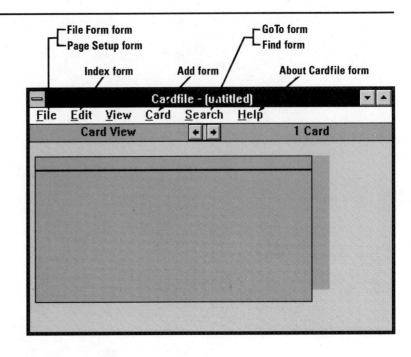

```
'Headers(CardIndex(n)) gives the header
'for the nth card alphabetically.
'
Global Length As Integer      ' The length of the three arrays.
Global AtFront As Integer     ' AtFront is an index to CardIndex().
'                               Its the index of the currently
'                               selected card.
'
' Example:
'
'Headers(CardIndex(AtFront)) gives the
'     header for the card which is
'     presently at the front.
'
'Cardfile-specific declarations

'Cardfile Page Setup

Global Header As String       ' Header and footer text used when printing
Global Footer As String
```

```
Global LeftMargin As Single      ' Margin values used when printing cards
Global RightMargin As Single

Global TopMargin  As Single
Global BottomMargin As Single

' Cardfile Form communication.

Global CancelOp As Integer' Global flag signifying cancellation
                          'multiple-form operation

'Cardfile Help constants.

Global Const CFHELP_KEYBOARD = &H1E
Global Const CFHELP_COMMANDS = &H20
Global Const CFHELP_PROCEDURES = &H21
```

NOTE

The Windows API includes libraries of functions that you can use in your Visual Basic applications. For example, one of the most useful Windows API functions is declared below: the **WinHelp** function. WinHelp displays Windows' powerful and extensive online help system that has been customized for the Cardfile application. The event procedure that calls this function is attached to five of the menu items found on the Cardfile form's Help menu: Index, Keyboard, Commands, Procedures, and Using Help. By clicking any one of these commands, you invoke the **Sub MNU_Help-Item_Click** event procedure, which displays the elaborate help system.

Since WinHelp returns a value (the appropriate help topic) when the event procedure is invoked, it is declared as a function. WinHelp takes four parameters, one of which is hWnd, a handle to Windows that refers to a unique integer value defined by the operating environment. The function also declares four constants. In Cardfile application's global module, this function is declared in the **Declare Function** line below. The **Lib** clause specifies the Windows API library that contains WinHelp, which is "User." I discuss using the Windows API in greater detail in Chapter 14. There I show you how to use another function called **StretchBlt** to create a dynamic "picture-in-picture" graphical effect.

```
,,,,,,,,,,,,,,,,,,,,,,
' General declarations '
,,,,,,,,,,,,,,,,,,,,,,


' WinHelp API declaration

    Declare Function WinHelp Lib "User" (ByVal hWnd As Integer, ByVal lpHelp
        File As String, ByVal wCommand As Integer, dwData As Any) As Integer

' WinHelp command constants

    Global Const HELP_CONTEXT = 1
    Global Const HELP_QUIT = 2
    Global Const HELP_INDEX = 3
    Global Const HELP_HELPONHELP = 4
' MsgBox() function command constants

    Global Const MB_OK = 1      'OK pressed
    Global Const MB_CANCEL = 2 'Cancel pressed
    Global Const MB_ABORT = 3   'Abort pressed
    Global Const MB_RETRY = 4   'Retry pressed
    Global Const MB_IGNORE = 5 'Ignore pressed
    Global Const MB_YES = 6     'Yes pressed
    Global Const MB_NO = 7      'No pressed


' Booleans

    Global Const TRUE = -1
    Global Const FALSE = 0


' Show parameters

    Global Const MODAL = 1
    Global Const MODELESS = 0


' System Colors

    Global Const DESKTOP = &H80000001              ' Desktop
    Global Const APPLICATION_WORKSPACE = &H8000000C ' Application Workspace
    Global Const WINDOW_BACKGROUND = &H80000005    ' Window Back ground
    Global Const WINDOW_TEXT = &H80000008          ' Window Text
    Global Const MENU_BAR = &H80000004             ' Menu Bar
    Global Const MENU_TEXT = &H80000007            ' Menu Text
    Global Const ACTIVE_TITLE_BAR = &H80000002     ' ActiveTitle Bar
    Global Const INACTIVE_TITLE_BAR = &H80000003   ' InactiveTitle Bar
```

```
Global Const TITLE_BAR_TEXT = &H80000009       ' Title BarText
Global Const ACTIVE_BORDER = &H8000000A        ' Active Border
Global Const INACTIVE_BORDER = &H8000000B      ' Inactive Border
Global Const WINDOW_FRAME = &H80000006         ' Window Frame
Global Const SCROLL_BARS = &H80000000          ' Scroll Bars
```

```
' Colors
```

```
Global Const BLACK = &H0&
Global Const RED = &HFF&
Global Const GREEN = &HFF00&
Global Const YELLOW = &HFFFF&
Global Const BLUE = &HFF0000
Global Const MAGENTA = &HFF00FF
Global Const CYAN = &HFFFF00
Global Const WHITE = &HFFFFFF
```

Module-Level Functions and Procedures

Module-level functions and procedures can be called by any form that is part of the application. In other words, these functions and procedures aren't limited to any specific form. These are found in CARDFILE.BAS:

```
Function TrimZeroTerm$ (S$)
'    Trims a null terminated string that has junk at the end.
'    e.g. S$ = "foobar" + chr$(0) + "This junk"
'         Print TrimZeroTerm(S$)
'      gives output:
'             foobar

    Dim Temp As String
    Dim NullSpot As Integer

    Temp = String$(1, 0)
    NullSpot = InStr(S$, Temp)

    If NullSpot = 0 Then
        TrimZeroTerm = S$
    Else
        TrimZeroTerm = Left$(S$, NullSpot - 1)
    End If

End Function
```

NOTE   The variable *NullSpot* is defined as the "null terminated string." This means that any text which might end with a null character (0) is automatically trimmed so you don't get a system error message.

```
Sub ShiftRight (A() As Integer, First As Integer, Last As Integer)
'   Shift the part of the array specified 1 to the right.
'
    ' A() is the array
    ' First is the index of the first element to be shifted.
    ' Last is the index of the last element to be shifted.

    Dim i As Integer

    For i = Last To First Step -1
        A(i + 1) = A(i)
    Next

End Sub

Sub ShiftLeft (A() As Integer, First As Integer, Last As Integer)
'   Shift the specified region of the array 1 to the left.
'
    ' A() is the array
    ' First is the index of the first element to be shifted.
    ' Last is the index of the last element to be shifted.

    Dim i As Integer

    If First < 2 Then First = 2

    For i = First To Last
        A(i - 1) = A(i)
    Next

End Sub

Function Min (A As Integer, B As Integer)

    If A < B Then Min = A Else Min = B

End Function
```

```
Function PadToWord$ (S As String)
' Pad the string with zeroes so that it fits in a long word.
    If Len(S) Mod 2 = 1 Then
        PadToWord = S + String$(1, 0)
    Else PadToWord = S
    End If

End Function

Sub ResetLB (theLB As Control)

    Dim i As Integer

    IsVisible = theLB.Visible
    theLB.Visible = FALSE

    For i = 1 To theLB.ListCount
        theLB.RemoveItem 0
    Next

    theLB.Visible = IsVisible

End Sub

Function StringCompare$ (S1 As String, S2 As String)
'    Compares two strings lexicographically.
'
'    Case S1 = S2     :    StringCompare = "="
'    Case S1 < S2     :    StringCompare = "<"
'    Case S1 > S2     :    StringCompare = ">"

    Dim Len1 As Integer, Len2 As Integer
    Dim Caps1 As String, Caps2 As String
    Dim CommonLen As Integer, i As Integer
    Dim GotIt As Integer
    Dim AsciiValue1, AsciiValue2 As Integer

    Len1 = Len(S1)
    Len2 = Len(S2)
    Caps1 = UCase$(S1)
    Caps2 = UCase$(S2)

    CommonLen = Min(Len1, Len2)

    For i = 1 To CommonLen
```

```
        AsciiValue1 = Asc(Mid$(Caps1, i, 1))
        AsciiValue2 = Asc(Mid$(Caps2, i, 1))
        If (AsciiValue1 < AsciiValue2) Then
            StringCompare$ = "<"
            GotIt = 1
            Exit For
        ElseIf (AsciiValue1 > AsciiValue2) Then
            StringCompare$ = ">"
            GotIt = 1
            Exit For
        End If
    Next i

    If (GotIt = 0) Then
        If (Len1 = Len2) Then
            StringCompare$ = "="
        ElseIf (Len1 > Len2) Then
            StringCompare$ = ">"
        Else StringCompare$ = "<"
        End If
    End If
End Function

Function DialogContinue () As Integer

    If Not CancelOp Then
        DialogContinue = TRUE
    Else
        DialogContinue = FALSE
        CancelOp = FALSE
    End If

End Function

Sub SelectText (aTextBox As Control)

' Select entire contents of a text box control

    aTextBox.SelStart = 0
    aTextBox.SelLength = Len(aTextBox.Text)

End Sub
```

The Cardfile Form

Form-level functions and procedures are only recognized by the particular form for which they written; in this case, only the Cardfile form recognizes the following 25 functions and procedures, in addition to the **Sub Form_Load, Sub Form_Resize**, and **Sub Form_Unload** event procedures shown in Figure 5.3.

FIGURE 5.3:

The Cardfile form calls 25 functions and general procedures in addition to its three event procedures shown

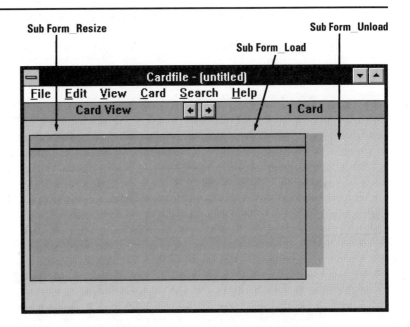

Sub Form_Resize

Sub Form_Load

Sub Form_Unload

The declarations section of the Cardfile form's general procedure contains the following variables and constants:

```
' Cardfile Form Constants
     Const UNTITLED - "(Untitled)"
     Const MAX_HEADER_LENGTH = 39

' View modes
     Const VIEW_LIST = 0
     Const VIEW_CARD = 1

' Miscellaneous variables global to the Cardfile form.
Dim FileName As String
```

```
Dim LastCard As Integer              'Number of cards which fit on
                                     'maximized form
Dim LastCardVisible As Integer       'Last card visible to user
Dim PixelWidth As Integer            'Dimensions of current display's
                                     'pixels
Dim PixelHeight As Integer
Dim WhatView As Integer              'Either VIEW_LIST or VIEW_CARD
Dim CardChanged As Integer           'Whether user has modified current
                                     'card
Dim NeedToSave As Integer            ' Whether user has modified current
                                     'file
Dim SearchString As String           'The last string that a "Find..." was done on.
'Placed in the Find dialog box when the user requests multiple Search_Find's
```

The main control that appears on the Cardfile form shown in Figure 5.4 is the **TXT_CardBody** text box on which you enter information. Behind the text box is a picture box control called **PIC_BackCard**, which gives the appearance that more than one file card exists. Behind both of these controls is another picture box control called **PIC_CardsClip**, which provides the background color for the form.

FIGURE 5.4:

The Cardfile form's controls

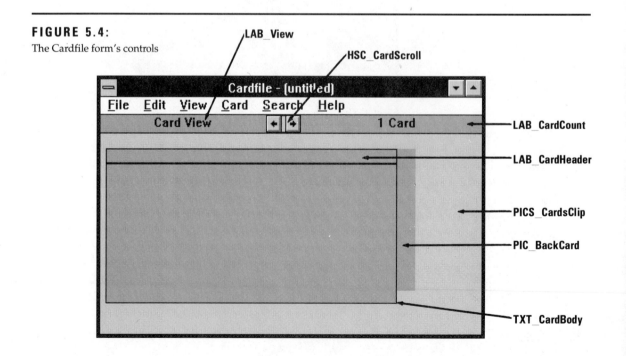

104

The properties that give the Cardfile form its size are set to the following dimensions:

Left: 1185

Top: 1530

Width: 6450

Height: 4215

The **Sub Form_Resize** event procedure changes the dimensions of all the controls that are affected by minimizing or maximizing the size of the window:

```
Sub Form_Resize ()
Static OldHeight As Integer, OldWidth As Integer
Dim DesiredHeight As Integer

If WindowState <> 1 Then ' Check whether form is minimized
    If OldHeight <> Cardfile.Height Then
        LBX_CardHeaders.Visible = FALSE
        PIC_CardsClip.Visible = FALSE
        OldHeight = Cardfile.Height
        LBX_CardHeaders.Height = Cardfile.ScaleHeight -
            PIC_StatusBar.Height
        PIC_CardsClip.Height = Cardfile.ScaleHeight -
            PIC_StatusBar.ScaleHeight
        PIC_Cards.Top = PIC_CardsClip.Height - PIC_Cards.Height

        ' List boxes are automatically sized vertically to prevent
        ' partial lines from being displayed, so make sure that the
        'form is sized flush to the bottom of LBX_CardHeaders
        If LBX_CardHeaders.Height < PIC_CardsClip.Height Then
            If WindowState <> 2 Then
                Cardfile.Height = Cardfile.Height -
                    (PIC_CardsClip.Height - LBX_CardHeaders.Height)
            Else
            LBX_CardHeaders.Height = LBX CardHeaders.Height +
                Cardfile.TextHeight("¦")
            End If
        End If
        LBX_CardHeaders.Visible = (WhatView = VIEW_LIST)
        PIC_CardsClip.Visible = (WhatView = VIEW_CARD)
    End If
    If OldWidth <> Cardfile.Width Then
        OldWidth = Cardfile.Width
        LBX_CardHeaders.Width = Cardfile.ScaleWidth
```

```
        PIC_CardsClip.Width = Cardfile.ScaleWidth
        SizeStatusBar
    End If
    CountVisibleCards
    If (WhatView = VIEW_CARD) And PIC_Cards.Visible Then
            TXT_CardBody.SetFocus
    End If
End Sub
```

The **Function GotoFun%** function returns an index to the next card that has Goto-String as a substring. In other words, the function returns 0 if no cards have the GotoString as a substring and 1 for the first card alphabetically:

```
Function GotoFun% (GotoStrg As String)
Dim GotoCaps As String, HeaderCaps As String
Dim Ans, i As Integer

GotoCaps = UCase$(GotoStrg)

' Search other card headers.
    i = Inc(AtFront)
    While (i <> AtFront) And (Ans = 0)
            HeaderCaps = UCase$(Headers(CardIndex(i)))
            If InStr(HeaderCaps, GotoCaps) > 0 Then Ans = i
            i = Inc(i)
    Wend
If Ans = 0 Then
    ' Search the front card header.
    HeaderCaps = UCase$(Headers(CardIndex(AtFront)))
    If InStr(HeaderCaps, GotoCaps) > 0 Then Ans = AtFront
End If
GotoFun = Ans
End Function
```

The **Sub OpenFile** procedure searches for a file card that matches a specific *filename* input string:

```
Sub OpenFile (FName As String)
    Dim Spot As Integer, Offset As Long
    Dim CardLen As Integer, i As Integer, NumCards As Integer
    Dim TheCard As String, TheHead As String, FileHeader As String * 3

    PIC_StatusBar.Refresh

    Open FName For Binary As 1
    ' Is this a valid Cardfile file? Look for 'MGC' file header.
```

```
    Get 1, 1, FileHeader

    If FileHeader <> "MGC" Then
        MsgBox "Not a valid card file.", 48, "Cardfile"
        Exit Sub
    End If

    ' Get the number of cards
    ' NumCards starts at the 4th byte
    Get 1, 4, NumCards

    TheHead = String$(MAX_HEADER_LENGTH, " ")

    For i = 1 To NumCards
        ' Get an index to the card contents.
        Spot = 12 + 52 * (i - 1)
        Get 1, Spot, Offset

        ' Read Header
        Get 1, Spot + 5, TheHead

        ' Get the length of the card.
        Get 1, Offset + 3, CardLen          ' Basic counts from 1, not 0

        ' Make a string of that length.
        TheCard = String$(CardLen, " ")

        ' Get the card body.
        Get 1, Offset + 5, TheCard    ' +5 -- 2 more than the last spot read
        InsertCard TrimZeroTerm(TheHead), TheCard
        LAB_CardCount.Refresh    ' Show user some activity (cardcount)
    Next
    Close 1

    FileName = FName

    SelectCard 1
    Form_Resize ' set LastCardVisible
    CardGraphics
End Sub
```

The **Sub FindString** procedure searches for a match to any input string:

```
Sub FindString (s As String)
' Parameters:
'    S:  The string to be searched for.
```

```
Static LastSearchString As String
Static LastCardFound As Integer
Static LastPositionFound As Integer

Dim Start As Integer
Dim FndSpot, SearchCard As Integer

If s <> "" Then                    '    void then exit.
     LastSearchString = SearchString
     SearchString = s
     SearchCard = AtFront

     ' Find where to start on first card.
     ' Will change to TXT_CardBody.SelStart or something.
     If (SearchString = LastSearchString) And (SearchCard = LastCardFound) Then
          Start = LastPositionFound + 1
     Else Start = 1
     End If

' Search the first card from the cursor.
     FndSpot = InStr(Start, Cards(CardIndex(SearchCard)), SearchString)

' Search the rest of the cards.
     SearchCard = Inc(SearchCard)
     While FndSpot = 0 And SearchCard <> AtFront
          FndSpot = InStr(1, Cards(CardIndex(SearchCard)), SearchString)
          If FndSpot > 0 Then
               AtFront = SearchCard
               SelectCard AtFront
          End If
          SearchCard = Inc(SearchCard)
     Wend
' Search the first card from the start.
     If FndSpot = 0 Then FndSpot = InStr(1, Cards(CardIndex(SearchCard)),
                         SearchString)
          If FndSpot > 0 Then
               LastCardFound = AtFront
               LastPositionFound = FndSpot
               TXT_CardBody.SelStart = LastPositionFound - 1
               TXT_CardBody.SelLength = Len(s)
          Else
               CantFind SearchString    'Tell user we couldn't find the    string
```

```
        End If
    End If
End Sub
```

The **Sub InitVars** procedure initializes variables that only have to be initialized once:

```
Sub InitVars ()
CancelOp = FALSE

NeedToSave = FALSE
WhatView = VIEW_CARD
ChangeLength 1
LastCard = 1
LastCardVisible = 1

LBX_CardHeaders.Left = 0 - PixelWidth
LBX_CardHeaders.Top = PIC_CardsClip.Top - PixelHeight
LBX_CardHeaders.Width = PIC_CardsClip.Width

LeftMargin = .75          'Margin values used when printing cards (inches)
RightMargin = .75
TopMargin = 1
BottomMargin = 1

Header = "&f"             ' Header and footer text used when printing
Footer = "Page &p"

' Find width & height of one pixel on current device, in twips
' (The thin border around a picture control is 1 pixel thick)
PixelWidth = (PIC_CardBorder.Width - PIC_CardBorder.ScaleWidth) / 2
PixelHeight = (PIC_CardBorder.Height - PIC_CardBorder.ScaleHeight) / 2
End Sub
```

The **Sub Form_Load** event procedure sets the properties of several Edit menu commands, and initializes the sizes and positions of the form's controls. It also calls the InitVars, ResetVars, and ResetDisplay procedures:

```
Sub Form_Load ()
    MNU_Edit_Undo.Caption = "&Undo" + Chr$(9) + "Alt+BkSp"
    MNU_Edit_Cut.Caption = "Cu&t" + Chr$(9) + "Shift+Del"
    MNU_Edit_Copy.Caption = "&Copy" + Chr$(9) + "Ctrl+Ins"
    MNU_Edit_Paste.Caption = "&Paste" + Chr$(9) + "Shift+Ins"
    TXT_CardBody.FontBold = FALSE
    LAB_CardHeader(1).FontBold = FALSE
```

```
    InitVars
    ResetVars
    ResetDisplay 1

 ' Initialize controls' sizes/positions
     ' Make PIC_Cards as large as a maximized screen. Then,
     ' when user resizes form, only PIC_Cards needs to move.
    PIC_Cards.Height = Screen.Height - (Cardfile.Height - Cardfile.ScaleHeight)
    PIC_Cards.Width = Screen.Width
    PIC_StatusBar.Width = Screen.Width + 2 * PixelWidth
    PIC_CardBorder.Top = PIC_Cards.Height - PIC_CardBorder.Height - 120
    LAB_CardHeader(1).Top = PIC_CardBorder.Top - LAB_CardHeader(1).Height +
            PixelHeight
    PIC_Cards.Top = PIC_CardsClip.Height - PIC_Cards.Height
End Sub
```

The **Sub ChangeHeader** procedure changes the current header to NewHeader, which is done by deletion and reinsertion to maintain the alphabetic index:

```
Sub ChangeHeader (NewHead As String)
    Dim OldHead As String, CardContents As String

OldHead = Headers(CardIndex(AtFront))

    If NewHead <> OldHead Then
        NeedToSave = TRUE

        ' Important to do these two stmts before data is destroyed.
        LBX_CardHeaders.RemoveItem AtFront - 1
        CardContents = Cards(CardIndex(AtFront))

        ' Remove from data structure.
        If Length = 1 Then
            Length = 0
        Else
            Remove AtFront
        End If

        ' Reinsert the card using the new header.
        AddCard NewHead, CardContents
    End If
End Sub
```

The **Function NthCard** function returns an index value to CardIndex () of the *n*th card that is displayed when AtFront is at the front:

```
Function NthCard (N As Integer)
'    e.g. Length = 5
'         AtFront = 2
'         N = 2         ----> NthCard = 3  (2 is 1st,  3 is 2nd)
'    e.g. Length = 5
'         AtFront = 5
'         N = 2         ----> NthCard = 1 (5 is 1st, 1 is 2nd)

Dim Ans As Integer

Ans = AtFront - 1 + N
If Ans > Length Then Ans = Ans - Length
     NthCard = Ans
End Function
```

The **Sub ResetVars** procedure is called when the user wants to reset back to the initial state:

```
Sub ResetVars ()
    LastCardVisible = 1
    AtFront = 1
    ChangeLength 1

    CardIndex(1) = 1
    Headers(1) = ""
    Cards(1) = ""


FileName = UNTITLED
End Sub
```

The **Sub ResetDisplay** procedure resets the card view display:

```
Sub ResetDisplay (OldLength As Integer)
    Dim i As Integer
    PIC_Cards.Cls

    If OldLength > 1 Then
        CardGraphics
        For i = 2 To Min(OldLength, LastCard)
            LAB_CardHeader(i).Visible = FALSE
            PIC_BackCard(i).Visible = FALSE
        Next
    End If

' Reset the Card View
```

```
    TXT_CardBody.Text = ""
    LAB_CardHeader(1).Caption = ""

' Reset List View display.
    ResetLB LBX_CardHeaders
    LBX_CardHeaders.AddItem ""
    LBX_CardHeaders.ListIndex = 0
End Sub
```

The **Sub Remove** procedure removes the element designated by Index from Card-Index():

```
Sub Remove (Index As Integer)
' Removes the element designated by Index
' from CardIndex().

'    Method:
'        * Copies stuff from the end of Cards() and Headers()
'            to the spots vacated. The spots vacated are:
'
'                Headers(CardIndex(Index))
'                    and
'                Cards(CardIndex(Index))
'
'        * Shifts left all of the CardIndex() stuff to the
'            right of the CardIndex() vacated spot.
'
'        * Updates Length and AtFront to reflect the deletion.
'
Dim OldSpotInHC As Integer, OldSpotInCardIndex As Integer
Dim Reference As Integer
    If Length = 1 Then

            CardIndex(1) = 1
            Headers(1) = ""
            Cards(1) = ""


    Else
            OldSpotInHC = CardIndex(Index)

            If OldSpotInHC <> Length Then
                ' Replace the Headers() and Cards() spots for
                ' the deleted item with what is at the end
                ' of those two arrays.
                ' Fix CardIndex() to reflect the change.
```

```
                    Headers(OldSpotInHC) = Headers(Length)
                    Cards(OldSpotInHC) = Cards(Length)

                    Reference = Lookup(OldSpotInHC)
                    OldSpotInCardIndex = Lookup(Length)
                    CardIndex(OldSpotInCardIndex) = OldSpotInHC
                End If

            ShiftLeft CardIndex(), (Reference + 1), Length

            Length = Length - 1
            If AtFront > Length Then AtFront = Length

        End If
End Sub
```

The **Sub SelectCard** procedure changes all of the text in the headers and in the cards, but not any line drawings:

```
Sub SelectCard (NewAtFront As Integer)
'    Changes all the text:
'        * All the headers
'        * The card body
'    (No line drawing.)

' Index is the number of the card that should be at front.
    AtFront = NewAtFront

    If WhatView = VIEW_CARD Then
        AssignHeaders
        LAB_CardHeader(1).Refresh
        TXT_CardBody.Text = Cards(CardIndex(AtFront))
        CardChanged = FALSE
    Else
        If LBX_CardHeaders.ListIndex <> AtFront - 1 Then
            LBX_CardHeaders.ListIndex = AtFront - 1
        End If
    End If
End Sub
```

The **Sub AssignHeaders** procedure assigns string values to all of the headers:

```
Sub AssignHeaders ()
    Dim i As Integer, Index As Integer
    Index = AtFront
    For i = 1 To Min(Length, LastCardVisible)
```

```
        For i = 1 To Min(Length, LastCardVisible)
             LAB_CardHeader(i).Caption = Headers(CardIndex(Index))
             Index = Inc(Index)
        Next
End Sub
```

The **Sub NewHeader** procedure creates a new header and a background card as long as the Index is greater than 1:

```
Sub NewHeader (Index As Integer)
If Index <> 1 Then
    If Index = 2 Then
        PIC_BackCard(2).Left = PIC_CardBorder.Left + PIC_CardBorder.Width
        PIC_BackCard(2).Top = LAB_CardHeader(1).Top
        PIC_BackCard(2).Height = PIC_CardBorder.Height
        PIC_BackCard(2).Visible = TRUE
    Else
        ' Create and position the edge of the next "card"
        Load PIC_BackCard(Index)
        PIC_BackCard(Index).BorderStyle = 0
        PIC_BackCard(Index).Left = PIC_BackCard(Index - 1).Left +
                PIC_BackCard(Index - 1).Width + PixelWidth
        PIC_BackCard(Index).Top = PIC_BackCard(Index - 1).Top -
                LAB_CardHeader(Index - 1).Height - PixelHeight
        PIC_BackCard(Index).Height = PIC_BackCard(Index - 1).Height
        PIC_BackCard(Index).Width = PIC_BackCard(2).Width - PixelWidth
        PIC_BackCard(Index).Visible = TRUE
    End If

    Load LAB_CardHeader(Index)
    LAB_CardHeader(Index).BorderStyle = 0
    LAB_CardHeader(Index).FontBold = FALSE
    LAB_CardHeader(Index).Visible = TRUE

' Place next card 300 twips to the right
    LAB_CardHeader(Index).Left = LAB_CardHeader(Index - 1).Left + 300
    LAB_CardHeader(Index).Top = LAB_CardHeader(Index - 1).Top - LAB_Card
                       Header(Index).Height - PixelHeight
    If Index = 2 Then
            LAB_CardHeader(Index).Top = LAB_CardHeader(Index).Top + PixelHeight
End If
End Sub
```

The **Sub CantFind** procedure tells the user that a specified string cannot be found:

```
Sub CantFind (s As String)
    MsgBox "Cannot find " + """" + s + """" + ".", 0, "Cardfile"
End Sub
```

The **Function InsertionPoint** function finds where the current card should be in the CardIndex() when the user inputs a header string. If one or more identical headers are already in the CardIndex(), then the function returns the index to the first header:

```
Function InsertionPoint (H As String)
Dim Relation As String
Dim i As Integer
For i = 1 To Length - 1
    Relation = StringCompare(H, Headers(CardIndex(i)))

        If Relation = "<" Or Relation = "=" Then
            InsertionPoint = i
            Exit Function
        End If
Next i
' If we haven't found an answer yet then...
InsertionPoint = Length
End Function
```

The **Function Lookup%** function finds the index to CardIndex() for the Index card in Headers() and Cards(). The function returns an index between 1 and Length, or 0 for not found:

```
Function Lookup% (Index As Integer)

Dim Count As Integer

Lookup% = 0

For Count = 1 To Length
    If CardIndex(Count) = Index Then Lookup% = Count
Next Count
End Function
```

The **Sub ChangeLength** procedure changes the number of cards in the current file and then updates the appropriate controls and variables:

```
Sub ChangeLength (NewLength As Integer)
Length = NewLength

HSC_CardScroll.Max = Length + 1     ' For wrapping.
```

```
If Length = 1 Then
    LAB_CardCount.Caption = "1 Card"
Else
    LAB_CardCount.Caption = Str$(Length) + " Cards"
End If
End Sub
```

The **Sub InsertCard** procedure inserts the card denoted by NewHead and New-Card, changing Headers(), Cards(), and CardIndex(). A new fake frame becomes visible:

```
Sub InsertCard (NewHead As String, NewCard As String)
' NewHead is a header
' NewCard is a card edit field.

Dim Spot As Integer

' Change Headers() and Cards().
Spot = Length + 1
Headers(Spot) = NewHead
Cards(Spot) = NewCard

' Change CardIndex(), Length and AtFront
ChangeLength Length + 1
AtFront = InsertionPoint(NewHead)
ShiftRight CardIndex(), AtFront, (Length - 1)
CardIndex(AtFront) = Spot

' Change the display.
LBX_CardHeaders.AddItem NewHead

    If Length <= LastCard Then ' Show fake card if it's already loaded
        LAB_CardHeader(Length).Visible = TRUE
        If Length > 1 Then PIC_BackCard(Length).Visible = TRUE

    Else ' Create a false background card if it fits on PIC_Cards.
    ' First, make sure we don't go past top or right edges of PIC_Cards
        If ((LAB_CardHeader(LastCard).Top > 0) And (LAB_CardHeader(Last Card)
        .Left < PIC_Cards.Width)) Then
            'Make sure we don't go past RIGHT edge of PIC_Cards
            'If ((PIC_BackCard(LastCard).Top + PIC_BackCard(LastCard).Height
            '> 0) And (PIC_BackCard(LastCard).Left + PIC_BackCard(LastCard)
            '.Width < PIC_Cards.Width)) Then
                LastCard = LastCard + 1
                NewHeader LastCard
```

```
            'End If
        End If
    End If
End Sub
```

The **Sub DrawCard** procedure draws a frame for the specified card. The Index should be between 2 and Length:

```
Sub DrawCard (Index As Integer, BorderColor As Integer
Dim LeftX As Integer, MidX As Integer, RightX As Integer
Dim TopY As Integer, MidY As Integer, BotY As Integer

LeftX = LAB_CardHeader(Index).Left - PixelWidth
TopY = LAB_CardHeader(Index).Top - PixelHeight

RightX = LeftX + LAB_CardHeader(Index).Width + PixelWidth
BotY = PIC_BackCard(Index).Top + PIC_BackCard(Index).Height

MidX = LAB_CardHeader(Index - 1).Left + TXT_CardBody.Width
MidY = LAB_CardHeader(Index - 1).Top

' Draw the outline.
PIC_Cards.ForeColor = BorderColor
PIC_Cards.Line (LeftX, MidY)-(LeftX, TopY)
PIC_Cards.Line (LeftX, TopY)-(RightX, TopY)
PIC_Cards.Line (RightX, TopY)-(RightX, BotY)
PIC_Cards.Line (RightX, BotY)-(MidX, BotY)
End Sub
```

The **Sub ShowHide** procedure shows or hides the cards' headers list, depending on the Boolean value (TRUE shows, FALSE hides):

```
Sub ShowHide (Bool As Integer)
If WhatView = VIEW_CARD Then
    PIC_Cards.Visible = Bool
    If Bool Then TXT_CardBody.SetFocus
Else
    LBX_CardHeaders.Visible = Bool
    If Bool Then LBX_CardHeaders.SetFocus
End If

HSC_CardScroll.Refresh
End Sub
```

The **Sub CardGraphics** procedure redraws all card borders for Card View:

```
Sub CardGraphics ()
```

```
Dim i As Integer

PIC_Cards.Cls

' Draw borders for all visible cards
For i = 2 To Min(LastCard, Length)
     DrawCard i, BLACK
Next
End Sub
```

The **Sub Form_Unload** event procedure gives the user a chance to save work or abort and exit:

```
Sub Form_Unload (Cancel As Integer)
If Not SaveChanges() Then
    Cancel = TRUE
Else
    HelpWorked = WinHelp(Cardfile.hWnd, "CARDFILE.HLP", HELP_QUIT, 0)
    End
End If
End Sub
```

The **Sub SizeStatusBar** procedure sizes the status bar and its child controls:

```
Sub SizeStatusBar ()
Dim LabelWidth As Integer

If Cardfile.WindowState <> 1 Then          ' 1 - Minimized

    LabelWidth = (Cardfile.Width - HSC_CardScroll.Width) \ 2

    HSC_CardScroll.Left = LabelWidth
    LAB_CardCount.Left = HSC_CardScroll.Left + HSC_CardScroll.Width
    LAB_View.Width = LabelWidth
    LAB_CardCount.Width = LabelWidth
End If
End Sub
```

The **Sub AddCard** procedure inserts a new card into the current card file, updating appropriate controls and variables:

```
Sub AddCard (NewHead As String, NewCard As String)
     InsertCard NewHead, NewCard
     SelectCard AtFront
     CardGraphics
End Sub
```

The **Sub Initialize** procedure resets the display and assorted variables to their startup conditions. As you can see, it also calls the ResetVars and ResetDisplay procedures:

```
Sub Initialize ()
    Dim OldLength As Integer

    CardChanged = FALSE
    NeedToSave = FALSE
    OldLength = Length
    ResetVars
    ResetDisplay OldLength
End Sub
```

The **Sub GetCardText** procedure updates Cards() and Headers() for the current card:

```
Sub GetCardText ()
    If CardChanged Then
        Cards(CardIndex(AtFront)) = TXT_CardBody.Text
        NeedToSave = TRUE
        CardChanged = FALSE
    End If
End Sub
```

The **Function Inc** function returns the index of the subsequent card in the card file:

```
Function Inc (N As Integer)

    If N = Length Then
        Inc = 1
    Else Inc = N + 1
    End If
End Function
```

The **Function SaveChanges** function gives the user the choice of saving changes to a card or cancelling the operation when the MNU_File_Save_Click event procedure is invoked:

```
Function SaveChanges () As Integer
    Dim Temp As Integer

    If NeedToSave Then
        Temp = MsgBox("Save current changes: " + FileName, 3 + 32, "Cardfile")
    End If
    SaveChanges = TRUE

    If Temp = MB_YES Then            ' User chose to save changes
```

```
        MNU_File_Save_Click
    ElseIf Temp = MB_CANCEL Then      ' User Cancelled operation
        SaveChanges = FALSE
    End If
End Function
```

The **Sub SaveFile** procedure saves the current card as a *binary* data file. Remember that a data file, such as the data contained on the card, is simply a physical location on your disk where information is stored. In this case, a binary file is treated as an *unformatted* sequence of individual bytes; that is, the file is not treated as a text file or a record file of fixed or varying length. The file is opened in *binary access* mode with the **Open** statement:

```
Open FileName For Binary As #1
```

This mode makes no assumptions about what the individual raw bytes of a file represent, which can be anything from ASCII text to a series of records. The advantage of using binary access mode is you can read or modify files saved in formats other than ASCII- or ANSI-format:

```
Sub SaveFile (FileName As String)
Dim FileHeader As String
Dim NextCardOffset As Integer ' All Integer variables are two bytes long
Dim CardLength As Integer
Dim Cursor As Integer
Dim Index As Integer
Dim Zero As Integer

Zero = 0

Open FileName For Binary As #1

FileHeader = "MGC"
Put #1, 1, FileHeader
Put #1, 4, Length
Put #1, 6, Zero

NextCardOffset = Length * 52 + 5

For Index = 0 To Length - 1
    Cursor = 12 + 52 * Index
    Put #1, Cursor, NextCardOffset
    Put #1, Cursor + 2, Zero
```

```
      Put #1, Cursor + 3, Zero
      If Len(Headers(CardIndex(Index + 1))) > MAX_HEADER_LENGTH Then
            Headers(Index + 1) = Left$(Headers(Index + 1), MAX_HEADER_LENGTH)
      Put #1, Cursor + 5, Headers(CardIndex(Index + 1))
      Put #1, , Zero

      CardLength = Len(Cards(CardIndex(Index + 1)))
      Put #1, NextCardOffset + 1, Zero
      Put #1, NextCardOffset + 3, CardLength
      Put #1, NextCardOffset + 5, Cards(CardIndex(Index + 1))
      NextCardOffset = NextCardOffset + CardLength + 4
Next Index
Close
End Sub
```

This procedure is called from both the **MNU_File_Save_Click** and **MNU_File-
_SaveAs_Click** event procedures that are attached to the Save and Save As commands on the File menu. All of the remaining procedures in the Cardfile application
are accessed through the various menus. (I show you how to design menu systems
in Chapter 10.) However, the other forms that comprise the Cardfile application are
discussed in the following sections.

The File Form Form

The File Form form is shown in Figure 5.5. This form is used as the basis for three
dialog boxes in Cardfile: Open, Save As, and File Merge. All of the dialog boxes are
accessed through the File menu. The Open dialog box is accessed when the Open
command is selected. The Save As dialog box is accessed when you select either the
Save or Save As command. The File Merge dialog box is accessed when the Merge
command is selected.

The text box control is called **TXT_TextBox,** in which the user enters a file name.
The file list box control is called **FIL_Files.** This control displays a list of file names
in the current directory. A user can either click or double-click on a file name to
select it. The **DIR_Dirs** directory list box control displays the directories on the current drive. A drive list box control called **DRV_Drives** displays the drives available.
The two command button controls, OK and Cancel, are called **BTN_OK_Click** and
BTN_Cancel_Click, respectively. The user invokes either one of them with a click
event.

FIGURE 5.5:

The File Form form is used as the basis for the Open, File Save As, and File Merge dialog boxes. Here you see all the event procedures associated with this form.

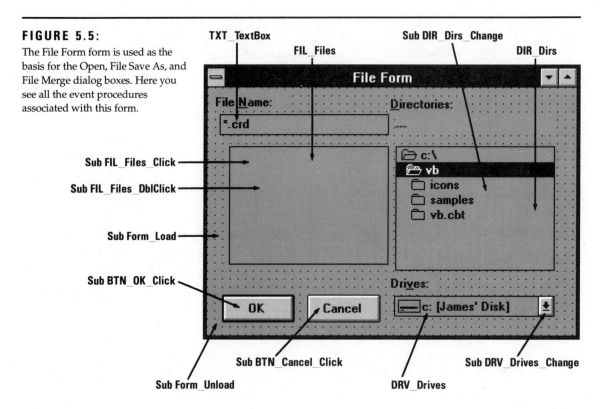

The properties that give the file form its size are set to the following dimensions:

Left: 1875

Top: 1320

Width: 5820

Height: 4140

The code below shows how the form's caption changes to reflect the particular command that has been selected:

```
Dim LastChange As Integer    'remember what changed last

Sub Form_Load ()
    LAB_CurrentDir.Caption = DIR_Dirs.path    'Show full path name in a label
    LastChange = 0                            'No controls have been modified
    DIR_Dirs.Height = FIL_Files.Height        'Align Drives box to Files box
```

```
End Sub

Sub Form_Unload (Cancel As Integer)

    Cancel = TRUE     ' Don't unload form, just hide it
    FileForm.Hide
    CancelOp = TRUE ' Notify Cardfile form of cancellation

End Sub

Function ProcessFileSpec (FileSpec As String) As Integer

' This function accepts a string which may be a directory name,
' a wildcard pattern, or a file name. The function returns TRUE
' if the string is a valid filename, and FALSE if the string is
' either an invalid filename or a directory specification. If the
' string specifies a directory, ProcessFileSpec() changes the
' current directory and updates the appropriate form controls.
'
' Note: This procedure expects FileForm's caption to be set to
'       one of "File Save As", "File Open" or "File Merge" in order
'       to prompt the user appropriately (eg - 'Replace existing
'       file?' during File Save As, or 'File not found' during
'       File Open/Merge).

Dim MsgBoxResponse As Integer
On Local Error Resume Next

If FileSpec <> "" Then
  Err = 0
  ChDir (FileSpec)
If Err Then        ' FileSpec is a filename or wildcard, not a dir
 If InStr(FileSpec, ".") = FALSE Then FileSpec = FileSpec + ".crd"
      If Len(FileSpec) > 12 Then
        MsgBox ("Filename too long: '" + FileSpec + "'")
        ProcessFileSpec = FALSE
      Else
        'Did user specify a new wildcard pattern?
        If InStr(FileSpec, "*") Or InStr(FileSpec, "?") Then
            FIL_Files.Pattern = FileSpec
         ProcessFileSpec = FALSE
        Else
         If FileSpec <> ".." Then
         'We're finished -- got a valid filename
          If Dir$(FileSpec) = "" Then
```

```
            If FileForm.Caption = "File Open" Or FileForm.Caption = "File
                    Merge" Then
              MsgBox "No such file: " + FileSpec, 0, "Cardfile"
              ProcessFileSpec = FALSE
            Else
              TXT_TextBox.Text = FileSpec
              ProcessFileSpec = TRUE
            End If
          Else
            If FileForm.Caption = "File Save As" Then
              MsgBoxResponse = MsgBox("Replace existing " + FileSpec + "?",
                      4 + 32 + 256, "Cardfile")
              If MsgBoxResponse = MB_YES Then
               Kill FileSpec
               TXT_TextBox.Text = FileSpec
               ProcessFileSpec = TRUE
              Else
                ProcessFileSpec = FALSE
              End If
             Else
               TXT_TextBox.Text = FileSpec
               ProcessFileSpec = TRUE
             End If
           End If
          End If
         End If
        End If
      Else    ' FileSpec was just a directory name
       ProcessFileSpec = FALSE
      End If
    Else
      ' The user only specified a new drive (handled in IsFileName)
      ProcessFileSpec = FALSE
    End If

End Function

Sub HighLightTextBox ()

    TXT_TextBox.SelStart = 0
    TXT_TextBox.SelLength = Len(TXT_TextBox.Text)
    TXT_TextBox.SetFocus

End Sub
```

```
Function IsFileName (FileSpec As String) As Integer

' This function accepts FileSpec, a string, as input, then
' checks to see if the string is a valid file path/expression.
' If FileSpec is valid, and specifies a new drive, pattern and/or
' directory, the directory and file list boxes are notified.
'
' If FileSpec contains a valid file name, the filename is placed
' in the form's text edit box and IsFileName() returns a value of
' TRUE. If FileSpec does not contain a valid file name (ie, it
' contains directory name and/or a new file pattern and/or an
' invalid file/path expression), IsFileName() returns FALSE.

    Dim Index As Integer
    Dim OldDir As String
    Dim NewDir As String

    On Local Error Resume Next

    OldDir = CurDir$                        'Remember current directory

    FileSpec = LCase$(FileSpec)

    If Mid$(FileSpec, 2, 1) = ":" Then   'Does it specify new drive?
        ChDrive (FileSpec)
        DIR_Dirs.path = CurDir$
        If Err Then
            MsgBox Error$(Err), 0, "Disk Error"
            ChDrive (OldDir)
            DIR_Dirs.path = CurDir$
            IsFileName = FALSE
            Exit Function
        Else FileSpec = Right$(FileSpec, Len(FileSpec) - 2)
        End If
    End If

    ChDir (FileSpec)
    If Err Then                         'Separate path/filename, try again
        While InStr(FileSpec, "\")      'Parse any directory info

            'NewDir gets text to the left of & including FileSpec's first "\"
            NewDir = NewDir + Left$(FileSpec, InStr(FileSpec, "\"))
```

```
            'FileSpec becomes the text to the right of the first "\"
            FileSpec = Right$(FileSpec, Len(FileSpec) - InStr(FileSpec, "\"))
        Wend

        If NewDir <> "" Then
          If Len(NewDir) > 1 Then NewDir = Left$(NewDir, Len(NewDir) - 1)
                   'Remove ending "\"
            Err = 0
            ChDir (NewDir)
            If Err Then
                MsgBox "Invalid path: '" + NewDir + "'", 0, "Cardfile"
                IsFileName = FALSE
            Else
                If ProcessFileSpec(FileSpec) Then
                    IsFileName = TRUE
                Else
                    If (InStr(FileSpec, "*") = 0) And (InStr(FileSpec, "?")
                         = 0) Then
                        ChDrive (OldDir)
                        ChDir (OldDir)
                    Else
                        DIR_Dirs.path = CurDir$      'Update file controls
                    End If
                    IsFileName = FALSE
                End If
            End If
        Else
            IsFileName = ProcessFileSpec(FileSpec)
        End If
    Else
        'User specified a new, valid dir; update the file controls
        DIR_Dirs.path = FileSpec
    End If

End Function
Sub BTN_Cancel_Click ()

    TXT_TextBox.SetFocus
    FileForm.Hide
    CancelOp = TRUE

End Sub
```

```
Sub DIR_Dirs_Change ()

    ' propogate directory changes to other controls
    FIL_Files.path = DIR_Dirs.path
    LAB_CurrentDir.Caption = DIR_Dirs.path
    ChDir DIR_Dirs.path

End Sub

Sub DIR_Dirs_Click ()

    LastChange = 2   'remember that the DIR_Dirs control changed

End Sub
Sub FIL_Files_Click ()
    'echo the selected name in the Text box
    TXT_TextBox.Text = FIL_Files.Filename

End Sub

Sub FIL_Files_DblClick ()

    'we have a final selection from the File Save dialog

    TXT_TextBox.Text = FIL_Files.Filename
    BTN_OK_Click

End Sub

Sub FIL_Files_PathChange ()

    'Show the current search pattern in the TXT_TextBox control
    TXT_TextBox.Text = FIL_Files.Pattern
    HighLightTextBox

End Sub

Sub FIL_Files_PatternChange ()
    TXT_TextBox.Text = FIL_Files.Pattern
    HighLightTextBox

End Sub

Sub BTN_OK_Click ()
```

```
    Dim FileSpec As String

    Select Case LastChange
        Case 0 To 1                 'Text box control was last changed
            LastChange = FALSE
            FileSpec = TXT_TextBox.Text
            If IsFileName(FileSpec) Then
                HighLightTextBox
                FileForm.Hide
            End If
        Case 2                      'Directory list control was last changed
            LastChange = FALSE
            DIR_Dirs.path = DIR_Dirs.List(DIR_Dirs.ListIndex)
        End Select

End Sub

Sub TXT_TextBox_Change ()

    LastChange = 1

End Sub

Sub DRV_Drives_Change ()

    ' change the DIR_Dirs control path, it will
    ' pass the change on to the FIL_Files control
    DIR_Dirs.path = DRV_Drives.Drive
    ChDrive (DRV_Drives.Drive)

End Sub
```

The Page Setup Form

The Page Setup form is shown in Figure 5.6. A user enters the text for headers and footers in the two text boxes called **TXT_Footer** and **TXT_Header.** Four other text box controls called **TXT_Left, TXT_Top, TXT_Right,** and **TXT_Bottom** enable the user to set margins for the card file text. These controls appear inside a frame control called **FRA_Margins.** There are also two command button controls called **BTN_OK_Click** and **BTN_Cancel_Click,** which a user invokes with a click event.

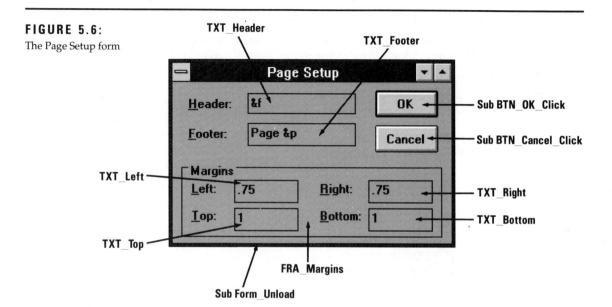

FIGURE 5.6:
The Page Setup form

The properties that give the file form its size are set to the following dimensions:

Left: 2355

Top: 2175

Width: 4425

Height: 2820

The Page Setup form doesn't have a separate Load procedure because it is automatically loaded when the main Cardfile form is loaded.

The **Sub Form_Unload** even procedure hides the Page Setup form when the user clicks on the OK command button:

```
Sub Form_Unload (Cancel As Integer)

    Cancel = TRUE    ' Don't unload form, just hide it
    PageForm.Hide
    CancelOp = TRUE ' Notify Cardfile form of cancellation

End Sub
```

The following event procedures with the GotFocus event all respond in the same manner: When the user clicks on a particular text box, that text box receives the form's current focus by displaying the blinking insertion bar:

```
Sub TXT_Bottom_GotFocus ()
    SelectText TXT_Bottom
End Sub

Sub TXT_Footer_GotFocus ()
    SelectText TXT_Footer
End Sub

Sub TXT_Header_GotFocus ()
    SelectText TXT_Header
End Sub

Sub TXT_Left_GotFocus ()
    SelectText TXT_Left
End Sub

Sub TXT_Right_GotFocus ()
    SelectText TXT_Right
End Sub

Sub TXT_Top_GotFocus ()
    SelectText TXT_Top
End Sub
```

These two even procedures give the user the option of either setting new Page Setup values or canceling the request:

```
Sub BTN_Cancel_Click ()
    TXT_Header.SetFocus
    PageForm.Hide
    CancelOp = TRUE
End Sub

Sub BTN_OK_Click ()
    TXT_Header.SetFocus
    PageForm.Hide
End Sub
```

The Index Form

The Index form is shown in Figure 5.7. The properties that give the Index form its size are set to the following dimensions:

Left: 1875

Top: 2610

Width: 5940

Height: 1425

The text box control called **TXT_NewHeader** allows the user to enter a text string that matches a new header entered on the Add form (described next). If the new header exists in the index, the new card file will appear. The command button controls OK and Cancel are called **BTN_OK_Click** and **BTN_Cancel_Click,** respectively. The user invokes either one of them with a click event:

```
Sub Form_Unload (Cancel As Integer)
    Cancel = TRUE    ' Don't unload form, just hide it
    IndexForm.Hide
    CancelOp = TRUE ' Notify Cardfile form of cancellation
End Sub

Sub BTN_Cancel_Click ()
    TXT_NewHeader.SetFocus
    IndexForm.Hide
    TXT_NewHeader.Text = ""
    CancelOp = TRUE
End Sub
```

FIGURE 5.7:
The Index form

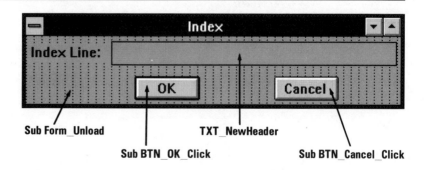

```
Sub TXT_NewHeader_KeyPress (KeyCode As Integer)
    If KeyCode = RETURN_KEY Then BTN_OK_Click
End Sub

Sub BTN_OK_Click ()
    TXT_NewHeader.SetFocus
    IndexForm.Hide
End Sub
```

The Add Form

The Add form is shown in Figure 5.8. This form enables the user to add a new header to a file card. The user enters the new header in the **TXT_NewHeader** text box control.

FIGURE 5.8:

The Add form

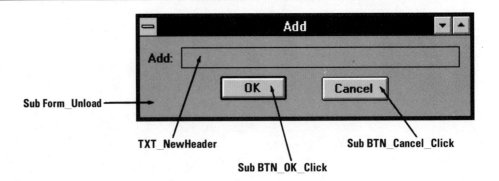

The properties that give the Add form its size are set to the following dimensions:

    Left: 1680

    Top: 2775

    Width: 5220

    Height: 1620

There are also two command button controls called **BTN_OK_Click** and **BTN-_Cancel_Click** that the user invokes with a click event:

```
Sub Form_Unload (Cancel As Integer)
    Cancel = TRUE    'Don't unload form, just hide it
    CancelOp = TRUE 'Notify Cardfile form of cancellation
    AddForm.Hide
End Sub

Sub BTN_Cancel_Click ()
    TXT_NewHeader.SetFocus
    TXT_NewHeader.Text = ""
    CancelOp = TRUE
    AddForm.Hide
End Sub

Sub TXT_NewHeader_KeyPress (KeyCode As Integer)
    If KeyCode = RETURN_KEY Then BTN_OK_Click
End Sub

Sub BTN_OK_Click ()
    TXT_NewHeader.SetFocus
    AddForm.Hide
End Sub
```

The Go To Form

The Go To form is shown in Figure 5.9. This form allows the user to enter a text string in the text box control called **TXT_SearchString**. If a header is found in the index that matches the text string, the file card appears.

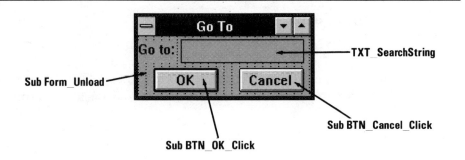

FIGURE 5.9:
The Go To form

The properties that give the Go To form its size are set to the following dimensions:

Left: 3165

Top: 2655

Width: 2790

Height: 1305

The two command button controls, OK and Cancel, are called **BTN_OK_Click** and **BTN_Cancel_Click,** respectively. They are also invoked with a click event:

```
Sub Form_Unload (Cancel As Integer)
    Cancel = TRUE    ' Don't unload form, just hide it
    GotoForm.Hide
    CancelOp = TRUE ' Notify Cardfile form of cancellation
End Sub

Sub BTN_Cancel_Click ()
    TXT_SearchString.SetFocus
    GotoForm.Hide
    TXT_SearchString.Text = ""
    CancelOp = TRUE
End Sub

Sub BTN_OK_Click ()
    TXT_SearchString.SetFocus
    GotoForm.Hide
End Sub

Sub TXT_SearchString_KeyPress (KeyCode As Integer)
    If KeyCode = RETURN_KEY Then BTN_OK_Click
End Sub
```

The Find Form

The Find form is shown in Figure 5.10. This form is used as the basis for the dialog boxes that appear when either the Find command or Find Next command is selected from the Search menu. The user enters a text string in the text box control called **TXT_SearchString**. If a match is found, the file card appears.

FIGURE 5.10:

The Find form is used as the basis for the dialog boxes that appear when either the Find or Find Next command is selected

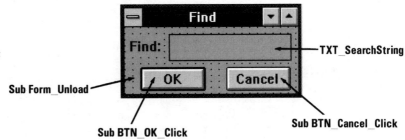

Sub Form_Unload

Sub BTN_OK_Click

TXT_SearchString

Sub BTN_Cancel_Click

The properties that give the Find form its size are set to the following dimensions:

Left: 3270

Top: 2595

Width: 2805

Height: 1410

The OK and Cancel command button controls are called **BTN_OK_Click** and **BTN_Cancel_Click,** respectively. The controls are each invoked with a click event:

```
Sub Form_Unload (Cancel As Integer)
    Cancel = TRUE    ' Don't unload form, just hide it
    FindForm.Hide
    CancelOp = TRUE ' Notify Cardfile form of cancellation
End Sub

Sub BTN_Cancel_Click ()
    TXT_SearchString.SetFocus
    FindForm.Hide
    TXT_SearchString.Text = ""
    CancelOp = TRUE
End Sub

Sub BTN_OK_Click ()
    TXT_SearchString.SetFocus
    FindForm.Hide
End Sub
```

```
Sub TXT_SearchString_KeyPress (KeyCode As Integer)
    If KeyCode = RETURN_KEY Then BTN_OK_Click
End Sub
```

The About Cardfile Form

The About Cardfile form is shown in Figure 5.11. This form simply displays information about the application. Each line of text is actually a label with a caption. The icon is called **PIC_Icon**, which is part of the extensive icon library that is available with Visual Basic.

The properties that give the About Cardfile form its size are set to the following dimensions:

Left: 1935

Top: 2160

Width: 5190

Height: 2565

The OK command button control is called **BTN_OK**. It is invoked with a click event. The other event procedures are as follows:

```
Sub BTN_OK_Click ()
    AboutBox.Hide
```

FIGURE 5.11:

The About Cardfile form

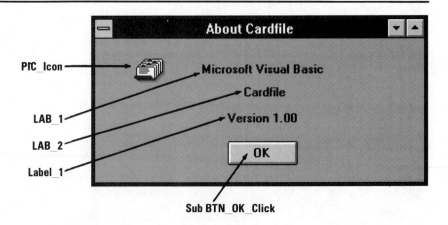

```
End Sub

Sub BTN_OK_KeyPress (KeyAscii As Integer)
    BTN_OK_Click
End Sub
```

Summary

As the developer, you need to put yourself in the place of users. Most of us learn best when we are actively engaged in tasks and are allowed to take risks. However, most of the time we only *react* to a computer in a highly structured way. Most applications present us with a limited set of options and prompt us for responses. Either we do something correctly or we don't continue.

In this way, the computer isn't letting us take risks and make mistakes. If we press the wrong key or make some other mistake, the computer either beeps at us or displays an error message. This puts the computer in the role of controlling an application, which goes against the Visual Basic philosophy. It is the user, not the computer, who initiates and *manipulates* all actions; users are always in control of an application.

The way in which you give users the feeling of controlling an application in Windows is to have them directly manipulate it, such as opening and closing an application; navigating within an application; and selecting objects. This control comes from using the mouse and the many other tools available in Visual Basic. Users should come to expect that their physical actions will get physical results.

When users select a menu, a list of commands pulls down; when they click on the minimize button, a window shrinks; when they click on text, they can highlight it and change its attributes. These are real results of their actions. Users should get immediate feedback from their work. This will help to continually reinforce the use of an application and give users a *reason* to use it.

The most direct way to control and manipulate an application is by using the mouse. When you create a new application and start with a blank page, the work area is visually and spatially oriented. The way everything is laid out—the title and menu bars, the control box, the maximize and minimze buttons, the scroll bars—always appears as a consistent and well-designed environment.

Visual Basic offers a rich environment in which you as the developer can make full use of its tools to create effective applications. At the same time, Visual Basic provides you with resources to create applications that feature a visually dynamic environment for users to complete tasks in, where they can follow nonlinear paths provided by objects. Users can interact directly with the screen, selecting objects and tasks they are interested in exploring by pointing at them.

Such a paradigm is very different from that of typing commands, which requires users to remember commands and type them in the computer. Therefore, a Visual Basic application practically eliminates the need for memorizing commands, which can be very disconcerting to users; the practice distracts them from tasks and focuses attention on the computer. When running an application, users should be able to select objects that embody commands and actions.

A visually-oriented environment like Windows is a difficult concept for many people to understand. In effect, Windows demands from users a willing suspension of disbelief before entering its graphical world. Likewise, as a developer you want users to embrace the premise of your application and to be drawn into the world you've created.

To aid in this acceptance, an application shouldn't bury anything deep in windows or dialog boxes that will be too difficult to uncover later. Everything should be presented on the screen right in front of users. The objects you include on screens should be there to help the user conceptualize tasks and navigate within the application. This will make an application much more engaging for users.

When an application isn't responding to user input or isn't behaving the way it should, the user needs to be told. Likewise, for users to feel in control of an application, they must be kept informed. While they're completing tasks, they need to be given feedback about their progress or on their status.

When you installed Visual Basic during the Setup program, you were frequently given information about choices you made and the percentage of the installation that had been completed. This was accomplished through dialog boxes. The messages were brief, direct, and expressed in a vocabulary that you could understand. Providing feedback on the screen in this manner is immediate and more effective than referring users to find the information somewhere else.

Using real-life metaphors that reflect common, everyday experiences is another way to help users feel in control of an application. Viewing an application in a window, opening an application, and closing an application are all familiar, concrete experiences.

Visual Basic's use of the *window* metaphor establishes a set of related actions and images that prepares users for all future tasks. By consistently utilizing one metaphor in this way, users become comfortable with using an application as the conveyor of information. It's this simple, yet powerful design principle that makes an application accessible to users and easy to use. It also aids in building a set of expectations that users can apply to using other Windows applications.

The standard elements found in one Windows application ensures consistency, ease of learning, and familiarity with other Windows applications. Users who are learning to use a new application build on prior experiences using the same Windows elements. Thus, users benefit from seeing consistency across different Windows applications.

Having learned a set of mouse conventions and navigational skills in Windows, users can transfer those skills to Visual Basic. Within an application, there should always be one coherent way for users to implement actions. Usually, this is accomplished with the mouse. Though some keyboard shortcuts may be provided, users should always be able to rely on familiar and straightforward ways to complete tasks. This puts the developer in the position of finding more commonly used solutions to the problems of designing an application. Consistency should be valued above cleverness.

Along these same lines, users will feel more comfortable using an application that remains understandable and familiar rather than unstable. For users to handle the complexity of a visually-oriented environment, they need some stable reference points.

To provide a *visual* sense of stability, a Visual Basic application provides a two-dimensional space on which objects are placed. It also defines a number of consistent graphic elements, such as the menu bar, the control box, and so on, to maintain the illusion of stability.

To provide a *conceptual* sense of stability, the interface provides a clear finite set of objects—text boxes, command buttons, icons, and graphics—and a clear set of actions to perform on those objects using a mouse. Even when particular actions are unavailable, they are not eliminated from a display, but are merely dimmed on menus.

It is the illusion of stability that is important, not stability in any strict physical sense. The application can—and should to some extent—change as users interact with it. But users should feel that they have a number of familiar "landmarks" to count on.

Users will make mistakes, so a Visual Basic application should forgive them. Most of the time their actions are reversible, but the developer must let users know about any that aren't. When tasks are presented clearly and feedback is appropriate and timely, however, learning is relatively error-free. Alert messages in dialog boxes should therefore be infrequent. If users are subjected to a barrage of alert messages, something is wrong with an application's design.

Visually confusing and unattractive applications detract from the effectiveness of the user-application interaction. An application depends on its visual appearance and users deserve and will appreciate an attractive environment. Consistent visual communication is very powerful in delivering complex messages and opportunities simply and directly. The purpose of visual consistency in an application is for the developer to construct a believable environment for users.

As much as possible, all commands, features, and parameters of an application—and all the important data—should appear as objects on its screens. Using objects gives the user options in choosing the appropriate one for a particular function. Manipulating objects gives users a sense of control over completing tasks.

In a Visual Basic application, everything users see and manipulate on the screen is graphical. The real point of an application's design, which comprises both graphics and text, is clear communication. I'll quote a familiar adage: "Good design must communicate, not just dazzle; it must inform, not just impress." If an application doesn't convey meaning effectively, users are lost in a graphical environment of random objects, and communication breaks down.

P A R T II

Programming in Visual Basic

Part II guides you through the steps of building an application called "Window$ to Wealth." As you learned from previous chapters, you need to begin formulating an application's purpose and objectives *before* building it. Furthermore, you need to decide *how* the program will achieve its objectives as a Windows application. Designing an application on paper is an appropriate first step, but actually programming an application, particularly a Windows application, is different because of the design issues involved.

The purpose of Window$ to Wealth is to help the user identify and set financial goals. The application's objectives are to guide the user through the steps of creating a personal financial statement and cash flow statement, and to demonstrate how the user can track particular investments. Terms like *assets*, *liabilities*, *income*, and *investments* are defined in the context of producing a "personal financial profile."

The strength of any Windows application is judged on how well it presents information in graphical terms; that is, how effectively it communicates *visually* rather than *textually*. As a developer, you can spend a lot of time considering the needs of users and how to best format data on a screen. You have to constantly question whether an application is communicating its intended message.

Visual Basic offers you many methods and properties that you can use to format screen output to achieve desired effects. You should take advantage of these resources to create applications that not only look good, but also communicate a clear and cohesive message.

CHAPTER

SIX

Creating Controls
and Setting Their Properties

6

- Creating Several Forms for an Application

- Setting Properties for Controls

- Saving a Project

The purpose of the *Window$ to Wealth* application is to help the user identify and set financial goals. As the saying goes, "It's not what you make that counts. It's what you save." The application's objectives are to guide the user through the steps of creating a personal financial statement and cash flow statement, and to demonstrate how the user can track particular investments. Terms like *assets, liabilities, income,* and *investments* are defined in the context of producing a "personal financial profile."

Window$ to Wealth may not make the user rich, but it will help the person set goals and plan for his or her financial future. After guiding a person through the process of figuring out just what he or she is worth, the results may be sobering. Furthermore, the process should help the user gain some insight into his or her financial priorities. Because the application identifies a person's assets and liabilities, the user can begin to make more informed decisions about future expenditures. Remember: if you don't have it, don't spend it!

As I stated in the previous chapter, you need to begin formulating an application's purpose and objectives *before* building it. Furthermore, you need to decide *how* the program will achieve its objectives as a Windows application. Designing an application on paper is an appropriate first step, but actually programming an application, particularly a Windows application, is different because of the design issues involved.

You might find it easier to create the controls on all forms first and then set the controls' properties once you've positioned them on the form. The coordinates you enter may differ, depending on your monitor. All the controls that comprise the menus will be discussed in a later chapter.

The Menu Form

The Menu form is shown in Figure 6.1. This form is the first form in the application, although it's not the "startup" form. In a later chapter, you will create a startup form that uses several of Windows' graphical features to create a dynamic effect.

There are four command buttons on the Menu form from which the user can choose where to navigate in the application: Personal Financial Statement, Cash Flow, Daily Stock Record, and Weekly Investment Tracker. You should make the effort to create the following forms and controls. All of the controls' properties are given, so you don't have any excuse!

FIGURE 6.1:

The Menu form. This is the first form in the application, from which the user decides which form to go to next.

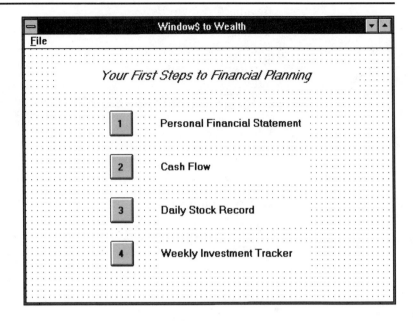

To create the Menu form, load Visual Basic and work on the default new form, Form1. Or select New Form from the File menu to bring up a new, blank form onscreen.

The form's properties are:

Caption: Window$ to Wealth

Left: 810

Top: 900

Width: 8010

Height: 5595

Command Buttons

The command buttons enable the user to navigate to other forms by invoking a particular control's click event. Their properties are:

Caption: 1

CtlName: Command1

Left: 1800

Top: 1200

Width: 495

Height: 495

TabIndex: 0

Caption: 2

CtlName: Command2

Left: 1800

Top: 2040

Width: 495

Height: 495

Caption: 3

CtlName: Command3

Left: 1800

Top: 2880

Width: 495

Height: 495

Caption: 4

CtlName: Command4

Left: 1800

Top: 3720

Width: 495

Height: 495

> **NOTE**
>
> The TabIndex property for the Command1 control has been set to 0, but the other controls do not have this property set. By setting the TabIndex property for this control to 0, the control will always have the focus each time the form is displayed. Focus is discussed in Chapter 8.

Labels

The largest label on the Menu form is used to present a "subtitle" for the form. Its properties are:

Caption: Your First Steps to Financial Planning

CtlName: SubTitle

Alignment: Center

FontSize: 12

FontItalic: True

FontBold: True

Left: 720

Top: 360

Width: 6375

Height: 375

ForeColor: &H00800000& (Blue)

The other labels are used to identify the names of each of the other forms that are accessed when the user clicks on the particular command button. Their properties are:

Caption: Personal Financial Statement

CtlName: Label1

FontSize: 9.75

Left: 2880

Top: 1320

Width: 3135

Height: 375

Caption: Cash Flow
CtlName: Label2
FontSize: 9.75
Left: 2880
Top: 2160
Width: 3135
Height: 375

Caption: Daily Stock Record
CtlName: Label3
FontSize: 9.75
Left: 2880
Top: 3000
Width: 3135
Height: 375

Caption: Weekly Investment Tracker
CtlName: Label4
FontSize: 9.75
Left: 2880
Top: 3840
Width: 3135
Height: 375

After you finish building the form, save it:

1. Select Save File from the File menu.

2. Save the form under the name **Menu**.

3. Select Save Project.

4. Save the project under the name **Wealth**.

The Personal Financial Statement Form

The Personal Financial Statement form, shown in Figure 6.2, is designed to help the user identify assets and liabilities. The form tallies values in both the Current Value and Amount columns as the user inputs values, simultaneously calculates and displays the sum of the values in the Total Assets and Total Liabilities text boxes, and calculates and displays the user's total net worth (Total Assets – Total Liabilities) in the Net Worth text box.

To create the Personal Financial Statement form, follow these steps:

1. Double-click on the Menu form's control box to close the form.

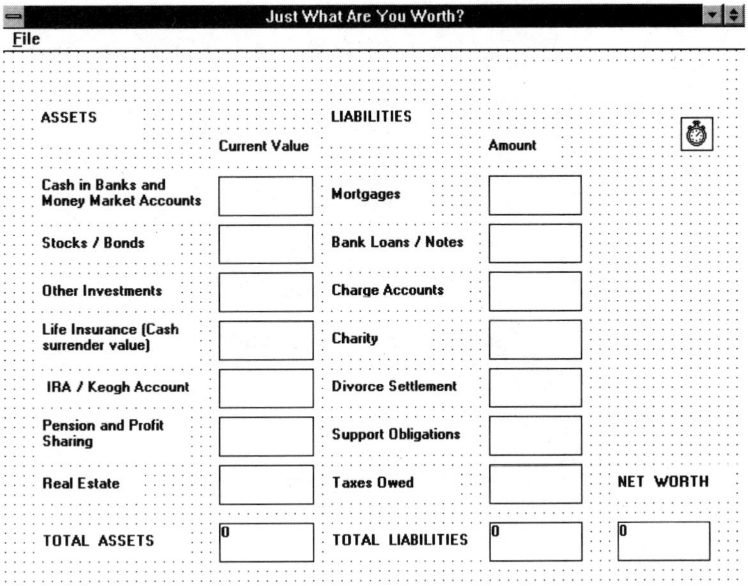

FIGURE 6.2:

The Personal Financial Statement form. Here the user enters assets and liabilities and calculates net worth.

2. Select New Form from the File menu.

3. Create the controls, which you will do in the next section.

When the form is loaded, as shown in Figure 6.2, the window is maximized. The properties for the form are:

Caption: Just What Are You Worth?

WindowState: Maximized

Labels

The labels help to introduce the user to accounting terms that are used to create a financial statement. The labels' properties are:

Caption: ASSETS
CtlName: Label1

Caption: Current Value
CtlName: Label2

Caption: Cash in Banks and Money Market Accounts
CtlName: Label3

Caption: Stocks/Bonds
CtlName: Label4

Caption: Other Investments
CtlName: Label5

Caption: Life Insurance (Cash surrender value)
CtlName: Label6

Caption: IRA/Keogh Account
CtlName: Label7

Caption: Pension and Profit Sharing
Ctlname: Label8

Caption: Real Estate
CtlName: Label9

Caption: TOTAL ASSETS
CtlName: Label10

Caption: LIABILITIES
CtlName: Label11

Caption: Amount
CtlName: Label12

Caption: Mortgages
CtlName: Label13

Caption: Bank Loans/Notes
CtlName: Label14

Caption: Charge Accounts
CtlName: Label15

Caption: Charity

CtlName: Label16

Caption: Divorce Settlement

CtlName: Label17

Caption: Support Obligations

CtlName: Label18

Caption: Taxes Owed

CtlName: Label19

Caption: TOTAL LIABILITIES

CtlName: Label20

Caption: NET WORTH

CtlName: Label21

Caption: (blank)

CtlName: DayAndTime

Left: 6360

Top: 240

Width: 2895

Height: 375

Alignment: Right Justify

NOTE The label control called DayAndTime is left blank; that is, its Caption property is blank. The current date is displayed in the label when the event for the Timer control, DayTime, is invoked.

Text Boxes

The Personal Financial Statement form uses two control arrays. The text boxes in the Current Value column comprise the control array, Value. The text boxes in the Amount column comprise the control array, Amount. A control array is a convenient and efficent method of setting properties and writing code for similar controls that serve the same function. In the case of both arrays, the text boxes accept user input, which is summed by the application. The totals are displayed in the text boxes at the bottom of each column.

All of the seven text boxes in the Value column have each of their CtlName properties set to Value and their Index properties set to 0–6 (0, 1, 2, 3, 4, 5, 6), respectively; the text boxes in the Amount column have each of their CtlName properties set to Amount and their Index properties set to 0–6, also. The properties for the text boxes are:

CtlName: Value

Index: 0–6 (Control Array)

Text: (blank)

CtlName: Amount

Index: 0–6 (Control Array)

Text: (blank)

CtlName: TotalAssets

Text: 0

CtlName: TotalLiabilities

Text: 0

CtlName: NetWorth

Text: 0

Timer

The event for the Timer control is invoked when the form is loaded. The event procedure displays the current date in the label; the label's Caption property is blank. The Timer's CtlName property is set to DayTime.

To save the form, follow these steps:

1. Select Save File from the File menu

2. Save the form under the name **Personal**.

3. Select Save Project to save the current changes you've made to the project.

The Cash Flow Form

The Cash Flow form is shown in Figure 6.3. The form helps the user to identify all sources of income for last year and to estimate all sources of income for next year.

To create the Cash Flow form, follow these steps:

1. Close the Personal Financial Statement form.

2. Select New Form from the File menu.

Like the Personal Financial Statement form, the window should be maximized when the form is loaded. The form's properties are:

Caption: Cash Flow

WindowState: Maximized

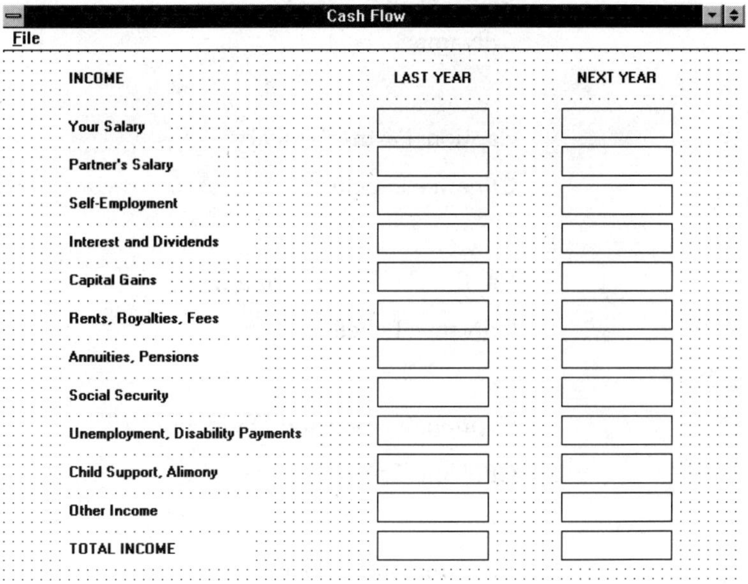

FIGURE 6.3:

The Cash Flow form. Here the user enters last year's income and estimates next year's income.

Labels

The labels for the Cash Flow form serve to identify the terms that are commonly used to designate sources of income. The label's properties are:

Caption: INCOME

CtlName: Label1

Caption: LAST YEAR

CtlName: Label2

Caption: NEXT YEAR

CtlName: Label3

Caption: Your Salary
CtlName: Label4

Caption: Partner's Salary
Ctlname: Label5

Caption: Self-Employment
CtlName: Label6

Caption: Interest and Dividends
CtlName: Label7

Caption: Capital Gains
CtlName: Label8

Caption: Rent, Royalties, Fees
CtlName: Label9

Caption: Annuities, Pensions
CtlName: Label10

Caption: Social Security
CtlName: Label11

Caption: Unemployment, Disability Payments
CtlName: Label12

Caption: Child Support, Alimony

CtlName: Label13

Caption: Other Income

CtlName: Label14

Caption: TOTAL INCOME

CtlName: Label15

Text Boxes

The Cash Flow form also uses two control arrays in the same manner as the Personal Financial Statement form. The text boxes in the Last Year column form the control array, LastYear. The text boxes in the Next Year column form the control array, Next Year:

CtlName: LastYear

Index 0–10 (Control Array)

Text: (blank)

CtlName: NextYear

Index: 0–10 (Control Array)

Text: (blank)

To save the form, follow these steps:

1. Select Save File from the File menu.

2. Save the form under the name **Cash**.

3. Select Save Project to save the current changes you've made to the project.

The Daily Stock Record Form

The Daily Stock Record form allows the user to keep a record of a specific stock, as shown in Figure 6.4. It could also be modified to allow the user to keep a record of other investments, such as mutual funds or bonds.

To create the Daily Stock Record form, follow these steps:

1. Close the Cash Flow form.

2. Select New Form from the File Menu.

The form is essentially a database record and saves each record to a random-access file. When the user clicks on the Save button, the name of each stock is automatically added to the combo box control. When the user clicks on the arrow to the right of the box, a drop-down list displays all of the names in the database. After the user selects a stock, the form displays a record of the information that was last saved, including the date on which it was saved.

FIGURE 6.4:
The Daily Stock Record form. Here the user can keep daily track of a specific stock or other investment, such as mutual fund or bond.

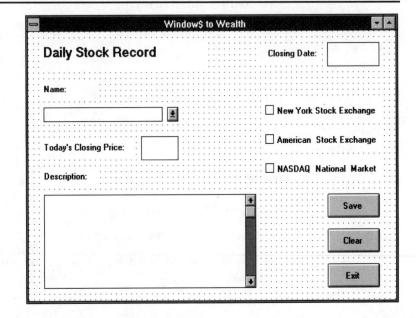

The form's properties are:

Caption: Window$ to Wealth

Left: 510

Top: 645

Width: 8670

Height: 5955

Labels

The labels correspond to the names of the fields in the database, which are defined in the form's data structure. (Creating a data structure will be discussed in the next chapter.) The properties for the labels are:

Caption: Daily Stock Record

CtlName: Label1

FontSize: 13.5

FontBold: True

Left: 360

Top: 240

Width: 4215

Height: 495

Caption: Closing Date:

CtlName: Label2

Left: 6600

Top: 360

Width: 1815

Height: 495

Caption: Name:

CtlName: Label3

Caption: Today's Closing Price:

CtlName: Label4

Caption: Description:

CtlName: Label5

Text Boxes

The text boxes are used as fields in which the user inputs both data and string values. Their values are:

CtlName: ClosePrice

Text: (blank)

Left: 2640

Top: 2160

Width: 855

Height: 495

CtlName: Description

Text: (blank)

ScrollBars: Vertical

MultiLine: True

Left: 360

Top: 3240

Width: 4935

Height: 1935

CtlName: CloseDate

Text: (blank)

FontSize: 9.75

Top: 6960

Left: 240

Width: 1215

Height: 495

Combo Box

To create a combo box, double-click on the Combo Box tool. The combo box is an interesting control because items are added to it each time a record is saved. The name of each stock appears on the control's drop-down list. Its properties are:

CtlName: StockName

Text: (blank)

Check Boxes

The check boxes are used to identify the type of stock in the record. The check box properties are:

CtlName: NewYork

Caption: New York Stock Exchange

Enabled: True

CtlName: American

Caption: American Stock Exchange

Enabled: True

CtlName: NASDAQ

Caption: NASDAQ National Market

Enabled: True

Command Buttons

When a command button is clicked, it invokes a specific event procedure to either save a record, clear a record, or exit the form and return to the menu. Their properties are:

Caption: Save

CtlName: SaveForm

Caption: Clear

CtlName: ClearForm

Caption: Exit

CtlName: ExitForm

To save the form, follow these steps:

1. Select Save File from the File menu.

2. Save the form under the name **Stock**.

3. Select Save Project to save the current changes you've made to the project.

The Weekly Investment Tracker Form

The Weekly Investment Tracker form is shown in Figure 6.5. This form records the closing prices for a stock over a five-day period (Monday to Friday). The form is a database that saves each of its records to a sequential file because of the sequential dates.

The Weekly Investment Tracker
form. Here the user records the
closing prices for a stock over
a five-day period. Each record is
saved to a file.

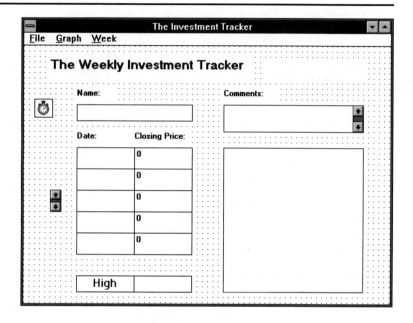

To create the Weekly Investment Tracker form, follow these steps:

1. Close the Daily Stock Record form.
2. Select New Form from the File menu.

After you have finished the program, when you load the form the current dates for
the five-day period are automatically displayed in a series of text boxes (a control
array). As the user inputs a specific day's closing price in each of the text boxes that
form another control array, the form displays the highest closing price for the five-
day period in a label at the bottom of the Closing Price column. A picture box also
displays a graph that shows the closing prices for each day of the five-day period.

The form's properties are:

Caption: The Investment Tracker

Left: 615

Top: 360

Width: 8550

Height: 6480

Labels

The labels identify the fields that are defined in the form's data structure (except for the label that identifies the name of the form itself). The label's properties are:

Caption: The Weekly Investment Tracker

CtlName: Label1

FontSize: 13.5

Left: 600

Top: 240

Width: 4575

Height: 495

Caption: (blank)

CtlName: DateViewed

Left: 5520

Top: 360

Width: 2295

Height: 375

Caption: Name

CtlName: Label3

Caption: Comments

CtlName: Label4

Caption: Date

CtlName: Label5

Caption: Closing Price

CtlName: Label6

Caption: High

CtlName: Label7

Alignment: Center

BorderStyle: Fixed Single

FontSize: 12

Caption: (blank)

CtlName: Total

Alignment: Center

BorderStyle: Fixed Single

FontSize: 12

Text Boxes

The text boxes accept user input of closing price information and display output of the current five-day period.

Two numeric arrays, StockOnScreen and StockOnDisk, which are declared in the form-level declarations section, are used to make sure that the current five-day period that is shown onscreen is also saved to disk. The series of text boxes on the left is the control array, WkDate. This control array displays the dates for the current five-day period. ClosePrice, the control array on the right, is a series of text boxes that displays the stock's closing price for each day of the five-day period.

This information is used to generate another chart that tracks a particular stock's performance over a ten-week period. The information can help the user make informed decisions about the investment's performance.

The properties for the text boxes are:

CtlName: InvestName

Text: (blank)

Left: 1200

Top: 1320

Width: 2655

Height: 375

CtlName: Comments

Text: (blank)

MultiLine: True

ScrollBar: Vertical

Left: 4560

Top: 130

Width: 3255

Height: 615

CtlName: WkDate:

Text: (blank)

Index: 0–4

CtlName: ClosePrice

Text: 0

Index: 0–4

Timer

The Timer control's event procedure is invoked when the form is loaded. The event procedure displays the current date in a label, which is also reflected in the stock graph. The Timer's CtlName property is DayTimer.

Vertical Scroll Bar

To create the Vertical Scroll Bar control, double-click on the Vertical Scroll Bar tool. This control enables the user to scroll forward or backward through a five-day period from the current date. When a user clicks on the up or down arrow, the new dates are displayed in the text boxes that form the WkDate control array; the corresponding closing prices are displayed in the text boxes that comprise the Close-Price control array. The control's CtlName property is ScrollWeek.

Picture Box

To create the Picture Box control, double-click on the Picture Box tool. The Picture Box control displays a graph called StockGraph. This graph shows the closing price for each day of the five-day period, reflecting the highest closing price for the period. The graph displays a vertical bar for each day that is proportional to the closing price. Its properties are:

CtlName: StockGraph

Left: 4560

Top: 2280

Width: 3255

Height: 3255

To save the form, follow these steps:

1. Select Save File from the File menu.

2. Save the form under the name **Tracker**.

3. Select Save Project to save the current changes you've made to the project.

Summary

Creating an interface is relatively easy with Visual Basic. By creating all the controls on a form first and then setting their properties, you can save yourself a lot of time. In this chapter, you created five forms: Menu, Personal Financial Statement, Cash Flow, Daily Stock Record, and Weekly Investment Tracker.

Attaching Code and Designating Events

- Using Random-Access and Sequential Modes

- Defining Data Types

- Identifying the Elements of a Record Structure

7

Now that you've created the controls for all the forms of Window$ to Wealth, it's time to write the functional code for the events and general procedures. You will create the menus that appear on some of the forms in Chapter 10. For now, follow along and enter the code as it appears on the following pages.

Global Module Declarations

The application's global module contains special declarations that are recognized by all of the forms that comprise the Window$ to Wealth application. A global module cannot contain procedures or functions.

In addition to declarations, the global module also contains definitions for several record types. **PersonalRecordType** identifies the two fields of a record stored in the database for the Personal Financial Statement form:

```
'WEALTH.GLO
'Global Declarations

'The record structure for Personal Financial Statement
Type PersonalRecordType
     ValueField As Double
     AmountField As Double
End Type
```

A random-access file is organized into individual units of data called *records*. Each record in a random-access file contains a structured group of data items known as a *field*. All the records in a given file have the same fixed length. (This is not true of other programming languages, which can have dynamic data structures of variable length.) Because of this characteristic, Visual Basic provides direct access to any record in a file. A record is identified by its *record number*, which is an integer ranging from 1 up to the number of records currently stored in the file.

Visual Basic's user-defined structure, also known as a record structure, is the ideal data structure to use in the definition and creation of a random-access file. A Type statement defines a record structure.

InvestRecType contains the four fields of a record stored in the database for the Weekly Investment Tracker form:

```
'The Tracker record type.
Type InvestRecType
```

```
        InvestNameField As String * 20
        CommentsField As String * 50
        WkDateField As Double
        ClosePriceField As Long
End Type
```

IndexType defines the two key fields of the index structure: the name field and the record number:

```
'The index record type.
Type IndexType
        InvestRef As String * 30
        RecNum As Integer
End Type
```

StockRecordType identifies the seven fields of a record stored in the database for the Daily Stock Record form:

```
'The record type definition for a stock record:
Type StockRecordType
        StockName As String * 20
        ClosePrice As Long
        Description As String * 125
        CloseDate As Double
        NewYork As Integer
        American As Integer
        NASDAQ As Integer
End Type
```

StockIndexType defines the two key fields of the index structure for this database: the stock name and the record number:

```
Type StockIndexType
        StockRef As String * 20
        RecNo As Integer
End Type
```

The remaining declarations are global constants:

```
'The path name for storing records.
Global Const PathName$ = "C:\Statemnt"

'The extension name for Window$ to Wealth files.
Global Const ExtName$ = "DAT"
Global Const TRUE = -1
```

```
Global Const FALSE = 0
Global Const MODAL = 1

'End of global declarations
```

Module-Level Declarations and Procedures

There is only one module-level procedure that has been written for the application. The **Sub ExitApplication** general procedure is called by two separate event procedures when the user invokes a click event by selecting an Exit command from two different menus:

```
Sub ExitApplication ()
    Msg$ = "Do you want to exit Window$ to Wealth?"
    If MsgBox(Msg$, 65, "Quit") = 1 Then
            End
    End If
End Sub
```

Obviously, it's more convenient (and less time-consuming) to write one general procedure that can be recognized by many event procedures than to write many separate event procedures that execute the same statements.

The Menu Form

The Menu form, as shown in Figure 7.1, contains the fewest number of event and general procedures of all the forms in the application. The form's interface consists of four command buttons and five labels.

You will notice on the figure that the form has a menu bar. The **Sub ExitCom_Click** event procedure is attached to the form's File menu. The event procedure calls the general procedure **ExitApplication**, which was just listed above:

```
Sub ExitCom_Click ()
    ExitApplication
End Sub
```

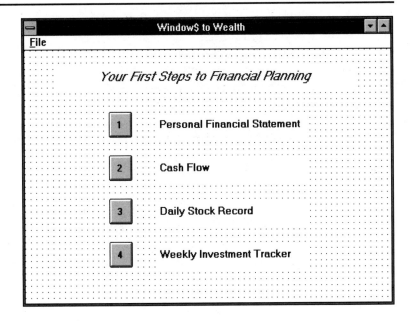

FIGURE 7.1:

The Menu form

Each of the four command buttons invokes an event procedure that *hides* the current form, which in this case is the Menu form, and *shows* the particular form that the user has selected:

```
Sub Command1_Click ()
     Form1.Hide
     Form2.Show
End Sub

Sub Command2_Click ()
     Form1.Hide
     Form3.Show
End Sub

Sub Command3_Click ()
     Form1.Hide
     Form4.Show
End Sub
```

```
Sub Command4_Click ()
     Form1.Hide
     Form5.Show
End Sub
```

The Personal
Financial Statement Form

The Personal Financial Statement form enables the user to calculate current assets and liabilities and then display his or her current net worth. After the user inputs all of the values, the contents of the form can be saved and printed. (I discuss formatting data to a printer in Chapter 12.)

Form-Level Declarations

All local variables and constants are contained in the Declarations section of the form's general procedure:

```
'PERSONAL.FRM
'Declarations
     Const False = 0
     Const True = Not False

     Dim CurIndex As Integer
     Dim CrLf$
     Dim Today As Long
```

In the beginning of this chapter, I described how the `Type PersonalRecordType` statement in the application's global module defined the form's record structure. The `Dim PersonalRecord As PersonalRecordType` statement below creates a corresponding record variable. As I stated earlier, a user-defined *type* is a compound structure representing multiple data fields. This data type is often referred to as a *record structure*. Two steps are necessary for defining a record variable. The first is to write a Type definition that outlines the field structure of the record type, which you saw in the global module. The second component is a Dim statement that declares a variable belonging to the defined record type. The declaration for a record variable may appear in a global module, the declaration section of a form or module, or a procedure, depending on the scope you want to establish for the variable. To declare a variable representing a single record, the DIM syntax is:

```
'The PersonalRecord structure.
'(The TYPE statement for this structure is in the
'global declarations module, WealthGlob.)

Dim PersonalRecord As PersonalRecordType      'A file record.
```

Event and General Procedures

The **Sub Form_Load** event procedure initializes the Personal Financial Statement form (shown on Figure 7.2) by setting the WindowState property of the form to maximized, which means that the window will appear maximized when the form is loaded. The event procedure also records today's date, which appears in the Day-AndTime label, and makes sure that the directory exists for storing the data on the form:

```
Sub Form_Load ()

       'When form is first loaded, initialize
       'the personal financial statement.
       Dim i%
       Const MAX = 2

       Form2.WindowState = MAX
       CrLf$ = Chr$(13) + Chr$(10)
```

> **NOTE**
>
> The **Int** function below converts any numeric expression to the largest integer that is less than or equal to the expression. The **Now** function returns a serial number that represents the current date and time according to the setting of your computer's system date and time. In the statement **Today = Int(Now),** The variable *Today* is assigned the current serial date value after the *Int* function converts the number returned by the *Now* function.

```
'Record today's serial date value.
Today = Int(Now)

'Make sure the directory exists for storing the
'Personal Financial Statement. If not, create it.
SearchForPath
DayTime_Timer

CurIndex = 0
ClearRecord_Click
```

```
End Sub
```

The **Sub DayTime_Timer** event procedure displays the current date in the Day-
AndTime label:

```
Sub DayTime_Timer ()

    'Display today's date at the top of the
    'Personal Financial statement.
    DayAndTime.Caption = Format$(Today, "mmmm dd, yyyy")

End Sub
```

> **NOTE**
>
> In the statement **DayAndTime.Caption = Format$(Today, " mmmm dd, yyyy")** above, the Format$ function converts the number assigned to the variable *Today* and formats it according to the instructions contained in the expression *" mmmm dd yyyy"*. The symbol *" mmmm"* displays the month as a full month name, which would be January to December. The symbol *"dd"* displays the day as a number from 01 to 31 (with a leading 0 for any one-digit number). The symbol *" yyyy"* displays the year as a four-digit number. In this example, the statement would display the date December 17, 1992 in the control *DayAndTime*.

The following two event procedures, **Sub Value_Change** and **Sub Amount- _Change,** have the same Index As Integer argument to indicate that they are both control arrays. Each one of the text boxes in both control arrays has its Index property set to a consecutive number, 0–6. Each event procedure calls a different general procedure that calculates and displays a value in a text box at the bottom of each column:

```
Sub Value_Change (Index As Integer)
    UpdateTotalAssets
End Sub

Sub Amount_Change (Index As Integer)
    UpdateTotalLiabilities
End Sub
```

The **Sub UpdateTotalAssets** general procedure keeps a "running total" by summing the values that the user inputs into each of the text boxes that comprise the Value control array. At the same time, the procedure displays the value of the total in the text box at the bottom of the Current Value column:

```
Sub UpdateTotalAssets ()

    For i% = 0 To 6
        CurrentValue = CurrentValue + Val(Value(i%).Text)
        TotalAssets.Text = Str$(CurrentValue)
    Next i%

End Sub
```

The **Sub UpdateTotalLiabilities** general procedure also keeps a running total of the values input into the text boxes that form the Amount control array. As the total is displayed in the text box at the bottom of the Amount column, the procedure also calculates and displays the current net worth by calling the function CalcNetWorth:

```
Sub UpdateTotalLiabilities ()

Dim Tot As Double, LineTot As Double, i%

For i% = 0 To 6
CurrentAmount = CurrentAmount + Val(Amount(i%).Text)
TotalLiabilities.Text = Str$(CurrentAmount)
Next i%
'Calculate total net worth.
LineTot = CalcNetWorth(i%)

'Display net worth value.
NetWorth.Text = Str$(LineTot)
Tot = Tot + LineTot

End Sub

Function CalcNetWorth (TotalValue As Integer) As Double

Dim T1 As Double, T2 As Double

T1 = Val(TotalAssets.Text)
T2 = Val(TotalLiabilities.Text)

CalcNetWorth = T1 - T2

End Function
```

The **Sub ClearRecord_Click** event procedure clears the values from all the text boxes and reinitializes the form:

```
Sub ClearRecord_Click ()

    'Clears all lines of the Personal Financial
    'statement.

    Dim i%

    For i% = 6 To 0 Step -1
        Value(i%).Text = ""
```

```
        Amount(i%).Text = ""
    Next i%

    TotalAssets.Text = "0"
    TotalLiabilities.Text = "0"
    NetWorth.Text = "0"

    If CurIndex <> 0 Then
        CurIndex = 0
        Value(CurIndex).SetFocus
    End If

End Sub
```

The **Sub SearchForPath** general procedure is called by the Form_Load event procedure. It searches for the directory in which the Personal Financial Statement files are to be stored. If the directory doesn't exist, the procedure creates the directory on Drive C:

```
Sub SearchForPath ()

    'Search for the directory in which Personal Financial
    'statement files are to be stored. Create the
    'directory (on drive C) if it does not exist yet.

    'Note: PathName$ is a global constant

    Dim CDir$
    'Record the current directory.
    CDir$ = CurDir$("C")

    'Set up an error-handling mode.
    On Error Resume Next

    'Attempt to change to the target directory.
    ChDir PathName$

    'If the directory doesn't exist, create it.
    MkDir PathName$

    'Restore the original directory.
    ChDir CDir$

End Sub
```

The **Function StateName$** function creates a file name from the current serial date. The TargetDate As Long argument returns a value to the SaveRecord_Click event procedure which calls it:

```
Function StatementName$ (TargetDate As Long)

    'Create a file name from a serial date.
    'Note: PathName$ and ExtName$ are global constants.
    Dim TempName$
    TempName$ = PathName$ + "\"
    TempName$ = TempName$ + Format$(TargetDate, "mm-dd-yy")
    StatementName$ = TempName$ + "." + ExtName$

End Function
```

The **SaveRecord_Click** event procedure saves the current record as a random-access file. The procedure uses the current date as the file's name by calling the StatementName$ function, which returns a serial date value:

```
Sub SaveRecord_Click ()

    'Save the current Personal Financial statement as
    'a random-access disk file. If a statement file
    'already exists for today, give the user the
    'option of appending to the existing file or
    'overwriting the existing file.

    Const YesNoCancel = 3
    Const Yes = 6
    Const No = 7
    Dim CurFile$, Answer As Integer
    Dim RecCount As Integer, NewRec As Integer

    'Create the file name, open the file and count its records.
    CurFile$ = StatementName$(Today)
    Open CurFile$ For Random As #1 Len = Len(PersonalRecord)
        RecCount = LOF(1) / Len(PersonalRecord)
        NewRec = 1

    'If any records exist, get the user's instructions.
    If RecCount > 0 Then
        Msg$ = "A financial statement file" + CrLf$
        Msg$ = Msg$ + "already exists for today. " + CrLf$ + CrLf$
        Msg$ = Msg$ + "Append to this file?" + CrLf$ + CrLf$
```

```
Msg$ = Msg$ + "    Click Yes to Append" + CrLf$
Msg$ = Msg$ + "    Click No to Replace"
Answer = MsgBox(Msg$, YesNoCancel, "Save Personal Financial
      Statement")

If Answer = Yes Then
      'Prepare to append to the end of the file.
      NewRec = RecCount + 1
ElseIf Answer = No Then

      'Erase the old file and create a new one.
      Close #1
      Kill CurFile$
      Open CurFile$ For Random As #1 Len = Len(PersonalRecord)
Else

      'Cancel the save operation.
      Close #1
      Exit Sub

End If
End If

'Save the valid record to the file
For i% = 0 To 6
      Put #1, NewRec, PersonalRecord
      NewRec = NewRec + 1
Next i%
Close #1

End Sub
```

The following form of the Open statement opens a file in the random-access mode:

```
Open CurFile$ For Random As #1 Len = Len(PersonalRecord)
```

In this syntax, *CurFile$* is the name of the file on disk, *#1* is an integer that identifies the open file in the subsequent I/O statements, and *PersonalRecord* is the name of the variable defined to represent records as they are read from the file or written to the file. This form of the Len clause defines the file's fixed record length to be equal to the length of the record variable. Visual Basic's Len function supplies the length, in bytes, of *PersonalRecord*. Once open, a random-access file is available for both reading and writing. At the outset a program typically needs to find out the number of records currently stored in the file. The following formula uses Visual Basic's LOF ("length of file") function to compute the record count:

```
RecCount = LOF(1) / Len(PersonalRecord)
```

The LOF function takes an integer argument, which is the file number of the open file, and returns the length, in bytes, of the file. Dividing this value by the length of the record structure gives the number of records in the file.

The Put statement writes a single record to a specified position in the open file:

```
Put #1, NewRec, PersonalRecord
```

If *NewRec* is equal to *RecCount* + 1, the Put statement appends a new record to the end of the open file. On the other hand, if *NewRec* is in the range from 1 to *RecCount*, Put writes the current contents of *PersonalRecord* over an existing record.

The **Sub ExitRecord_Click** event procedure exits the current form and returns to the Menu form:

```
Sub ExitRecord_Click ()
      Form2.Hide
      Form1.Show
End Sub
```

The Cash Flow Form

The Cash Flow form is structured like the Personal Financial Statement form, as shown in Figure 7.3. Remember to declare the constant MAX =2 in the declarations section of the form's general procedure. You also need to include the statement Form3.WindowState = MAX in the form's **Sub Form_Load** event procedure. This statement will set the form's WindowState property to maximized and cause the window to appear at full-screen size when the Cash Flow form is loaded.

Because all of the code for this form is similar to the Personal Financial Statement form mentioned above, I won't include it. If you want to write the functional code for the form's control arrays and the menu commands, refer to the code that I have included for the other form.

FIGURE 7.3:
The Cash Flow form

FIGURE 7.3:
The Cash Flow form

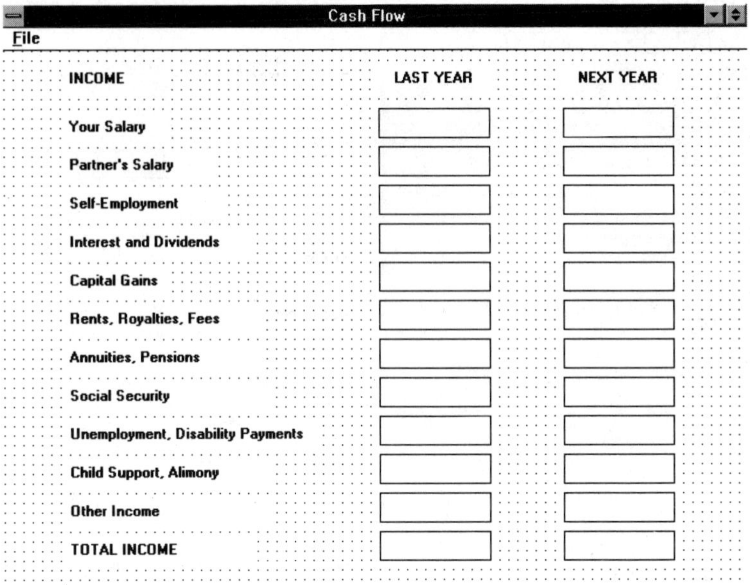

The Daily Stock Record Form

The Daily Stock Record form, as shown in Figure 7.4, organizes its records into a random-access file.

Form-Level Declarations

Among the constants and variables that are declared, the constant MaxRecords is set to the integer value of 200 to indicate the maximum number of records that the database can contain:

```
Const DateFormat = "d-mmm-yy"
Const StockDataBase = "C:\Stocks.DB"
Const MaxRecords = 200

'The StockRecord and StockList structures.
'(The TYPE statements for these structures are in the
'global declarations module, Wealth.Glo.)
Dim StockRecord As StockRecordType
```

FIGURE 7.4:

The Daily Stock Record form

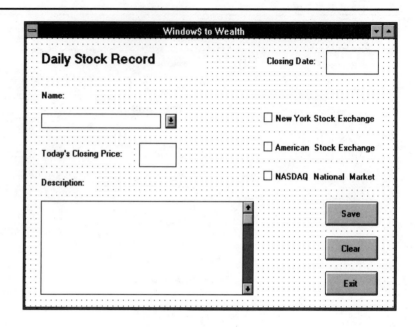

```
Dim StockList(MaxRecords) As StockIndexType
Dim RecCount As Integer
```

An array of records is defined, in which each array element represents a separate record. In this case, the Dim syntax is

```
Dim StockList(MaxRecords) As StockIndexType
```

for a static one-dimensional array.

Events and General Procedures

The **Sub Form_Load** event procedure initializes the closing date field and displays the current date by calling the InitializeDate general procedure. The form opens the database in which the records are stored, reads the existing records sequentially, and then sorts the index alphabetically by calling the SortStockList general procedure:

```
Sub Form_Load ()

    'When the form is first loaded, initialize
```

```
'the closing date field and its display.
InitializeDate

'Then open the stock database file and read
'the records sequentially.
Open StockDataBase For Random As #1 Len = Len(StockRecord)
RecCount = LOF(1) / Len(StockRecord)
```

> **NOTE**
>
> The **AddItem** method below simply adds an item to a list box or combo box at runtime. In the statement **StockName.AddItem StockRecord.StockName**, all the stock names in the database are displayed in the combo box control *StockName. StockName* has been defined as a field of the record *StockRecord.* When the user enters the name of a new stock and saves the record, the name is also added immediately to the combo box.

```
'Store the stock fields and the record number
'in the StockList index.
For i% = 1 To RecCount
    Get #1, i%, StockRecord
    StockName.AddItem StockRecord.StockName
    StockList(i%).StockRef = UCase$(StockRecord.StockName)
    StockList(i%).RecNo = i%
Next i%
Close #1

'Alphabetize the index.
SortStockList
```

```
End Sub
```

The **Get** statement reads a single record from a specified position in the open file:

```
Get #1, i%, StockRecord
```

The value of *#1* ranges from 1 up to the current *RecCount.* As a result of this statement, the entire record stored at the *#1* position in the file is assigned to the fields of *StockRecord.* A For loop is used to read a random-access file sequentially:

```
For i% = 1 To RecCount
    Get #1, i%, StockRecord
    StockName.AddItem StockRecord.StockName
    StockList(i%).StockRef = UCase$(StockRecord.StockName)
```

```
        StockList(i%).RecNo = i%
Next i%
```

The **UCase$** function above simply returns a string in which all the letters have been converted to uppercase. In the statement **StockList(i%).StockRef = UCase$(StockRecord.StockName)**, the names of all the stocks that appear in the combo box control StockName are converted to uppercase and assigned to eht StockList index file. If the file is called by a Prnt statemen, the names will appear formatted in uppercase letters.

The **Sub InitializeDate** general procedure sets the date field to the current date:

```
Sub InitializeDate ()

    'Initialize the date field to today's date.
    StockRecord.CloseDate = Now

     'Display the date in standard date format.
    CloseDate.Text = Format$(StockRecord.CloseDate, DateFormat)

End Sub
```

The **Sub SortStockList** general procedure builds the index by sorting the list of stocks alphabetically. The procedure uses a pair of nested For loops to compare the name of each stock in the index list with the name of each stock after it. Whenever two names are out of order, they are swapped. At the end of the looping, the names in the list are sorted in alphanumeric order:

```
Sub SortStockList ()

    'Alphabetize the database index.
    Dim TempStockRec As StockIndexType
    For i% = 1 To RecCount - 1
        For j% = i% + 1 To RecCount
            If StockList(i%).StockRef > StockList(j%).StockRef Then
                TempStockRec = StockList(i%)
                StockList(i%) = StockList(j%)
                StockList(j%) = TempStockRec
            End If
        Next j%
    Next i%
```

```
End Sub
```

The **Sub StockName_Click** event procedure displays the name of the stock that the user selects from the combo box control, and retrieves the stock's record:

```
Sub StockName_Click ()

    'Retrieve a stock name record when the user
    'selects a stock from the StockName combo box.
    GetRec% = SearchStockRecord%((StockName.Text))
    If GetRec% <> 0 Then
        Open StockDataBase For Random As #1 Len = Len(StockRecord)
        Get #1, GetRec%, StockRecord
        Close #1

        'Copy the fields of the stock record to the
        'appropriate controls on the input form.
        CloseDate.Text = Format$(StockRecord.CloseDate, DateFormat)
        ClosePrice.Text = Str$(StockRecord.ClosePrice)
        Description.Text = StockRecord.Description
        NewYork.Value = StockRecord.NewYork
        American.Value = StockRecord.American
        NASDAQ.Value = StockRecord.NASDAQ
    End If

End Sub
```

> **NOTE**
>
> The **Value** property simply determines the state of a control. In the example above, the three check boxes have been declared as fields in the database for the record *StockRecord*. By clicking one of the check boxes, you set its property to 1 for "on." When the check box is checked, it is designated as the current selection. When none of the check boxes is selected (that is, all are unchecked), their properties are set to 0 for "off," which is the default setting for a check box.

Visual Basic recognizes a special format for references to individual fields in a record variable. In this format, the record variable name (StockRecord) is followed by a period and the field name:

```
Format$(StockRecord.CloseDate, DateFormat)
```

```
Str$(StockRecord.ClosePrice)
StockRecord.Description
StockRecord.NewYork
StockRecord.American
StockRecord.NASDAQ
```

The **Function SearchStockRecord**% function searches for the name of a stock in the database index and returns the record number if the name is found. If the name isn't found, the function returns a value of 0:

```
Function SearchStockRecord% (InStockName$)

    'Search for a stock name in the database index
    StockFound% = 0
    StartPos% = 1
    EndPos% = RecCount

    Do While ((StockFound% = 0) And (StartPos% <= EndPos%))
        CenterPos% = (StartPos% + EndPos%) \ 2
        Select Case UCase$(InStockName$)
            Case StockList(CenterPos%).StockRef
                StockFound% = StockList(CenterPos%).RecNo
            Case Is > StockList(CenterPos%).StockRef
                StartPos% = CenterPos% + 1
            Case Else
                EndPos% = CenterPos% - 1
        End Select
    Loop

    'Return the record number if the address was found;
    'otherwise, return a value of zero.
    SearchStockRecord% = StockFound%

End Function
```

The **Sub ClearForm_Click** event procedure clears each field on the form and resets the focus to the StockName combo box control:

```
Sub ClearForm_Click ()

    'Clear all the string and numeric text boxes
    'and reinitialize the date field.
    StockName.Text = ""
    InitializeDate
    ClosePrice.Text = ""
    Description.Text = ""
```

```
      NewYork.Value = False
      American.Value = False
      NASDAQ.Value = False
      StockName.SetFocus

  End Sub
```

NOTE

The **SetFocus** method sets the focus to the specified control, which in the case above is the combo box *StockName*. When the user clicks the Clear command on the File menu, the data entered in all of the controls are cleared. The combo box is given the focus so the user can begin to input a new record by entering the name of a stock.

When the user enters the seven fields of the new stock record and then clicks the Save button, the **Sub SaveForm_Click** event procedure writes the record to the database. This procedure needs a way to distinguish between a new record that the user wants to append to the stock database and a revised record that the user wants to write over an existing record. To find out which of these is the case, the program searches through the index for the current StockName field. If the name already exists, the program assumes this is a revision; if not, this is a new record.

NOTE

The **LTrim$** function displays on the monitor screen an image of a string with its leftmost spaces removed. The **RTrim$** function has the opposite effect and displays a string with its rightmost spaces removed. In the statement **Stock$ = LTrim$(RTrim$(StockName.Text))** below, the string variable *Stock$* is assigned the name of the stock entered in the combo box control *StockName* after the left and right spaces have been stripped from the name. The *StockName* field is defined as a string of 20 characters in the database record. The **LTrim$** and **RTrim$** functions strip the unused characters (which include spaces) from the string before assigning the name to *Stock$*.

```
Sub SaveForm_Click ()

    'Save a new stock name in the database.
```

```
Dim Msg$, CurRec%, Stock$

Stock$ = LTrim$(RTrim$(StockName.Text))
If Stock$ = "" Then

    'Do not try to save without a stock field.
     Msg$ = "Stock record cannot be saved with a name."
    MsgBox Msg$, 48, "Save Stock Record"
    StockName.SetFocus

Else
    StockRecord.StockName = Stock$

    'Find out if this record exists already.
    CurRec% = SearchStockRecord%(StockRecord.StockName)

    'If not, create a new record.
    If CurRec% = 0 And RecCount < MaxRecords Then

        'First add the stock to the index.
        RecCount = RecCount + 1
        StockList(RecCount).StockRef = UCase$(StockRecord.StockName)
        StockList(RecCount).RecNo = RecCount
        SortStockList

        'Add the address to the combo box list.
        StockName.AddItem StockRecord.StockName
        CurRec% = RecCount

    ElseIf CurRec% = 0 And RecCount + MaxRecords Then

        'Display a message if the database is full,
        'and go no further with the Save operation.
        Msg$ = "The database has reached its maximum length. "
        Msg$ = Msg$ + "You cannot add this new record."
        MsgBox Msg$, 48, "Daily Stock Record"
        Exit Sub
    End If

    'Read the fields that have not already been read.
    StockRecord.Description = Description.Text
    StockRecord.NewYork = NewYork.Value
    StockRecord.American = American.Value
    StockRecord.NASDAQ = NASDAQ.Value
```

```
        'Write the record to the database. If this is a
        'new record, CurRec% is the new length of the
        'database. For revising a record, CurRec% is the
        'numeric position of the existing record.
        Open StockDataBase For Random As #1 Len = Len(StockRecord)
            Put #1, CurRec%, StockRecord
        Close #1
    End If

End Sub
```

A call to the **SearchStockRecord%** function searches for the current stock entry in the index:

```
CurRec% = SearchStockRecord%(StockRecord.StockName)
```

The SearchStockRecord% function performs an efficient operation known as a *binary search.* This process continually divides the sorted stock list into smaller and smaller pairs of sections, always focusing the search on the section in which the target stock name will ultimately be found if it exists. This approach minimizes the number of actual comparisons during the search. If the routine finds the stock name in the index list, SearchStockRecord% returns the corresponding record number; that is, it returns the position of the record in the database. If the stock name isn't found, the function returns a value of 0. The **Sub SaveForm_Click** event procedure stores this return value in the CurRec% variable.

The **Sub CloseDate_LostFocus** event procedure simply validates the user's date entry. It attempts to convert the date that the user inputs to a serial date. If the conversion attempt is unsuccessful, the application reinitializes the date field to the current date:

```
Sub CloseDate_LostFocus ()

    'Validate the user's date entry.
    DateError% = False
    On Error GoTo BadDate

        'Attempt to convert the date input to a serial
        'date.
        StockRecord.CloseDate = DateValue(CloseDate.Text)

        'If an error occurs in the conversion attempt,
        'reinitialize the date field to today's date.
        If DateError% Then InitializeDate
```

> **NOTE** The statement **Error GoTo 0** below disables error handling once the error handler accomplishes its task.

```
On Error GoTo 0

'Record the program's standard date format.
CloseDate.Text = Format$(StockRecord.CloseDate, DateFormat)
Exit Sub

BadDate:

    'If the user has entered an invalid date, display
    'an error message and toggle the DateError flag to
    'True.
    MsgBox "Illegal Date", 48, "Input Error"
    DateError% = True

Resume Next

End Sub
```

The following three event procedures, **Sub ClosePrice_GotFocus, Sub Description_GotFocus,** and **Sub CloseDate_GotFocus,** call the **Sub HighlightEntry** general procedure. This procedure sets the form's focus to the particular text box that the user clicks, highlighting whatever integer or string value is inside the text box:

```
Sub ClosePrice_GotFocus ()
    'Highlight the contents of the text box.
    HighlightEntry ClosePrice

End Sub

Sub Description_GotFocus ()
    'Highlight the contents of the text box.
    HighlightEntry Description
End Sub

Sub CloseDate_GotFocus ()
    'Highlight the contents of the text box.
    HighlightEntry CloseDate
End Sub

Sub HighlightEntry (TextBox As Control)
```

```
'Highlight the contents of the text box
'that has just received the focus.
TextBox.SelStart = 0
TextBox.SelLength = Len(TextBox.Text)
End Sub
```

The **Sub ClosePrice_LostFocus** event procedure validates the stock's closing price when the user moves the focus to another text box control:

```
Sub ClosePrice_LostFocus ()

    'Validate the closing price when the user
    'moves the focus to another control.
    StockRecord.ClosePrice = Val(ClosePrice.Text)
    ClosePrice.Text = LTrim$(Str$(StockRecord.ClosePrice))

End Sub
```

When the user clicks the Exit button, the **Sub ExitForm_Click** event procedure is invoked. This procedure hides the Daily Stock Record form and shows the main Menu form:

```
Sub ExitForm_Click ()

    'Exit the form and return to the menu.
    Form4.Hide
    Form1.Show

End Sub
```

The Weekly Investment Tracker Form

The Weekly Investment Tracker form, shown in Figure 7.5, enables the user to track an investment over a five-day period. The data that the user enters are saved to a database on disk, giving the user a permanent chronological record of investment data from Monday through Friday. The application saves the investment database as a series of small files rather than one large random-access file. Each file contains the investment data for the five-day period. The program also builds bar graphs representing investment information for a given five-day period or for a series of consecutive weeks.

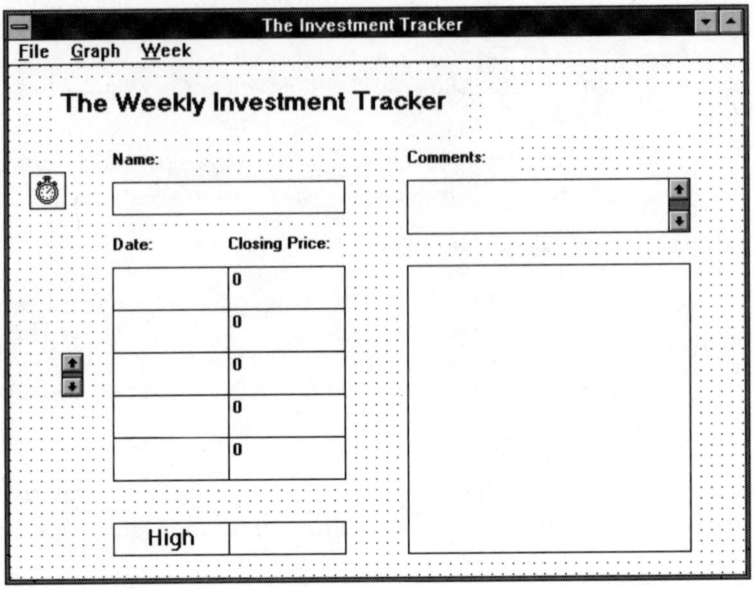

FIGURE 7.5:

The Weekly Investment Tracker form

Form-Level Declarations

The declarations section of the form's general procedure contains the following constants and variables:

```
'Declarations.
'The directory for weekly stock prices.
Const InvestmentDataBase = "C:\INVEST.DB"
Const InvestFile$ = "C:\Investmt"
Const ExtName$ = "DAT"
Const IndexFile = "C:\Invest.NDX"
Const InvestInfo = "C:\Invest.RTN"

'Boolean values
Const False = 0
Const True = Not False

Const DateFormat = "mmmm d, yyyy"

'Keyboard navigation keys.
Const PgDn = &H22
Const PgUp = &H21
```

```
Const Up = &H26
Const Down = &H28

'The maximum number of investment records.
Const MaxRecords = 100

'Serial number and file name for the current week.
Dim WeekRef&, FileName$
Dim CrLf$
Dim Today As Long

'Position of current week in trend graph.
Dim BackWeeks As Integer

Dim InvestRec As InvestRecType            'Investment record.
Dim InvestIndex(MaxRecords) As IndexType  'The index array.
Dim InvestCount As Integer                'Current number of records.
Dim InvestStr$                            'Abbreviation for name of
                                          'investment.
```

Two important arrays are also declared in this section:

```
'Arrays for current week's stock prices.
Dim StockOnDisk(4), StockOnScreen(4)
```

As you can infer from their names, these numeric arrays represent a five-day period's investment data as currently stored on disk and as displayed on the screen.

Event and General Procedures

The following event and general procedures are used for the Weekly Investment Tracker.

The **Sub Form_Load** event procedure initializes the date field and the current date. It also initializes the form's variables, menu options, and database:

```
Sub Form_Load ()

    'When the form is first loaded, initialize
    'the date field and its display.
    Today = Int(Now)

    'Initialize variables and menu options, and
    'check the length of the investment database.
```

```
'Carriage-return, line feed.
CrLf$ = Chr$(13) + Chr$(10)

'Initialize this week's serial number
'and show the week's graph.
Dim i%
DayTimer_Timer
SearchForPath
WeekRef& = Int(Now)
ShowWeek

'Initialize the position value
'for the trend graph.
BackWeeks = 45

'Open the database file and find
'out how many records it contains.
Open InvestmentDataBase For Random As #1 Len = Len(InvestRec)
InvestCount = LOF(1) / Len(InvestRec)

'Store the investment name field and the record
'number in the InvestIndex index.
For i% = 1 To InvestCount
    Get #1, i%, InvestRec
    InvestName.AddItem InvestRec.InvestNameField
    InvestIndex(i%).InvestRef = UCase$(InvestRec.InvestNameField)
    InvestIndex(i%).RecNum = i%
Next i%
Close #1

'Alphabetize the index.
SortInvestIndex

End Sub
```

As you can see from the previous example, the **Sub Form_Load** event procedure calls the **Sub SortInvestIndex** general procedure. This procedure alphabetizes the index of stock records for the Weekly Investment Tracker. You should note that the procedure first dimensions the TempInvestRec variable as the index array. This array is static; that is, the array can only sort the current number of records, which can be a maximimum of 100 records:

```
Sub SortInvestIndex ()

    'Alphabetize the index.
```

```
    Dim TempInvestRec As IndexType

  For i% = 1 To InvestCount - 1
     For j% =i% + 1 To InvestCount
        If InvestIndex(i%).InvestRef > InvestIndex(j%).InvestRef Then
            TempInvestRec = InvestIndex(i%)
            InvestIndex(i%) = InvestIndex(j%)
            InvestIndex(j%) = TempInvestRec
        End If
     Next j%
  Next i%

End Sub
```

The **Sub ShowWeek** general procedure is called from the Sub Form_Load event procedure. It displays the data for the current five-day period and builds the file name for the new five-day period's data by reading the data from disk:

```
Sub ShowWeek ()

   'Display the data for a new week.

   'Calculate the serial value for the first day
   'of the week, and display the day captions.
   WeekStart& = WeekRef& - (Weekday(WeekRef&) - 2)
   For i% = 0 To 4
       WkDate(i%).Text = Format$(WeekStart& + i%, "ddd m/d")
   Next i%

   'Build the file name for the new week's data
   'and read the data from disk.
   FileName$ = PathName$ + "\" + Format$(WeekStart&, "mm-dd-yy") + ".DAT"
   ReadNewWeek

End Sub
```

The **Sub ReadNewWeek** general procedure is called from the Sub ShowWeek general procedure. It uses an error trap to determine whether a data file exists yet for the currently selected five-day period. The **Open** statement normally causes a runtime error if an attempt is made to open a nonexistent file for input. The file exists if the CannotRead variable still has a value of False after this passage:

```
Sub ReadNewWeek ()

    'Read data from disk for the newly selected week.
```

```
'First check to see if the week's file exists yet.
CannotRead = False
On Error GoTo FileProblem
    Open FileName$ For Input As #1
On Error GoTo 0

'If the file exists, read it and display individual
'data values in the ClosePrice text boxes. Otherwise,
'display a value of zero in each box.
For i% = 0 To 4
    If CannotRead Then
        ClosePrice(i%).Text = "0"
    Else
        Input #1, PriceText$
        ClosePrice(i%).Text = PriceText$
    End If
    StockOnDisk(i%) = Val(ClosePrice(i%).Text)
    StockOnScreen(i%) = StockOnDisk(i%)
Next i%
Close #1

'Redraw the graph.
UpdateHigh
Exit Sub

'Error trap to handle nonexistent file.
FileProblem:
    CannotRead = True
Resume Next

End Sub
```

After displaying the investment data, **Sub ReadNewWeek** sets the values of the arrays **StockOnDisk** and **StockOnScreen**. At this point, the two arrays contain the same values (before the user has had the opportunity to make changes in the data):

```
StockOnDisk(i%) = Val(ClosePrice(i%).Text)
StockOnScreen(i%) = StockOnDisk(i%)
```

When the user selects a new week, the **Sub SaveCurWeek** general procedure uses these two arrays to determine whether the current five-day period needs to be updated on disk; that is, it determines whether there are any new data values to save:

```
Sub SaveCurWeek ()

    'Save the revised data for the current week.
```

```
'First check to see if there are any new data to save.
StockToSave% = False
For i% = 0 To 4
    If StockOnScreen(i%) <> StockOnDisk(i%) Then StockToSave% = True
Next i%

'If there are any new data, save the entire
'week's data as a sequential text file.
If StockToSave% Then
    Open FileName$ For Output As #1
    For i% = 0 To 4
        Print #1, ClosePrice(i%).Text
        StockOnDisk(i%) = Val(ClosePrice(i%).Text)
    Next i%
    Close #1
End If

End Sub
```

The **Sub ReadNewWeek** and **Sub SaveNewWeek** procedures uses Visual Basic's **Open**, **Input#**, **Print#**, and **Close#** statements to manage the form's sequential-access data files on disk. Read and write operations in the data files are performed *sequentially*—that is, one value at a time from the beginning to the end of the file. To open a data file for a reading operation, the form uses the **Open** statement as follows:

```
Open FileName$ For Input As #1
```

FileName$ is the name of an existing file on disk and *#1* is an integer that you use to identify the open file in subsequent I/O statements.

The **Input#** statement reads the individual data values from a text file for reading:

```
Input #1, PriceText$
```

where *#1* is the number assigned to the open file in the corresponding Open statement. *PriceText$* consists of a variable name, with a data type corresponding to the data expected from the file.

To open a file for writing, you use the **Open** statement in this form:

```
Open FileName$ For Output As #1
```

The Output mode relates a new file and opens it for writing. The **Print#** statement sends individual data items to a file that is open in this mode:

```
Print #1, ClosePrice(i%).Text
```

The **Close#** statement closes an open file:

```
Close #1
```

The **Sub SearchForPath** general procedure searches for the directory in which the investment data records are to be stored. It also creates the directory on Drive C if it doesn't exist:

```
Sub SearchForPath ()

    'Search for the directory in which weekly investment
    'records are to be stored. Create the directory (on
    'drive C) if it does not exist yet.
    'Note: InvestFile$ is declared at the declarations level
    'of the Investment Tracker form.
    Dim CDir$

    'Record the current directory.
    CDir$ = CurDir$("C")

    'Set up an error-handling mode.
    On Error Resume Next

    'Attempt to change to the target directory.
    ChDir InvestFile$

    'If the directory doesn't exist, create it.
    MkDir InvestFile$

    'Restore the original directory.
    ChDir CDir$

End Sub
```

The **Sub DrawAxes** general procedure draws the horizontal and vertical axes for the investment graph **StockGraph** that appears on the picture box:

```
Sub DrawAxes ()

    'Draw the horizontal and vertical axes
    'in the graph box.
    StockGraph.Cls
```

```
       StockGraph.DrawWidth = 2
       StockGraph.Line (20, 20)-(20, 90), RGB(0, 128, 0)
       StockGraph.Line (20, 90)-(90, 90), RGB(0, 128, 0)
```

End Sub

The **DrawWidth** property displays the line width for the output from any graphics method, which in the example above is the **Line** method. In the statement **Stock-Graph.DrawWidth = 2,** the screen output displays a solid line. Since the default setting for DrawWidth is 1 (for one pixel), any value greater than 1 always results in a thicker solid line.

The RGB (Red%, Green%, Blue%) function above returns a long integer value representing an RGB color. In this case, the function uses the arguments 0, 128, and 0 to return a value of green.

The **Sub DrawWeekGraph** general procedure draws the bar graph for a five-day period, displaying the highest closing price during the period:

```
Sub DrawWeekGraph ()

    'Draw the graph for one week's data.
    Const MaxHeight = 70
    Dim MaxDay, x%, y%, i%

    'Find the largest single day's stock price.
    MaxDay = StockOnScreen(0)
    For i% = 0 To 4
        If StockOnScreen(i%) > MaxDay Then MaxDay = StockOnScreen(i%)
    Next i%

    'Draw the five bars on the graph.
    If MaxDay <> 0 Then
        For i% = 0 To 4
            x% = 22 + i% * 10
            y% = -(StockOnScreen(i%) / MaxDay) * MaxHeight

            'Display the x-axis label.
            StockGraph.Line (x%, 90)-Step(8, y%), RGB(0, 128, 0), BF
            StockGraph.CurrentX = x%
            StockGraph.CurrentY = 92
            StockGraph.Print Left$(WkDate(i%).Text, 1);
        Next i%

    'Display y-axis label and title.
```

```
        StockGraph.CurrentX = 1
        StockGraph.CurrentY = 18
        StockGraph.Print MaxDay;
        StockGraph.CurrentX = 25
        StockGraph.CurrentY = 7
        StockGraph.Print "The Week of"; Mid$(WkDate(0).Text, 4);
```

```
    End If
```

```
End Sub
```

The **Sub ClosePrice** event procedure is called whenever the user selects a new text box in the control array. The object of the event in this case is the text box that *previously* had the focus. The program uses this event as an opportunity to read and validate the number in the previously selected text box and to update the total and the graph if the value represents a new or revised closing price entry:

```
Sub ClosePrice_LostFocus (Index As Integer)

    'Read a new daily stock price listing from a text box.
    Dim CurVal

    'Read the text value and convert it to a number.
    CurVal = Val(ClosePrice(Index).Text)

    'Eliminate any invalid characters from the display.
    ClosePrice(Index).Text = LTrim$(Str$(CurVal))

    'Update the graph only if this is a new input value.
    If CurVal <> StockOnScreen(Index) Then
        StockOnScreen(Index) = CurVal
        UpdateHigh
    End If

End Sub
```

The **Sub DrawTrendGraph** general procedure draws the ten-week trend graph for the form:

```
Sub DrawTrendGraph ()

    'Draw the ten-week trend graph for Investment Tracker.
    Const MaxHeight = 70
    Dim CurWeekStart As Long, MaxTrendWeek
    Static TrendWeeks(9), WeekChar$(9)
```

```
SaveCurWeek
WeekStart& = WeekRef& - (Weekday(WeekRef&) - 1)
MaxTrendWeek = 0
For i% = 0 To 9

    'Build the file name for each week's data.
    CurWeekStart = WeekStart& - (BackWeeks - (i% * 7))
    TrendFileName$ = PathName$ + "\" + Format$(CurWeekStart,
            "mm-dd-yy")
    TrendFileName$ = TrendFileName$ + ".DAT"

    'Determine the x-axis label for the week.
    If CurWeekStart = WeekStart& Then
        WeekChar$(i%) = "^"
    ElseIf CurWeekStart < WeekStart& Then
        WeekChar$(i%) = Format$(i% + 1, "#")
    Else
        WeekChar$(i%) = Format$(i%, "#")
    End If

    'Check to see if file exists. Cancel error checking.
    FileFound% = True
    On Error GoTo NoTrendFileName
        Open TrendFileName$ For Input As #1
    On Error GoTo 0

    'Read the file and display the highest
    'closing price for the week.
    TrendWeeks(i%) = 0
    If FileFound% Then
        For j% = 1 To 5
            Input #1, dayVal
            TrendWeeks(i%) = TrendWeeks(i%) + dayVal
        Next j%
        Close #1
        If TrendWeeks(i%) > MaxTrendWeek Then MaxTrendWeek =
                        TrendWeeks(i%)
    End If
Next i%

'Draw the bar for each week.
If MaxTrendWeek <> 0 Then
    For i% = 0 To 9
        x% = 22 + i% + 7
        y% = -(TrendWeeks(i%) / MaxTrendWeek) * MaxHeight
```

```
            StockGraph.Line (x%, 90)-Step(5, y%), , BF
            StockGraph.CurrentX = x%
            StockGraph.CurrentY = 92
            StockGraph.Print WeekChar$(i%);
        Next i%

    'Display the y-axis label and the title.
        StockGraph.CurrentX = 1
        StockGraph.CurrentY = 18
        StockGraph.Print MaxTrendWeek;
        StockGraph.CurrentX = 28
        StockGraph.CurrentY = 7
        StockGraph.Print "Ten Week Trend";
    End If
    Exit Sub

'The error trap for a nonexistent file.
NoTrendFileName:
    FileFound% = False
Resume Next

End Sub
```

The following four event procedures are accessed from the Week menu, which will be discussed and created in Chapter 10. The **Sub OneWeek_Click** event procedure displays the graph for a five-day period; **Sub TenWeeks_Click** displays the ten-week graph; **Sub ThisWeek_Click** displays the investment data and graph for the current five-day period; and **Sub LastWeek_Click** displays the investment data and graph for last week:

```
Sub OneWeek_Click ()
    'Display the graph for one week's data.
    OneWeek.Checked = True
    TenWeeks.Checked = False
    UpdateHigh
End Sub

Sub TenWeeks_Click ()
    'Switch to the ten-week trend graph.
    TenWeeks.Checked = True
    OneWeek.Checked = False
    UpdateHigh
End Sub

Sub ThisWeek_Click ()
```

```
        'Display the current week's data and graph.
        WeekRef& = Int(Now)
        ShowWeek
End Sub

Sub LastWeek_Click ()
        'Display last week's data and graph.
        WeekRef& = Now - 7
        ShowWeek
End Sub
```

The next three event procedures are invoked when the user clicks on the vertical scroll bar. The **Sub ScrollWeek_Change** event procedure scrolls backward or forward to a new week; the **Sub Backward_Click** event procedure scrolls back to the previous five-day period; the **Sub ForwardWeek_Click** event procedure scrolls forward one week:

```
Sub ScrollWeek_Change ()

        'Scroll backward or forward to a new week.
        'ScrollWeekMin (0) is the setting for an
        'up-arrow click and ScrollWeek.Max(2) is
        'the setting for a down-arrow click. The
        'neutral ScrollWeek.Value setting is 1.

        If ScrollWeek.Value = ScrollWeek.Min Then
            Backward_Click
        ElseIf ScrollWeek.Value = ScrollWeek.Max Then
            Forward_Click
        End If

        'Reset the ScrollWeek value.
        If ScrollWeek.Value <> 1 Then
            ScrollWeek.Value = 1
            ClosePrice(0).SetFocus
        End If
End Sub

Sub Backward_Click ()
        'Scroll back to the previous week.
        WeekRef& = WeekRef& - 7
        ShowWeek
End Sub

Sub Forward_Click ()
```

```
        'Move forward by one week.
        WeekRef& = WeekRef& + 7
        ShowWeek
End Sub
```

When a new text box receives the focus, the **Sub ClosePrice_GotFocus** event procedure highlights the entire text currently stored in the box:

```
Sub ClosePrice_GotFocus (Index As Integer)

        'Extend the highlight over the entire text
        'entry when the user selects an input box.
        ClosePrice(Index).SelStart = 0
        ClosePrice(Index).SelLength = Len(ClosePrice(Index).Text)

End Sub
```

The following event procedures respond to specific keyboard input, such as pressing the ↑ or ↓ key, rather than to mouse input:

```
Sub ClosePrice_KeyDown (Index As Integer, KeyCode As Integer, Shift As Integer)

    'Respond to navigation keys for selecting the daily
    'values in a week's data, and for scrolling through weeks.
    Select Case KeyCode

        'Scroll back to the previous week.
        Case PgUp
        ScrollWeek.Value = ScrollWeek.Min

        'Scroll forward to the next week.
        Case PgDn
        ScrollWeek.Value = ScrollWeek.Max

        'Select the previous day's text box.
        Case Up
            If Index = 0 Then
                ClosePrice(4).SetFocus
            Else
                ClosePrice(Index - 1).SetFocus
            End If

        'Select the next day's text box.
        Case Down
            If Index = 4 Then
                ClosePrice(0).SetFocus
```

```
        Else
            ClosePrice(Index + 1).SetFocus
        End If
    End Select

End Sub
```

The **Sub UpdateHigh** general procedure displays the highest closing price for any five-day period in the label at the bottom of the Closing Price column. Each time the user inputs a new value, the procedure compares the value against the current high value:

```
Sub UpdateHigh ()

    Dim MaxDay

    'Display week's highest closing price.
    Total.Caption = "0"
    MaxDay = StockOnScreen(0)
    For i% = 1 To 4
        If StockOnScreen(i%) > MaxDay Then MaxDay = StockOnScreen(i%)
    Next i%
    Total.Caption = Str$(Val(Total.Caption) + MaxDay)

    'Redraw the graph.
    DrawAxes
    If OneWeek.Checked Then DrawWeekGraph

End Sub
```

The **DayTimer_Timer** event procedure initializes the date field to the current date:

```
Sub DayTimer_Timer ()

    'Initialize the date field to today's date.
    DateViewed.Caption = Format$(Now, DateFormat)

End Sub
```

When the user clicks the Quit command on the File menu, the **Sub Quit_Click** event procedure is invoked. This procedure hides the Weekly Investment Tracker form and displays the Menu form:

```
Sub Quit_Click ()

    'Exit form.
    Form5.Hide
    Form1.Show
```

```
End Sub
```

Summary

This chapter presented the functional code for all the forms in the *Window$ to Wealth* application. The chapter covered many statements and functions, including the following:

- The **Int** function converts any numeric expression to the largest integer that is less than or equal to the expression.

- The **Now** function returns a serial number that represents the current date and time according to the setting of your computer's system date and time.

- The **Format$** function converts any number assigned to a variable and formats it according to the instructions given.

- The **AddItem** method simply adds an item to a list box or combo box at runtime.

- The **UCase$** function returns a string in which all the letters have been converted to uppercase.

- The **Value** property determines the state of a control.

- The **SetFocus** method sets the focus to the specified control.

- The **LTrim$** function displays on the monitor screen an image of a string with its leftmost spaces removed. The **RTrim$** function has the opposite effect and displays a string with it rightmost spaces removed.

- The **DrawWidth** property displays the line width for the output from any graphics method.

CHAPTER

EIGHT

Getting Keyboard and Mouse Input

- Learning the Importance of Setting a Control's Focus

- Assigning Keyboard and Mouse Events and Properties

8

Most Windows applications accept some form of user input, whether by entering text in a textbox or selecting any other control with a mouse. A well-designed application should allow the user to enter information from the keyboard, make selections with a mouse, or use a combination of both. However, before the user can input any information, an application must first indicate where the *point of insertion* for the information is located. In other words, the application must tell the user where information can be entered, either from the keyboard or with the mouse. The point of insertion for both keyboard and mouse input is commonly referred to as a control's *focus*.

A Windows application provides a user with two methods of moving the focus from one control to another: by pressing the Tab key and by clicking the mouse. However, users become so accustomed to using the mouse that they probably don't consider using the Tab key method—and why should they? Clicking with a mouse is so much faster than pressing the Tab key and then the Enter key. (After a user presses Tab to change a control's focus, Enter must also be pressed to execute the command or to toggle a selection.)

Using both methods isn't an either/or proposition, however. Most Windows applications offer both, although using a mouse is usually more convenient. Furthermore, you always know the location of the current focus when you click on a particular control with the mouse. When you have many controls to choose from, the current focus can be difficult to locate by pressing the Tab key.

For example, when you select the Run command from the Program Manager's File menu and open the Run dialog box, you see a blinking bar in the Command Line text box. This bar indicates the dialog box's current focus; that is, this is where text is entered from the keyboard. When a user clicks on the Run Minimized check box to select it, the focus moves from the text box to the check box. Finally, the user has the option of clicking on either the OK or Cancel button to confirm or cancel the selection.

Accessing Controls from the Keyboard and with a Mouse

The user can make any selection by using the Tab, arrow, and Enter keys in place of using a mouse. For example, when you display the Run dialog box, you can press the Tab key to move the focus from (1) the text box to (2) the check box to (3) the OK button to (4) the Cancel button. When the user presses the Tab key to move the focus around, the controls' captions will appear outlined in turn to indicate when each is the focus. Pressing the Enter key confirms or toggles the selection. For most controls, the combination of pressing the Tab key and then the Enter key achieves the same results as clicking with the mouse. (To access menu commands, you have to use the up and down arrow keys.)

The following nine controls are accessed from the keyboard and with the mouse at runtime.

Text Box Control

Using the text box control enables the user to input text in a text box. To input multiple lines of text in a text box at runtime, the MultiLine property must be set to True. To display numeric input in a text box, the Val function must be used; it returns the numeric value of a string of characters.

Check Box Control

A check box control allows the user to check one or more options that may be displayed on a form. When the user tabs to a check box, the control will appear outlined to indicate that it has the focus. Pressing the Enter key selects the check box. By contrast, clicking on a check box with the mouse immediately gives the control the focus and indicates that it has been selected; clicking on the check box again deselects it.

Option Button Control

The option button control is similar to the check box control except that the user can only select one option button at a time. When the user selects an option button, any other option button on the form is cancelled.

Combo Box Control

The user types text into the combo box or selects an item from the list below it. When the user tabs or clicks the control to give it the focus, an I-beam will appear to indicate the insertion point for text.

Command Button Control

A command button performs a specific task when the user chooses it. The user either clicks on the control with the mouse or presses the Tab key.

List Box Control

Using a list box control enables the user to scroll up or down a list of items that may appear inside the control. However, the items can only be identified through code; they appear at runtime only.

File List Box Control

Using a file list box control enables the user to open a file from a list of available files in the current directory. The user makes a selection simply by clicking on a file, thus giving the file the focus.

Drive List Box Control

Using a drive list box control enables the user to open a file from a list of available files on a disk or a different drive. The user makes a selection by clicking on the file.

Directory List Box Control

Using a directory list box control enables the user to open a file from a list of available directories. The user makes a selection by clicking on the file.

Keyboard and Mouse Events and Properties

Most events and properties for the keyboard and mouse can be selected during design time. By selecting properties and changing their settings on the Properties bar, you practically eliminate the need for writing code to achieve the same results. Since you can also designate a desired event for a control by selecting it from the Procedure list box in a control's code window, you again eliminate the need for writing code.

There may be times, however, when you want to write code that establishes certain keyboard and mouse behavior, especially when you want to achieve dynamic effects at runtime. For example, you may want to include a statement in an event procedure that causes the mouse pointer to change its shape when it is over a particular area of a form or control.

Most of the following events and properties can be designated at design time.

Click Event

The Click event applies to the following controls:

- Check box
- Combo box
- Command button
- Directory list box
- File list box
- Form
- Label
- List box
- Menu
- Option button
- Picture box

This event occurs when the user presses and then releases a mouse button over a control.

For a form, this event occurs when the user clicks either a blank area of the form or a disabled control.

For a control, this event occurs when the user does either of the following: clicks a control with any mouse button; selects an item in a combo box or list box, whether by pressing the arrow keys or by clicking the mouse button; presses the spacebar when a command button, option button, or check box has the focus; presses the Enter key when the form has a command button with its Default property set to True (–1); or presses the Escape key when a form has a Cancel button—a button with its Cancel property set to True (–1).

The event procedure for this event is given the name **Sub *Ctlname*_Click.**

DblClick Event

The DblClick event applies to the following controls:

- Combo box
- Directory list box
- File list box
- Form
- Label
- List box
- Option button
- Picture box

This event occurs when the user clicks a mouse button, then clicks it quickly again over a control.

For a form, the DblClick event occurs when the user double-clicks a disabled control or a blank area of the form.

For a control, it occurs when the user does any of the following: double-clicks a control; double-clicks an item in a combo box (only if the Style property is set to 1), file list box, or list box; changes the path property for a directory list box from code; sets a file list box's FileName property in code to a valid existing file name (with no wildcard characters).

The event procedure for this event is given the name **Sub *Ctlname*_DblClick.**

DragDrop Event

The DragDrop event applies to the following forms:

- Check box
- Combo box
- Command button

- Directory list box
- Drive list box
- File list box
- Form
- Frame
- Horizontal scroll bar
- Label
- List box
- Option button
- Picture box
- Text box
- Vertical scroll bar

This event occurs when a drag-and-drop operation is completed as a result of (1) dragging a control over a form or another control and releasing the mouse button or (2) using the Drag method. (By using the Drag method, you begin, end, or cancel dragging a control.)

The event procedure for this event is given the name **Sub *Ctlname*_DragDrop.**

DragOver Event

The DragOver event applies to the following controls:

- Check box
- Combo box
- Command button
- Directory list box
- Drive list box
- File list box
- Form
- Frame

- Horizontal scroll bar
- Label
- List box
- Option button
- Picture box
- Text box
- Vertical scroll bar

This event occurs when a drag-and-drop operation is in progress. You can use this event to recognize when the mouse pointer enters, leaves, or is directly over a form or control. The mouse pointer position determines which control receives this event.

The event procedure for this event is given the name **Sub *Ctlname*_DragOver.**

DropDown Event

The DropDown event applies to the combo box only. This event occurs when a list portion of the combo box is about to drop down. You should note that this event does not occur for a combo box control with its Style property set to 1 (Simple).

The event procedure for this event is given the name **Sub *Ctlname*_DropDown.**

Enabled Property

The Enabled property applies to the following controls:

- Check box
- Combo box
- Command button
- Directory list box
- Drive list box
- File list box
- Form
- Frame

- Horizontal scroll bar
- Label
- List box
- Menu
- Option button
- Picture box
- Text box
- Timer
- Vertical scroll bar

This property determines if the form or control can respond to user-generated events such as keypresses and mouse events. The property has two settings:

True (–1), which is the default. This setting allows the control to respond to events.

False (0), which prevents the control from responding to events.

For example, the statement `Text1.Enabled = True` would allow a user to input text into the control Text1. Setting the value to False would disable the control and not allow the user to input text.

GotFocus Event

The GotFocus event applies to the following controls:

- Check box
- Combo box
- Command button
- Directory list box
- Drive list box
- File list box
- Form
- Horizontal scroll bar

- Label
- List Box
- Option button
- Picture box
- Text box
- Vertical scroll bar

This event occurs when the control *perceives* the focus—that is, either by user action or by changing the focus in code through the SetFocus method. For example, when the user clicks or tabs to the control, the GotFocus event is invoked—the control has the focus.

The event procedure for this event is given the name **Sub** *Ctlname*_**GotFocus.**

KeyDown and KeyUp Events

These events apply to the following controls:

- Check box
- Combo box
- Command button
- Directory list box
- Drive list box
- File list box
- Form
- Horizontal scroll bar
- List box
- Option button
- Picture box
- Text box
- Vertical scroll bar

These events occur when the user presses (KeyDown) or releases (KeyUp) a key while a control or form has the focus. These events detect all the keys on the keyboard, although they are generally used for extended keys.

For either event, the control with the focus receives all keystrokes. However, a form can have the focus only if it has no visible and enabled controls.

The event procedures for these events are given the names **Sub Ctlname_KeyDown** and **Sub Ctlname_KeyUp.**

KeyPress Event

This event applies to the following controls:

- Check box
- Combo box
- Command button
- Directory list box
- Drive list box
- File list box
- Form
- Horizontal scroll bar
- List box
- Option button
- Picture box
- Text box
- Vertical scroll bar

This event occurs when the user presses and releases an ASCII key. The control with the focus receives the event. However, a form can receive the event only if it doesn't have any visible and enabled controls. A KeyPress event can involve any printable keyboard character. For example, the Ctrl key can be combined with a character from the standard alphabet or one of a few special characters such as the Enter or Backspace key.

The event procedure for this event is given the name **Sub *Ctlname*_KeyPress.**

LargeChange and SmallChange Properties

These properties apply to the horizontal and vertical scroll bars. The LargeChanges property determines the amount of change to report in a scroll bar control when the user clicks between the scroll box and the scroll arrow. The scroll bar's Value property increases or decreases by this amount.

The SmallChange property determines the amount of change to report in a scroll bar control when the user clicks a scroll arrow. The scroll bar's Value property increases or decreases by this amount.

For example, the statement `HScroll1.LargeChange = 30` would move the scroll bar the equivalent of 30 clicks; the statement `VScroll1.SmallChange = 15` would move the scroll bar 15 clicks.

LostFocus Event

The LostFocus event applies to the following controls:

- Check box
- Combo box
- Command button
- Directory list box
- Drive list box
- File list box
- Form
- Horizontal scroll bar
- List box
- Option button
- Picture box
- Text box
- Vertical scroll bar

This event occurs when an object loses the focus, either by user action or as a result of changing the focus in code through the SetFocus method. For example, when the user clicks or tabs to the form or another control, the previous control loses the focus.

The event procedure for this event is given the name **Sub** *Ctlname*_**LostFocus.**

MouseDown and MouseUp Events

These events apply to the following controls:

- File list box
- Form
- Label
- List box
- Picture box

Both of these events occur when the user presses a mouse button (MouseDown) or releases a mouse button (MouseUp).

The event procedures for these events are given the names **Sub** *Ctlname*_**Mouse-Down** and **Sub** *Ctlname*_**MouseUp.**

MouseMove Event

The MouseMove event applies to the following controls:

- File list box
- Form
- Label
- List box
- Picture box

This event occurs when the user moves the mouse anywhere on a form or over a control.

The event procedure for this event is given the name **Sub** *Ctlname*_**MouseMove.**

MousePointer Property

The MousePointer property applies to the following controls:

- Check box
- Combo box
- Command button
- Directory list box
- Drive list box
- File list box
- Form
- Frame
- Horizontal scroll bar
- Label
- List box
- Option button
- Picture box
- Screen object
- Text box
- Vertical scroll bar

This property displays the value of the type of mouse pointer that has been designated when the mouse pointer is over a form or control at runtime.

There are 13 settings which display the following shapes:

0 Default shape is determined by the control

1 Arrow

2 Cross (cross hair)

3 I-Beam

4 Icon (small square within a square)

5 Size (four-pointed arrow pointing north, south, east, west)

6 Size NE SW (double arrow pointing northeast and southwest)

7 Size NS (double arrow pointing north and south)

8 Size NW SE (double arrow pointing northwest and southeast)

9 Size WE (double arrow pointing west and east)

10 Up arrow

11 Wait (hourglass)

12 No drop

For example, the statement `Label1.MousePointer = 3` would display an I-Beam when the mouse pointer was over the control Label1.

Pointer Property

The Pointer property applies to the following controls:

- Check box
- Combo box
- Command button
- Directory list box
- Drive list box
- File list box
- Form
- Frame
- Horizontal scroll bar
- Label
- List box
- Option button
- Picture box
- Text box
- Vertical scroll bar

This property is similar to the MousePointer property except that this event displays the value of the type of mouse pointer designated when the mouse is over a *particular* part of a form or control at runtime. In other words, this property controls the shape of the mouse pointer when it is over a particular control. In this way you can customize the shape of the mouse pointer to correspond to the function of a particular type of control.

There are 12 settings, which display the following shapes:

0   Arrow pointer (default)

1   Arrow

2   Cross (cross hair)

3   I-Beam

4   Icon (small square within a square)

5   Size (four-pointed arrow pointing north, south, east, west)

6   Size NE SW (double arrow pointing northeast and southwest)

7   Size NS (double arrow pointing north and south)

8   Size NW SE(double arrow pointing northwest and southeast)

9   Size WE (double arrow pointing west and east)

10 Up arrow

11 Wait (hourglass)

For example, the statement `Command1.Pointer = 4` would display the icon shape when the mouse pointer was over the control Command1.

TabIndex Property

The TabIndex property applies to the following controls:

- Check box
- Combo box
- Command button
- Directory list box

- Drive list box
- File list box
- Form
- Frame
- Horizontal scroll bar
- Label
- List box
- Option button
- Picture box
- Text box
- Vertical scroll bar

This property returns the value of a control's position in the tab order within a form, starting with 0. By default, Visual Basic assigns tab order to the controls in the order in which they are drawn on a form. Each new control is placed last in the tab order. If you change the value of a control's TabIndex property to adjust the default tab order, Visual Basic automatically renumbers the TabIndex of other controls to reflect insertions and deletions. All controls except menus and timers are included in the tab order.

For example, suppose there were four text box controls on a form. The statement `Text1.TabIndex = 3` would place the control Text1 in the fourth position of the tab order. The tab order positions of the three other controls on the form would have been set to 0, 1, and 2, respectively.

TabStop Property

The TabStop property applies to the following controls:

- Check box
- Combo box
- Command button
- Directory list box
- Drive list box

- File list box
- Form
- Horizontal scroll bar
- List box
- Option button
- Picture box
- Text box
- Vertical scroll bar

This property determines if tabbing stops at a particular control. The TabStop property has two values:

True (–1), which is the default value and designates the control as a tab stop.

False (0), which causes the control to be bypassed when the user is tabbing, although the control still holds its place in the actual tab order.

For example, the statement `Combo1.TabStop = False` would cause the combo box control, Combo1, to be bypassed when the user is tabbing.

Summary

You need to give some consideration to how you want users to input information in an application. By default, Visual Basic enables you to create an application that will respond to both keyboard and mouse input. However, you can disable most controls on a form to not respond to input. You can also select events and properties for controls at design time, thus eliminating the need to write code. However, when you have a need to display the result of an event dynamically at runtime, you can write the code that will achieve the same result.

CHAPTER
NINE

Displaying Screen Output

- Formatting Text

- Setting a Control's Dimensions

- Selecting Background and Foreground Colors

9

Imagine a world without formatted data. Books, magazines, newspapers, and other print material would be unreadable. Graphics and text would appear like blobs on a page. Written communication would be lost in a mishmash of ink.

Likewise, imagine computer output that wasn't formatted on a screen. Gone are the days of only the monochrome monitor. Now we can see everything in a countless number of dithered colors. Gone are the days of only the Courier typeface. We no longer have to be satisfied with formatting documents with a limited number of typefaces and fonts. Now we have Windows TrueType font technology. We can select fonts that appear the same on the screen as they appear on a page.

Formatting screen output is often painstaking work. The strength of an application is judged on how well it presents information in graphical terms; that is, how effectively it communicates *visually* rather than *texturally*. As a developer, you can spend a lot of time considering the needs of users and how to best format data on a screen. You have to constantly question whether an application is communicating its intended message.

Formatting Text and Controls

Visual Basic offers you many methods and properties that you can use to format screen output to achieve desired effects. You should take advantage of these resources to create applications that not only look good, but also communicate a clear and cohesive message. The following methods and properties are useful when formatting text and graphics.

Alignment Property

The Alignment property only applies to the Label control. The Alignment property has three settings: 0–left justify, which is the default setting; 1–right-justify; and 2–center. The statement `Label1.Alignment = 1` would cause the label control's caption to appear right-justified.

AutoRedraw Property

The AutoRedraw property applies to a form and picture box control. This property sets or returns the output from the graphics methods Circle, Cls, Line, Point, PSet, and Print. It has two settings: True (–1), which enables the automatic repainting of a form or picture box with a permanent graphic; and False (0) for temporary graphics, which disables automatic repainting of an object and writes graphics or print output only to the screen.

AutoSize Property

The AutoSize property applies to a label and a picture box. This property determines whether a control is automatically resized to fit its contents. The property has two settings: True (–1) automatically resizes the control to fit its contents; False (0), which is the default setting, keeps the size of the control constant. The contents will appear clipped when they exceed the area of the control. The statement `Picture1.AutoSize = True` will automatically resize the picture box to fit its contents.

BackColor Property

The BackColor property applies to a form, check box, combo box, command button, directory list box, drive list box, file list box, frame, label, list box, option button, picture box, printer object (any data that are outputted to the printer), and text box. The BackColor property sets or returns the *background* color of an object. The statement `Label1.BackColor` = would change the background color of the control Label1 to the designated hue.

BorderStyle Property

The BorderStyle property applies to the form, label, picture box, and text box controls. This property sets the border style for a control. For a form, the settings are:

0 None (no border or related border elements)

1 Fixed Single (optional control box, title bar, maximize button, and minimize button; can be resized only with those buttons)

2 Sizeable, which is the default setting (border can be resized with any of the optional border elements listed previously)

3 Fixed Double (non-sizable border; optional control box, optional title bar, no minimize or maximize buttons)

For a label, text box, and picture box, the settings are:

0 None (default for label)

1 Fixed Single (default for picture box and text box)

Caption Property

The Caption property applies to the form, check box, command button, frame, label, menu, and option buttons. For a form, the caption specifies the text displayed in the form's title bar. When the form is minimized, this text is displayed below the form's icon. For a control, the caption specifies the text in or next to a control. The statement Label1.Caption = "Welcome" would display "Welcome" on the control Label1.

Circle Method

The Circle method draws a circle, ellipse, or arc.

Cls Method

The Cls method clears runtime-generated graphics and text output from a form or picture box.

ControlBox Property

The ControlBox property applies only to a form. This property determines whether a control box appears on a form at runtime; the control box is read-only at runtime. This property has two settings: True (–1), which is the default, displays the control box; and False (0) removes the control box. To display a control box, you must also set the form's BorderStyle property to Fixed Single, Sizeable, or Fixed Double.

CurrentX and CurrentY Properties

The CurrentX and CurrentY properties apply to the form, picture box, and printer object. These two properties set or return the current horizontal (x) and vertical (y) screen or page coordinates for output from any of the *graphics methods* (such as the Circle and Line methods); they are not available at design time. The other graphics methods are Cls, Pset, and Point.

DrawMode Property

The DrawMode property applies to the form, picture box, and printer object. This property sets or returns the appearance of output from any of the graphics methods.

DrawStyle Property

The DrawStyle Property applies to the form, picture box, and printer object. This property sets the line style for output from graphics methods. There are seven settings:

0 Solid (default)

1 Dash

2 Dot

3 Dash-Dot

4 Dash-dot-dot

5 Invisible

6 Inside solid

The statement `Picture1.DrawStyle = 1` would display a dashed line around the picture box.

DrawWidth Property

The DrawWidth property applies to the form, picture box, and printer object. This property sets the line width for output from any of the graphics methods. The default setting is set to 1 for *pixel*, the smallest unit of resolution on a monitor.

External Dimension Properties

These properties apply to the following controls: form, check box, combo box, command button, directory list box, drive list box, file list box, frame, horizontal scroll bar, label, list box, option button, picture box, text box, vertical scroll bar, and printer object. These properties set or return the dimensions of a form or control:

The **Height** property determines the external height of the form or control; for a form, the height includes the total area, including the borders and title bar.

The **Width** property determines the external width of the form or control; for a form, the width includes the total area, including the borders and the title bar.

The **Left** property determines the distance between the internal left edge of an object and the top edge of its container.

The **Top** property determines the distance between the internal top edge of an object and the top edge of its container.

FillColor Property

The FillColor property (not to be confused with the ForeColor property) applies to the form, picture box, and printer object. This property sets the color used to fill in circles and boxes created with the Circle and Line graphics methods. The FillColor property refers to a filling technique, not a color property (which would be set with the ForeColor and BackColor properties).

FillStyle Property

The FillStyle property applies to the form, picture box, and printer object. This property sets or returns the pattern used to fill in circles and boxes created with the Circle and Line graphics methods. There are eight settings:

0 Solid

1 Transparent (default)

2 Horizontal line

3 Vertical line

4 Upward diagonal

5 Downward diagonal

6 Cross

7 Diagonal cross

Font Properties

The following properties determine the font styles for formatting text:

FontBold

FontItalic

FontStrikethru

FontTransparent

FontUnderline

These properties apply to the form, check box, combo box, command button, directory list box, drive list box, file list box, frame, label, list box, option button, picture box, text box, and printer object.

The FontTransparent property determines whether background text or graphics are included along with the characters in a particular font; this property applies only to forms, picture boxes, and the printer object.

All of these properties have two settings: True (–1) that turns on the formatting in a particular style; and False (0) that turns off the formatting in that style.

FontName Property

The FontName property applies to the form, check box, command button, combo box, directory list box, drive list box, file list box, frame, label, list box, option button, picture box, text box, and printer object. The following fonts are available, depending on your system configuration:

Arial	Courier	Courier New
Fixedsys	Modern	MS Sans Serif
MS Serif	Roman	Script
Small Fonts	Symbol	System
Terminal	Times New Roman	

FontSize Property

The FontSize property applies to the form, check box, command button, combo box, directory list box, drive list box, file list box, frame, label, list box, option button, picture box, text box, and printer object. This property sets or returns the size of the font to be used for text displayed in a control or a runtime drawing or printing operation. This property offers six sizes:

8.25

9.75

12

13.5

18

24

The statement `Command1.FontSize = 24` would display the caption on a label in 24-point type.

ForeColor Property

The ForeColor property applies to a form, check box, combo box, command button, directory list box, drive list box, file list box, frame, label, list box, option button, picture box, printer object, and text box. The ForeColor property sets or returns the *foreground* color used to display text and graphics. When you select this property, the Color Palette is displayed, from which you can choose the desired color. The statement `Command1.ForeColor =` would cause the command button's caption to appear in the designated color.

Hide Method

The Hide method applies to the form only. This method "hides" a form, but doesn't unload it. The statement `Form1.Hide` would cause the form Form1 to disappear.

Internal Dimension Properties

These scale-related properties apply only to the form, picture box, and printer object. The following properties are used for operations or calculations based only on a control's internal scale. For example, you would use the scale-related properties to calculate the internal dimensions of a control that you had drawn or moved within a form:

The **ScaleLeft** property sets or returns the *horizontal coordinates* that describe the left corner of the control's internal area.

The **ScaleTop** property sets or returns the *vertical coordinates* that describe the top corner of the control's internal area.

The **ScaleHeight** property sets or returns the range of the *vertical axis* for a control's internal coordinate system in terms of its current dimensions. The coordinate system is used to position controls on forms and picture boxes.

The **ScaleWidth** property sets or returns the range of the *horizontal axis* for a control's internal coordinate system in terms of its current dimensions. The coordinate system is used to position controls on forms and picture boxes.

Line Method

The Line method draws lines and rectangles on a form, picture box, or printer object.

MaxButton Property

The MaxButton property applies to the form only. This property determines whether a form has a maximize button in the upper-right corner; the button is read-only at runtime. There are two settings: True (–1), the default setting, which places a maximize button on a form; and False (0), which removes the button.

MinButton Property

The MinButton applies to the form only. This property determines whether a form has a minimize button in the upper-right corner; the button is read-only at runtime. There are two settings: True (–1), the default setting, which places a minimize button on a form; and False (0), which removes the button.

MultiLine Property

The MultiLine property applies to a text box only. This property determines whether a text box can accept and display multiple lines of text. The MultiLine property has two settings: True (–1), which allows multiple lines of text; and False (0), the default, which ignores carriage returns and restricts data to a single line. The statement `Text1.MultiLine = True` would display multiple lines of text as you entered them in a text box.

Show Method

The Show method applies to the form only and has the opposite effect of the Hide method. The Show method displays or shows a form. The statement `Form1.Show` would display the form Form1.

Summary

After you create all the controls on a form, you need to give some consideration as to how they are to be formatted. Fonts, window-size dimensions, border styles, and colors are a few of the properties you can set to change the appearance of an application dramatically.

A control's properties are easy to format, and you don't have to write code in order to achieve the desired results. By selecting properties from the Properties bar, you can format a control to appear the way you want on the screen at design time rather than waiting until runtime. You'll immediately see the results of selecting a control's properties, such as choosing the type and size of a font, changing the background and foreground colors, and setting the height and width. If you don't like the look of a property, you can change its appearance immediately. Visual Basic makes it very convenient to make formatting changes quickly.

Creating Menus for Forms

- Examining the Menu Design Window

- Determining Access Keys

- Choosing Shortcut Keys

10

Creating menus for your applications is easy with Visual Basic. By using Visual Basic's Menu Design window, you can create pulldown menus and commands, and set shortcut and access keys.

A *shortcut key* is a single function key or combination of keystrokes that you designate at design time. By pressing a shortcut key, you execute a menu command immediately by invoking the event procedure attached to the command. This action is the same as clicking directly on the command.

For example, Visual Basic's File menu contains the following shortcut keys:

Add File…	Ctrl-F12
Save File	Shift-F12
Save File As…	F12

These shortcut keys are unique to Visual Basic. However, Visual Basic also contains several standard shortcut keys that are used by *all* Windows applications. For example, the Edit menu contains the following shortcut keys:

Cut	Shift-Del
Copy	Ctrl-Ins
Paste	Shift-Ins
Delete	Del

NOTE   Most Windows applications provide an Edit menu that allows you to cut and copy data to the Clipboard. Using the same shortcut keys provides consistency among all Windows applications and gives you a convenient way to move data between documents. As you gain more experience programming in Visual Basic, you need to consider building applications that conform to Windows API standards.

These shortcut keys always respond to user action in the same manner, whether you use Microsoft Excel, Microsoft Word for Windows, ToolBook, CorelDRAW, or any other Windows application.

An *access key* is a single letter that you also designate at design time. For example, in the menu listings above, all of the command names on the left have a single letter that is displayed with an underscore (_). After you pull down a menu, you can select a particular command by typing the designated letter that you've assigned to it. By pressing the access key, you invoke a command's event procedure in the same way as you would by clicking on it.

Exploring the Menu Design Window

The Menu Design window, shown in Figure 10.1, is one of Visual Basic's best features simply because it's so convenient to use. This window contains the options for defining the commands, properties, and characteristics of an entire menu bar, with one or more pulldown menus.

SHORTCUT You can also bring up the Menu Design window by pressing Alt-W, M.

FIGURE 10.1:
The Menu Design window allows you to create menus and commands easily

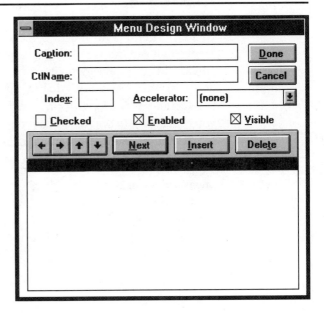

Let's take a closer look at this window's features. To display the window, first make sure that a form is displayed. (If a form is not displayed, the command to access the window will appear disabled.) You can display one of the forms from the Window$ to Wealth application or display a new form. Follow these steps:

1. Open the Window menu.

2. Choose the Menu Design Window command. The window will appear.

The Menu Design window enables you to create menu controls; each entry in the top half of the window defines one menu control. Like any control, a menu control has properties that you set during the design of the menu.

The **Caption text box** is where you enter the Caption property of each menu control. The caption is the name of the menu as it appears on the menu bar or the name of any command that appears in the menu list. As you enter the name of the menu or command, the name will appear automatically in the window below.

The **CtlName text box** is where you input the corresponding control property of each menu control. The control name is the special identifier that you assign to each menu and command entry, which will be used for writing the event procedure code that you attach to the menus and commands.

The **Index text box** allows you to input a value for a menu control's Index property. After you enter an index property for a menu control, the control automatically becomes part of a control array. This option gives you a powerful tool for creating menus that can grow and shrink. For example, many Windows applications allow you to add and delete menu items dynamically at runtime. Microsoft Word for Windows, for instance, adds a document's file name to the File menu after you create the document. You simply click on the file name to open the particular document; you don't have to open the File menu, select the Open command, and then choose the desired file name from a dialog box. When you delete the file, the file name is removed automatically from the menu.

The **Accelerator combo box** displays a complete listing of all shortcut keys and key combinations that you can designate for menu commands. You should note that you cannot use the same shortcut key twice on the same menu. Visual Basic will display an error message indicating that you must select another shortcut key.

The **Checked check box** can be selected if you want to display a check mark next to a command after you select it. Selecting this option creates an on/off toggle to indicate whether a command is in effect. By default, this property's value is set to False; by selecting this property, you set its value to True.

The **Enabled check box** is always checked by default to indicate that its value is set to True. When a menu command is enabled, it responds by executing the event procedure code attached to it. If the command is disabled, its Enabled property value is set to False. The command will appear dimmed and won't respond when you select it.

The **Visible check box** is also checked by default to indicate that its value has been set to True. To make a menu command invisible, deselect the Visible check box. Deselecting this option sets the property's value to False. This action disables the command and removes it from the menu.

The bottom half of the Menu Design window displays the hierarchy of a form's menu system as you create it. This part of the window is actually a list box control, which displays all of the menu and command name entries. I'll discuss the use of the other controls in the window while you create the menus for all the Window$ to Wealth forms.

Creating Menus with the Menu Design Window

Although you can use the access and shortcut keys to select menu commands, it's usually much faster to use the mouse. All menu commands are invoked with a Click event procedure by default. After you create a menu, you write the code that will be executed when the particular event procedure is invoked.

NOTE You write an event procedure for a menu command in the same way as you do for any control. The control name that you give each menu command in the Menu Design window is used as part of the control's event procedure name.

Designing the Menu Form's Menu

The menu on the Menu form allows you to exit the Window$ to Wealth application.

Creating the File Menu

To create the menu for the Menu form, follow these steps:

1. Display the Wealth project window.

2. Double-click on the Menu form file. The form will appear.

3. Open the Menu Design window.

4. In the Caption text box, type **&File.** The ampersand indicates that the next character, which in this case is *F*, will be the access key for the File menu and will appear underlined.

5. Enter **FileMenu** in the CtlName text box. This control name will be used as part of the event procedure name.

6. Click the Next button to move the highlight bar down.

7. Click the → button to indent the next entry. This action designates that the next entry is a command within the menu. An ellipsis appears at the beginning of the command.

8. Type **E&xit** in the Caption text box. This will be the name of the command; *x* will be the access key.

9. Enter **ExitCommand** in the CtlName text box, as shown in Figure 10.2. This name will also be used as part of the name for the command's event procedure.

10. Click the Done button when you have finished. The File menu will appear on the Menu form, as shown below.

11. Select Save File from the File menu to save your work.

12. Select Save Project to save the project.

FIGURE 10.2:

The Menu Design window shows the entries that are necessary to create the Menu form's File menu

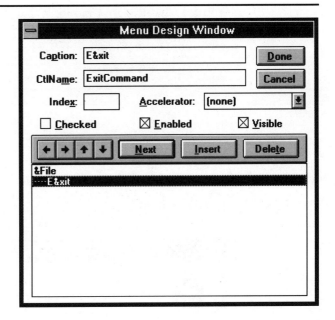

If you have several form menus that you need to create, you'll probably want to design the menus first and then write all of the event procedures later. For now, however, I'll show you the code for each menu's event procedures after going through the steps for designing the menus.

The File Menu Code

The **Sub ExitCommmand_Click** event procedure is attached to the File menu's Exit command. The event procedure calls the general procedure **ExitApplication**. Type the following code:

```
Sub ExitCommand_Click ()

     ExitApplication

End Sub
```

You may recall from Chapter 7 that the **ExitApplication** general procedure was designated as a module-level procedure because two forms call it from separate menu control event procedures. The following code displays the dialog box shown below, which appears when the user selects the Exit command on the Menu form's File menu:

```
Sub ExitApplication ()

       Msg$ = "Do you want to exit Window$ to Wealth?"
       If MsgBox(Msg$, 65, "Quit") = 1 Then
              End
       End If

End Sub
```

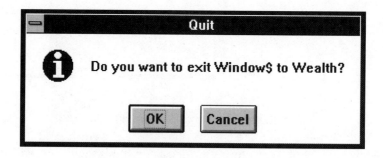

Designing the Personal Financial Statement Form's Menu

The menu on the Personal Financial Statement form allows you to clear your entries on the form, save your entries, or exit to the Menu form.

Creating the File Menu

To create the menu for the Personal Financial Statement form, follow these steps:

1. Display the Wealth project window.

2. Double-click on the Personal form file. The form will appear.

3. Open the Menu Design window.

4. In the Caption text box, type **&File.**

5. Enter **FileMenu** in the CtlName text box. This control name will be used as part of the event procedure name.

6. Click the Next button to move the highlight bar down.

7. Click the → button to indent the next entry.

8. Type **&Clear** in the Caption text box. This will be the name of the command; C will be the access key.

9. Enter **ClearRecord** in the CtlName text box. This name will also be used as part of the name for the command's event procedure.

10. Click the Next button to move the highlight bar down for the next entry. The entry will appear indented automatically; you don't have to click the → button.

11. Type – (a hyphen) in the Caption text box. Entering a hyphen will create a *separator bar* between commands. Using this control (and it *is* a control) is an effective way to display and organize commands on a menu.

12. Enter **Separator1** in the CtlName text box.

13. Click the Next button.

14. Type **&Save** in the Caption text box.

15. Enter **SaveRecord** in the CtlName text box.

16. Move the highlight bar down for the next entry by clicking the Next button.

17. Type – in the Caption text box.

18. Enter **Separator2** in the CtlName text box.

19. Click the Next button.

20. Type **E&xit** in the Caption text box.

21. Enter **ExitRecord** in the CtlName text box. The window should now look like Figure 10.3.

22. Click the Done button when you have finished. The File menu will appear on the Personal Financial Statement form, as shown below.

23. Save your work.

FIGURE 10.3:

The Menu Design window shows the entries that are necessary to create the Personal Financial Statement form's File menu

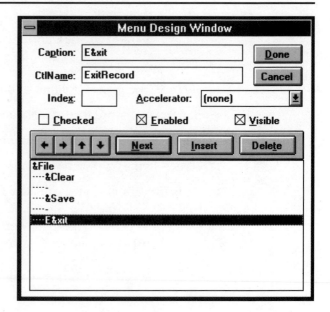

The File Menu Code

The **Sub ClearRecord_Click** event procedure clears the values from all the text boxes and reinitializes the form. Enter the following code for the event procedure:

```
Sub ClearRecord_Click ()

        'Clears all lines of the Personal Financial
        'statement.

        Dim i%

        For i% = 6 To 0 Step -1
             Value(i%).Text = ""
             Amount(i%).Text = ""
        Next i%

        TotalAssets.Caption = "0"
        TotalLiabilities.Caption = "0"
        NetWorth.Caption = "0"

        If CurIndex <> 0 Then
             CurIndex = 0
             Value(CurIndex).SetFocus
        End If

End Sub
```

> **NOTE**
>
> When the Clear command is selected, all the controls on the form which constitute a record are cleared of their current values. When CurIndex (above) is assigned the value 0, the statement **Value(CurIndex).SetFocus** sets the Index property of the Value control array to 0. The text box that has its Index property value set to 0 receives the focus. The insertion bar will appear in the first text box under the " Current Value" column.

The **SaveRecord_Click** event procedure saves the current record as a random-access file. The procedure uses the current date as the file's name by calling the

StatementName$ function, which returns a serial date value:

```
Sub SaveRecord_Click ()

    'Save the current Personal Financial Statement as
    'a random-access disk file. If a statement file
    'already exists for today, give the user the
    'option of appending to the existing file or
    'overwriting the existing file.

    Const YesNoCancel = 3
    Const Yes = 6
    Const No = 7
    Dim CurFile$, Answer As Integer
    Dim RecCount As Integer, NewRec As Integer

    'Create the file name, open the file and count its records.
    CurFile$ = StatementName$(Today)
    Open CurFile$ For Random As #1 Len = Len(PersonalRecord)
        RecCount = LOF(1) / Len(PersonalRecord)
        NewRec = 1

    'If any records exist, get the user's instructions.
    If RecCount > 0 Then
        Msg$ = "A financial statement file" + CrLf$
        Msg$ = Msg$ + "already exists for today. " + CrLf$ + CrLf$
        Msg$ = Msg$ + "Append to this file?" + CrLf$ + CrLf$
        Msg$ = Msg$ + "    Click Yes to Append" + CrLf$
        Msg$ = Msg$ + "    Click No to Replace"
        Answer = MsgBox(Msg$, YesNoCancel, "Save Personal Financial Statement")

        If Answer = Yes Then
            'Prepare to append to the end of the file.
            NewRec = RecCount + 1

        ElseIf Answer = No Then
            'Erase the old file and create a new one.
            Close #1
            Kill CurFile$
            Open CurFile$ For Random As #1 Len = Len(PersonalRecord)
        Else
```

```
                'Cancel the save operation.
                Close #1
                Exit Sub
        End If
  End If

  'Save the valid record to the file
  For i% = 0 To 6
        Put #1, NewRec, PersonalRecord
        NewRec = NewRec + 1
  Next i%
  Close #1

End Sub
```

> **NOTE**
>
> When you select the Save command, the value entered in each text box control of both the Value and Amount control arrays is assigned to *NewRec*. This variable has been declared as part of the PersonalRecord data structure, which was declared in the global module. The **Put** statement immediately above writes from a record variable (*NewRec*) to the disk file PersonalRecord.

The **Sub ExitRecord_Click** event exits the current form and returns you to the Menu form:

```
Sub ExitRecord_Click ()

      Form2.Hide
      Form1.Show

End Sub
```

I won't bother to show you how the Cash Flow form's menu was designed because it is identical to the menu for the Personal Financial Statement form. The Daily Stock Record form doesn't include a menu bar; command buttons are used to perform save, clear, and exit functions.

Designing the Menus for the Cash Flow and Daily Stock Record Forms

I haven't included the steps for creating the Cash Flow form's menu, because the form's File menu is similiar to the File menu for the Personal Financial Statement form. When you display the Cash Flow form, you will certainly want to write an event procedure that enables the user to exit and return to the Menu form. If you want to see examples of event procedures that you can attach to the File menu's commands, refer to the previous section on creating the same menu for the Personal Financial Statement form.

The Daily Stock Record form doesn't include a menu. You will recall that I used command button controls to handle the Save, Clear, and Exit functions. However, you could modify the form by creating a menu and then adding the commands to perform these actions. The event procedures for each of the command button controls can just as easily be used for the menu commands.

Designing the Weekly Investment Tracker Form's Menus

The Weekly Investment Tracker form includes three menus: **File, Graph,** and **Week.**

Creating the File Menu

To create the File menu, follow these steps:

1. Display the Wealth project window.
2. Double-click on the Tracker form file. The form will appear.
3. Open the Menu Design window.
4. In the Caption text box, type **&File.**
5. Enter **FileMenu** in the CtlName text box.
6. Click the Next button to move the highlight bar down.
7. Click the → button to indent the next entry. An ellipsis will appear.
8. Type **Sea&rch** in the Caption text box.

9. Enter **SearchInvest** in the CtlName text box.

10. Click the Next button.

11. Type **&Save** in the Caption text box.

12. Enter **SaveInvest** in the CtlName text box.

13. Click the Accelerator combo box.

14. Select Ctrl+S from the list.

15. Click the Next button.

16. Type **&Clear** in the Caption text box.

17. Enter **ClearInvest** in the CtlName text box.

18. Click the Accelerator combo box.

19. Select Ctrl+C from the list.

20. Click the Next button.

21. Type **&Print** in the Caption text box.

22. Enter **PrintInvest** in the CtlName text box.

23. Select Ctrl+P from the Accelerator combo box list.

24. Click the Next button.

25. Type – (a hyphen) in the Caption text box.

26. Enter **Separator1** in the CtlName text box.

27. Click the Next button.

28. Type **E&xit** in the Caption text box.

29. Enter **Quit** in the CtlName text box.

30. Choose Ctrl+X from the Accelerator combo box list. The window should now look like Figure 10.4.

31. Click the Done button when you have finished. The File menu will look like that below.

32. Save your work by selecting the Save File command from the File menu.

33. Save the project by selecting Save Project.

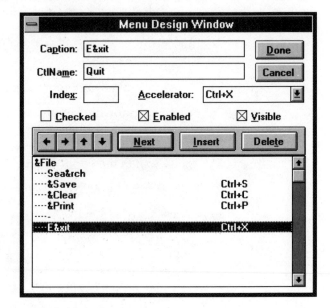

FIGURE 10.4:

The Menu Design window shows the entries necessary to create the Weekly Investment Tracker form's File menu

The File Menu Code

Most of the event procedures for the File menu's commands are similar to those that you wrote for the other form menus. However, let's look at the event procedures for the Search and Save commands to understand what they accomplish. I will discuss the event procedure for the Print command in Chapter 12.

NOTE I haven't included the code for the Weekly Investment Tracker form's Clear, Print, and Exit menu commands. If you want to see examples of event procedures written for other Clear and Exit menu commands, you can look at them in the section that discusses the Personal Financial Statement form. I have written an event procedure for the Personal Financial Statement form's Print command, which is discussed in Chapter 12.

The **SearchInvest_Click** event procedure searches for an investment record in the form's database. If the record doesn't exist, the application informs the user:

```
Sub SearchInvest_Click ()

    'Search for the current investment in the database.

    Dim TargetPos%

    'Find the name in the index, and read the record's
    'position. (A return value of zero indicates that
    'the record is not in the database.)

    TargetPos% = SearchIndex%((InvestName.Text))
    If TargetPos% <> 0 Then

        'Read the record.
        Open InvestFile For Random As #1 Len = Len(InvestRec)
            Get #1, TargetPos%, InvestRec
        Close #1

        'Display the fields of the record in
        'the appropriate text boxes.
        Comments.Text = InvestRec.CommentsField
        ClosePrice.Text = Format$(InvestRec.ClosePriceField)
```

```
            'If the record doesn't exist, inform the user.
        Else
            Msg$ = InvestName.Text
            Msg$ = Msg$ + " is not in the database."
            MsgBox Msg$, 48, "Investment File"
        End If

End Sub
```

The **Sub SearchInvest_Click** event procedure calls the **SearchIndex%** function. If the function returns a value of 0, then the investment record doesn't exist in the database:

```
Function SearchIndex% (SearchName$)

    'Search through the index for the name of the stock
    'that the user has entered into the InvestName combo box.

    Dim InvestFound%, StartPos%, LastPos%, CenterPos%, SearchName$

    InvestFound% = 0
    StartPos% = 1
    LastPos% = InvestCount

    'Build the target name in the format used in the index.

    Do While ((InvestFound% = 0) And (StartPos% <= LastPos%))
        CenterPos% = (StartPos% + LastPos%) \ 2
        Select Case UCase$(SearchName$)
            Case InvestIndex(CenterPos%).InvestRef
                InvestFound% = InvestIndex(CenterPos%).RecNum
            Case Is > InvestIndex(CenterPos%).InvestRef
                StartPos% = CenterPos% + 1
            Case Else
                LastPos% = CenterPos% + 1
        End Select
    Loop

    'Return the record number if the name was found,
    'or a value of zero if the name was not found.

    SearchIndex% = InvestFound%

End Function
```

The dialog box below appears when an investment record cannot be found after the Sub SearchInvest_Click event procedure is invoked. If the user doesn't enter a name in the form's Name text box and clicks the Search command, a blank will appear between the exclamation point and the word *is*.

The **Sub SaveInvest_Click** event procedure saves the current investment record in the database:

```
Sub SaveInvest_Click ()

    'Save the current investment record in the database
    'as a random-access file. If the record already
    'exists, give the user the option of appending to the
    'existing file or overwriting the existing file.

    Const YesNoCancel = 3        'Type of message box.
    Const Yes = 6                'Return value of yes.
    Const No = 7                 'Return value of no.

    Dim Msg$, CurRec%, Investment$
    Dim CurFile$, Answer As Integer
    Dim NewRec As Integer

    'Create the file name, open the file, and count its
    'records.
    CurFile$ = InvestmentName$(Today)
    Open CurFile$ For Random As #1 Len = Len(InvestRec)
```

```
RecCount = LOF(1) / Len(InvestRec)
NewRec = 1

Investment$ = LTrim$(RTrim$(InvestName.Text))
If Investment$ = "" Then

    'Don't save a blank record.
    Msg$ = "Investment record cannot be saved "
    Msg$ = Msg$ + "without a name."
    MsgBox Msg$, 48, "Investment File"
    InvestName.SetFocus
Else
    InvestRec.InvestNameField = Investment$
End If


CurRec% = SearchIndex%(InvestRec.InvestNameField)

'If any record exists, get the user's instructions.
If InvestCount > 0 Then
    Msg$ = "An investment record already exists" + CrLf$
    Msg$ = Msg$ + "for today. " + CrLf$ + CrLf$
    Msg$ = Msg$ + "Append to this file?" + CrLf$ + CrLf$
    Msg$ = Msg$ + "      Click Yes to Append" + CrLf$
    Msg$ = Msg$ + "      Click No to Replace"
    Answer = MsgBox(Msg$, YesNoCancel, "Save Investment Record")

    If Answer = Yes Then
        'Prepare to append to the end of file.
        InvestCount = InvestCount + 1
        InvestIndex(InvestCount).InvestRef =
            UCase$(InvestRec.InvestNameField)
        InvestIndex(InvestCount).RecNum = InvestCount
        SortInvestIndex

        'Add the investment name to the combo box list.
        InvestName.AddItem InvestRec.InvestNameField

    ElseIf Answer = No Then
        'Erase the old file and create a new one.
        Close #1
        Kill CurFile$
```

```
        Open CurFile$ For Random As #1 Len = Len(InvestRec)
    Else

        'Cancel the save operation.
        Close #1
        Exit Sub
    End If

    'Read the fields that have not already been read.
    InvestRec.CommentsField = Comments.Text

End If

'Save the valid record to the file.
For i% = 0 To 4

    'Call the Valid Line function to determine
    'whether a record is complete. If so, the
    'function fills the global InvestRec variable.
    If ValidLine(i%) Then
        Put #1, NewRec, InvestRec
        NewRec = NewRec + 1
    End If
Next i%
Close #1

End Sub
```

The **Sub SaveInvest_Click** event procedure calls two functions: **Investment-Name$** and **ValidLine.** After the user inputs the data for the current investment record and invokes the event procedure for the Save command, the application searches the database to check if the record already exists. The procedure creates the file name, opens the random-access file, and counts the number of existing records. Using the argument *Today,* the function **InvestmentName$** is assigned to the variable *CurFile$.* The function uses the current date to see whether the current file name exists for an earlier date. (Remember that the current date is the name of a file.) If the file does exist, the application displays a dialog box, giving the user the option of appending or overwriting it:

```
Function InvestmentName$ (TargetDate As Long)

    'Create a file name from an investment name.
```

```
Dim TempName$

TempName$ = InvestFile$ + "\"
TempName$ = TempName$ + Format$(TargetDate, "mm-dd-yy")
InvestmentName$ = TempName$ + "." + ExtName$
```

End Function

The function **ValidLine** is called by the event procedure to determine quickly whether the record is complete; that is, it checks to make sure that the user has inputted data in the Closing Price field. The record isn't complete until this important information is entered. The form wouldn't serve any real purpose if a stock's closing price wasn't saved for the current date. How else would you be able to track the stock to determine its performance? If the record isn't complete, a dialog box alerts the user. When the record is completed, the fields of the global variable *InvestRec* are filled in and the record is saved:

```
Function ValidLine (LineNum As Integer) As Integer

    'Determine whether a line is complete.
    'If so, save it as an InvestRec.

    'To be complete, a line must contain a Closing Price.

    OkLine = WkDate(LineNum).Text <> " "
    OkLine = OkLine And ClosePrice(LineNum).Text <> " "

    'If the record is complete, fill in the fields
    'of global InvestRec variable.

    If OkLine Then
        InvestRec.WkDateField = Val(WkDate(LineNum).Text)
        InvestRec.ClosePriceField = Val(ClosePrice(LineNum).Text)
    End If

    'Return a value of true or false.
    ValidLine = OkLine

End Function
```

The dialog box shown below will appear when you click the Save command but haven't yet entered a name in the form's Name text box.

Creating the Graph Menu

The Weekly Investment Tracker form's Graph menu allows the user to display the current period or a ten-week period. To create the form's Graph menu, open the Menu Design window and move the highlight bar below the Exit command option. Follow these steps:

1. In the Caption text box, type **&Graph.** (Do not indent this line, or else *Graph* will be added to the File menu.)

2. Enter **GraphMenu** in the CtlName text box.

3. Click the Next button to move the highlight bar down.

4. Click the → button to indent the next entry. An ellipsis will appear.

5. Type **&One Week** in the Caption text box.

6. Enter **OneWeek** in the CtlName text box.

7. Select F7 from the Accelerator text box list.

8. Select the Checked check box option. When this command is clicked, a check mark will appear to the left of the command's name to indicate that it has been selected.

9. Click the Next button.

10. Type **&Ten Week Trend** in the Caption text box.

11. Enter **TenWeeks** in the CtlName text box.

12. Select F8 from the Accelerator text box list.

13. Select the Checked check box option.

14. Click the Done button when you have finished. The menu should look like the one below.

15. Save your work.

The Graph Menu Code

The **Sub OneWeek_Click** event procedure displays the graph for a five-day period; the **Sub TenWeeks_Click** event procedure displays the ten-week graph. Type the following code:

```
Sub OneWeek_Click ()

    'Display the graph for one week's data.
    OneWeek.Checked = True
    TenWeeks.Checked = False
    UpdateHigh

End Sub
```

NOTE

Both the **Sub OneWeek_Click** and **Sub TenWeek_Click** event procedures call the **UpdateHigh** general procedure. This procedure displays the highest closing price for a five-day period.

```
Sub TenWeeks_Click ()

    'Switch to the ten-week trend graph.
    TenWeeks.Checked = True
    OneWeek.Checked = False
    UpdateHigh

End Sub
```

Creating the Week Menu

The Weekly Investment Tracker form's Week menu allows the user to display the current or previous five-day period and to move forward or backward one week at a time. To create the form's Week menu, open the Menu Design window and move the highlight bar after &Ten Week Trend. Follow these steps:

1. In the Caption text box, type **&Week.**

2. Enter **WeekMenu** in the CtlName text box.

3. Click the Next button to move the highlight bar down.

4. Click the → button to indent the next entry. An ellipsis will appear.

5. Type **&This Week** in the Caption text box.

6. Enter **ThisWeek** in the CtlName text box.

7. Select F5 from the Accelerator text box list.

8. Click the Next button.

9. Type **&Last Week** in the Caption text box.

10. Enter **LastWeek** in the CtlName text box.

11. Select F6 from the Accelerator text box list.

12. Click the Next button.

13. Type – (a hyphen) in the Caption text box.

14. Enter **Separator2** in the CtlName text box.

15. Click the Next button.

16. Type **Move &Backward** in the Caption text box.

17. Enter **Backward** in the CtlName text box.

18. Click the Next button.

19. Type **Move &Forward** in the Caption text box.

20. Enter **Forward** in the CtlName text box.

21. Click the Done button when you have finished. The menu should look like the one below.

22. Save your work.

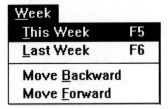

The Week Menu Code

The **Sub ThisWeek** event procedure displays the investment data and graph for the current five-day period; the **Sub LastWeek** event procedure displays the investment data and graph for last week:

```
Sub ThisWeek_Click ()

    'Display the current weeks data and graph.
    WeekRef& = Int(Now)
    ShowWeek

End Sub
```

> **NOTE**
>
> Both event procedures call the **ShowWeek** general procedure as the form's reference point. This procedure references the **WeekRef&** serial date variable as the starting point for displaying the current five-day period. When the user clicks the This Week command, the **Sub ThisWeek_Click** event procedure is invoked; when the user clicks the Last Week command and invokes the **Sub LastWeek_Click** event procedure, **WeekRef&** is again referenced. Seven days are subtracted from today's date, which results in the display of last week's data and graph.

```
Sub LastWeek_Click ()

    'Display last week's data and graph.
    WeekRef& = Now - 7
    ShowWeek

End Sub
```

The **Sub Backward_Click** event procedure scrolls back to the previous five-day period; the **Sub ForwardWeek_Click** event procedure scrolls forward. These are accessed from the newly created menu commands, Move Backward and Move Forward:

```
Sub Backward_Click ()
    'Scroll back to the previous week.
    WeekRef& = WeekRef& - 7
    ShowWeek
End Sub

Sub Forward_Click ()
    'Move forward by one week.
    WeekRef& = WeekRef& + 7
    ShowWeek
End Sub
```

Summary

Creating a menu is an easy task with Visual Basic. You simply open the Menu Design window from the Window menu and enter the pertinent information for each menu and command name. To design menus that appear and behave like menus found in other popular Windows applications like Microsoft Excel and Microsoft Word, note the following:

- An *access key* is a single letter that you designate in a menu or command name with an underscore (_). To create an access key, open the Menu Design window. As you enter a name in the Caption text box, type an & (ampersand) *before* the letter that you are designating as the access key. The designated letter will appear in a menu or command name with the underscore. To open a menu, press the Alt key and the access key. To execute a command, press the command name's access key. Once you designate an access key for one command, you cannot use the same access key on the same menu.

- A *shortcut key* is a function key or a keystroke combination that you designate for a command in the Menu Design window. To create a shortcut key, enter the information for the command and then open the Accelerator combo box. Select a shortcut key from the list that appears. Note that you cannot use the same short key twice on the same menu.

- A *separator bar* is a graphical control that is displayed as a line across a menu. For example, you might want to separate the Exit command on a File menu from the other commands. Using a separator bar is a convenient way to group similar commands. To create a separator bar, type a hyphen (–) in the Caption text box. Give the control a unique name, such as Separator1, Separator2, etc.

PART III

Using Advanced Visual Basic Features

Part III introduces several advanced Visual Basic features that can enhance your applications by extending their functionality.

After you build an application and write the code, you need to debug it. One of Visual Basic's most powerful features is its ability to trap those pesky syntax errors that somehow find their way into your applications as you write code. As any Windows programmer can tell you, syntax errors that weren't detected during design time can occur during runtime. No matter how hard you strive to write perfect code, compile-time and runtime errors are unavoidable. However, by using Visual Basic's context-sensitive help and other error-handling features, you can shorten debugging time significantly.

The task of printing the contents of a form is another task that is very easy to accomplish in Visual Basic. By using the PrintForm method, you can send a bit-for-bit image of the form to the printer. The result is similar to sending a Print Screen command to the printer, except that PrintMethod prints the *entire* form even if only a portion of the form appears on the screen. All the information that appears on the form is outputted; this information includes all the controls and any input you enter on the form.

One of the most powerful aspects of applications running under Windows is the ability to share data. The Windows *dynamic data exchange* is simply a mechanism that enables two applications to exchange data automatically and continuously. In other words, DDE is the way for two applications to "talk" to each other. You automate the communication mechanism by which the applications will exchange and update data. However, before you can initiate any data exchange, or *conversation,* you must designate one application as the "server" and the other application as the "client."

The process of DDE is analogous to a conversation between two people. Before the client can begin a conversation with a server, it has to specify the name of the server, the topic, and the item that it going to be exchanged between the two applications.

A *link* is another way to refer to a DDE conversation. Here the two applications are "linked" by the data they are exchanging at any given moment. There are two types of links: *hot links* and *cold links.* A hot link is a way for the server to pass new data to the client every time the data changes. A cold link is the way the server passes new data to the client only when the client requests it.

CHAPTER

ELEVEN

Tapping the Power of Windows' Dynamic Data Exchange

- Creating a Client Link or Server Link at Design Time

- Examining Link Properties

- Loading the CONSTANT.TXT File in an Application's Global Module

- Making an Executable File

11

A powerful aspect of running applications under Windows is the ability to share data among them. For example, using the Windows Clipboard is a convenient way to move data from one application to another. You can place data in the Clipboard from, say, a Microsoft Word for Windows document and paste it into another document. You may have also discovered how easy it is to copy code written in one Visual Basic form and paste it into another form. You can save yourself a lot of programming time by reusing code in this way.

Using the Clipboard, however, has its limitations. All you're doing is *storing* data in the Clipboard's buffer so that you can paste the same data into another document. Furthermore, you're doing the work manually by accessing the Cut, Copy, and Paste commands from each of the application's Edit menus. What if you wanted to give one Windows application the ability to share data *automatically* with another application? How would you create the mechanism that allowed the exchange of data to occur *continuously* so that each time you modified the data in one document it would be updated in the other document? You would have to use Windows' Dynamic Data Exchange (DDE) feature to accomplish these tasks.

NOTE | You need to be aware that not all Windows programs support Dynamic Data Exchange. You should read the documentation that accompanies the program to find out if this is the case.

Putting Dynamic Data Exchange to Work

Dynamic Data Exchange is simply a mechanism that enables two applications to exchange data automatically and continuously, hence the name "dynamic." In other words, DDE is the way for two applications to "talk" to each other. This automates the mechanism by which applications can exchange and update data. However, before initiating any data exchange, or *conversation*, you must designate one application as the "server" and the other application as the "client."

The process of DDE is analogous to a conversation between two people. The application that initiates the conversation is called the *client* and the application that responds to the client is called the *server*. The subject of the conversation is called— you guessed it—the *topic*. Before the client can begin a conversation with a server, it has to specify the name of the server, the topic, and the item that is going to be exchanged between the two applications. This *item* refers to specific data that both applications recognize. An item can change at any time, but it won't affect the conversation. Examples of items are the text in a text box control, the caption in a label control, and the picture in a picture box control.

You might ask yourself how an exchange takes place after you've identified the client/server relationship, the topic of the conversation, and the item(s) exchanged during the conversation. All this information is passed between the two applications through links. A *link* is another way to refer to a DDE conversation. In other words, the two applications are "linked" by the data they are exchanging at any given moment.

There are two types of links: *hot links* and *cold links*. A hot link is a way for the server to pass new data to the client every time the data change. A cold link is the way the server passes new data to the client only when the client requests it. Furthermore, link properties have values that you can set. Like all properties, you can set link properties at design time or at runtime.

Creating Design-Time Links

There will be times when you want to create data links between applications while you are designing a form. This is a convenient way to set link properties without writing code. When you run the application, the links that you have established will be recognized by the client and server.

Making a Client Link

A Visual Basic application can be either a client or a server. If you want your Visual Basic application to receive data from another application, such as a Microsoft Excel worksheet, you have to create a *client link*. In other words, the Visual Basic application (the client) is the one requesting the information from the Excel worksheet (the server). Before you try this, however, both applications must be running.

For example, follow the steps below to create a client link at design time. This exercise involves creating a client link between the Personal Financial Statement form and an Excel worksheet:

1. Open the Wealth project.

2. Double-click on the Personal Financial Statement form to open it.

3. Minimize Visual Basic.

4. Display the Program Manager.

5. Open Microsoft Excel to display a worksheet.

6. Format the worksheet to look like the Personal Financial Statement form. You can replicate the form by entering the same labels in cells.

7. Resize the spreadsheet and form so that they both appear on the screen, as shown in Figure 11.1.

8. While you are in the worksheet, select the first cell (data item) under the "Current Value" column in the Excel spreadsheet. In this example, the cell is C9.

9. Choose the Copy command from Excel's Edit menu.

10. Select the text box control on the form that corresponds to the cell in the worksheet. Selection handles will appear around the control.

11. Choose the Paste Link command on Visual Basic's Edit Menu. A cell delimiter will appear automatically in the text box.

NOTE   A cell *delimiter* is always sent to a control when you interact with Excel. It is used to separate data from different cells in the worksheet. This means that you can send data from more than one cell to a control. A delimiter makes it easy to specify a range of data that has been passed to a control.

Making a Server Link

A Visual Basic application can also pass data to other applications. To make this happen, you have to create a *server link*. A server link is used by the other application (the client) to request data from the Visual Basic application (the server). The

FIGURE 11.1:

Before you can create a client link at design time, two applications must be open at the same time. Here an Excel spreadsheet (bottom) and the Personal Financial Statement form (top) are displayed.

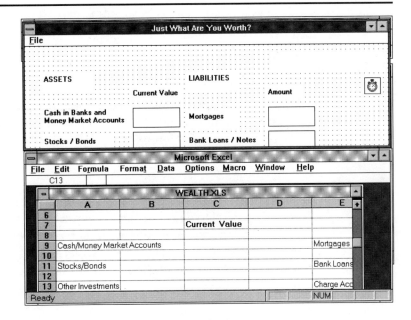

process of creating a server link at design time is similar to the process you followed to create a client link. Before you begin the process, both the Visual Basic application and the other application must be running.

In the example below, I again use the Personal Financial Statement form and the same Excel worksheet created earlier. To create a server link, follow these steps:

1. Open the Wealth project.

2. Double-click on the Personal Financial Statement form to open it.

3. Minimize Visual Basic.

4. Display the Program Manager.

5. Open Microsoft Excel to display a worksheet.

6. Format the worksheet to look like the form.

7. Resize the spreadsheet and form so that they both appear on the screen.

8. Select the second text box control under the "Current Value" column in the Visual Basic form. Selection handles will appear around the control.

9. Choose the Copy command from Visual Basic's Edit menu.

10. Select the cell in the worksheet that corresponds to the text box on the form.

11. Choose the Paste Link command from Excel's Edit Menu. A zero will appear automatically in the cell. The edit line will also display the formula in the cell, as shown in Figure 11.2.

The formula

```
{=WEALTH|Form2!'Value(0)'}
```

is used by Excel to define the link between the server (the Personal Financial Statement form) and the client (the worksheet). The cell's formula identifies the server in the conversation in this way: The server is **WEALTH**, the topic is **Form2,** and the item is **Value(0).** While the link is active, the cell in the worksheet displays the Text property setting of the text box control Value. Remember that each of the text boxes under the "Current Value" column in the Personal Financial Statement form is part of a control array.

FIGURE 11.2:

When an Excel spreadsheet is designated as a *client* application, the edit line will always display the link's formula. All applications that support DDE use their own conventions to show how a link was created.

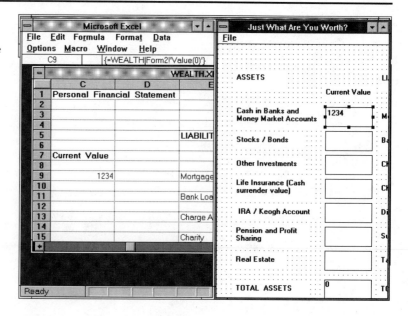

As you can see, it's not difficult to create a client or server link at design time. To initiate a data exchange, follow these steps:

1. Click the text box on the form.

2. Select the Text property from the Properties bar. The current setting will appear blank.

3. Type a number, say **1234**.

4. Press the Enter key to confirm.

5. The number will appear automatically in the corresponding cell on the worksheet, as in Figure 11.2.

Limitations of Design-Time Links

The biggest limitation to using the Copy and Paste Link commands to start any data exchange during design time is that you have to do the work manually. If you were concerned only with establishing a DDE conversation between applications that only involved a few data items, then you could be satisfied with creating links in this manner. However, you would really have your work cut out for you if you had a complex application that involved the exchange of many data items.

For example, if the conversation established previously by the Personal Financial Statement form and the Excel worksheet involved an exchange of data between all the text boxes on the form and the corresponding cells in the worksheet, creating the links during design time would be inefficient and very time-consuming. Furthermore, you wouldn't be able to set up DDE conversations with applications that didn't offer Copy and Paste Link command options. A better way to establish links between applications is to write the code that will accomplish this task.

NOTE

Although many Windows applications don't offer Copy and Paste Link commands, they might still support DDE. In these cases, you would have to write code to establish the data links necessary for a communication exchange. You should read the documentation that accompanies a program to find out if this is possible.

Creating Runtime Links

To establish runtime data links between applications, you must write an event procedure that includes the code to handle this task. The event procedure initiates the exchange; in other words, the conversation can only begin when the event procedure is invoked. This process is analogous to calling someone on the telephone. When the person at the other end of the line picks up the phone and says, "Hello," the conversation can begin. If a wrong number has been dialed, which results in a termination of the conversation, the line is broken. This can occur in a runtime DDE exchange. When an event procedure is invoked, the applications involved try to establish a conversation. If the applications can't establish a link and a connection isn't made, Visual Basic will respond with an error message telling you that communication link failed.

Suppose you wanted the Personal Financial Statement form to request data from an Excel worksheet. In this case, the form would be the client and the worksheet would be the server. The worksheet could supply the current date to the form's label control **DayAndTime.** The code for establishing this data exchange could be written as follows. Type the code as it appears below:

```
Sub Form_Click ()
    Const Hot = 1, None = 0
    DayAndTime.LinkMode = None
    DayAndTime.LinkTopic = "EXCEL¦C:\EXCEL\SHEET1.XLS"
    DayAndTime.LinkItem = "R1C6"
    DayAndTime.LinkMode = Hot
```

Three Link properties are set in the event procedure: LinkMode, LinkTopic, and LinkItem.

The **LinkMode** property has three settings: Hot (1), Cold (2), and None (0). Setting the LinkMode property activates the link between applications. The default setting for LinkMode is None, which means that nothing will happen until the setting is changed to either Hot or Cold. In the previous example, LinkMode is set initally to None by the statement `DayAndTime.LinkMode = None`. When the statement `DayAndTime.LinkMode = Hot` is executed, Visual Basic immediately tries to establish a conversation that is specified by the LinkTopic property. This *hot link* enables the server to pass data to the client.

The **LinkTopic** property simply specifies the application that is engaged in the dynamic data exchange. In other words, the statement `DayAndTime.LinkTopic = "EXCEL¦C:\EXCEL\SHEET1.XLS"` contains the name of the server application and the topic of the conversation. In this case, the server application is Excel and the topic is C:\EXCEL\SHEET1.XLS. Remember that you must separate the name of the server and the name of the topic with a pipe (¦).

The **LinkItem** property specifies the particular data item that is involved in the exchange between the applications. Depending on the application, the data item name must appear between quotes in the statement that sets the property. In the previous example, the statement DayAndTime.LinkItem = "R1C6" sets the DayAndTime label control's LinkItem property. Since an Excel worksheet is the topic of this data exchange, the location of the data item is specified by R1C6, which stands for Row 1, Column 6. (The cell's location is actually F1.) You can, however, set the LinkItem property to any location that you desire.

> **NOTE**
>
> Every Windows application that supports Dynamic Data Exchange will use a different naming convention when you set the server application's LinkItem property. In this example, an Excel spreadsheet is the server application. Instead of using cell names line A1 or G34, the LinkItem property must designate a row and column number.

If you wanted to use a *cold link* to establish a conversation between the applications, you would simply set the LinkMode property to Cold. The following code accomplishes this by also including the LinkRequest method. If you want to try using a cold link, type the following code:

```
Sub Form_Click ()
    Const Cold = 2, None = 0
    If DayAndTime.LinkMode = None Then
        DayAndTime.LinkTopic = "EXCEL¦C:\EXCEL\SHEET1.XLS"
        DayAndTime.LinkItem = "R1C6"
        DayAndTime.LinkMode = Cold
    End If
    DayAndTime.LinkRequest
End Sub
```

In this example, when you use a cold link, the DayAndTime label control does not automatically receive data from the worksheet until a request is made. The LinkRequest method handles this task with the statement DayAndTime.LinkRequest. Each time the event procedure is invoked with the Click event, the control can request new data.

In the previous two event procedures, the constants Hot, Cold, and None were declared. In the next example, the constant Server is declared. All of these constants (and others) which are needed for using DDE are found in the CONSTANT.TXT file that is included with Visual Basic. You must copy this file in an application's global module before you can establish any DDE conversations with other applications. The directions for copying this file are shown in the next section.

Now suppose you wanted the Personal Financial Statement form to supply the current date to the worksheet. In this case, the form would be the server and the worksheet would be the client.

> **NOTE**
>
> You need to be aware that only a *form* can be designated as a server in an exchange. Although any control can supply data to the client, a control cannot be the server. You simply set the control's LinkMode property to Server, which means that the form is the server. You set the control's LinkItem property to the application that will receive the data.

The following code would enable you to click on the form to check whether a DDE exchange had been established between the form's **DayAndTime** label control and the worksheet (with the form acting as the server):

```
Sub Form1_Click ()
    Const Server = 1, None = 0
    If LinkMode = None Then
        LinkTopic = "DayAndTime"
        LinkMode = Server
    Else
        LinkMode = None
    End If
End Sub
```

Loading the CONSTANT.TXT File in the Global Module

Many important DDE constants are defined and contained in the CONSTANT.TXT file. Therefore, you have to copy this file into an application's global module to make sure that these constants are present before you start any data exchange. Otherwise, when you run an application, Visual Basic will respond with error messages, telling you that specific constants you are using have not been defined in the particular procedure.

To copy all of the declarations found in the file to the Window$ to Wealth application's global module, follow these steps:

1. Open the global module to display the code window.

2. Position the text insertion bar where you want to merge the file.

3. Select the Load Text command from the Code menu. A dialog box will appear.

4. Highlight the CONSTANT.TXT file that is found in the Visual Basic directory.

5. Click on the Merge button. The file will appear in the code window.

The contents of the file includes all of the following global constants:

```
' Some constants are commented out because they have duplicates (for
' example, NONE appears in several places).

'========='
' General '
'========='

' Booleans
Global Const TRUE = -1
Global Const FALSE = 0

'=================='
' Event parameters '
'=================='

' Button and Shift (KeyDown, KeyUp, MouseDown, MouseMove, MouseUp)
Global Const SHIFT_MASK = 1
Global Const CTRL_MASK = 2
Global Const ALT_MASK = 4
Global Const LEFT_BUTTON = 1
Global Const RIGHT_BUTTON = 2
Global Const MIDDLE_BUTTON = 4

' ErrNum (LinkError)
```

```
Global Const WRONG_FORMAT = 1
Global Const REQUEST_WITHOUT_INIT = 2
Global Const DDE_WITHOUT_INIT = 3
Global Const ADVISE_WITHOUT_INIT = 4
Global Const POKE_WITHOUT_INIT = 5
Global Const DDE_SERVER_CLOSED = 6
Global Const TOO_MANY_LINKS = 7
Global Const STRING_TOO_LONG = 8
Global Const INVALID_CONTROL_ARRAY_REFERENCE = 9
Global Const UNEXPECTED_DDE = 10
Global Const OUT_OF_MEMORY = 11
Global Const SERVER_ATTEMPTED_CLIENT_OPERATION = 12


' KeyCode (KeyDown, KeyUp)
Global Const KEY_LBUTTON = &H1
Global Const KEY_RBUTTON = &H2
Global Const KEY_CANCEL = &H3
Global Const KEY_MBUTTON = &H4              ' NOT contiguous with L & RBUTTON
Global Const KEY_BACK = &H8
Global Const KEY_TAB = &H9
Global Const KEY_CLEAR = &HC
Global Const KEY_RETURN = &HD
Global Const KEY_SHIFT = &H10
Global Const KEY_CONTROL = &H11
Global Const KEY_MENU = &H12
Global Const KEY_PAUSE = &H13
Global Const KEY_CAPITAL = &H14
Global Const KEY_ESCAPE = &H1B
Global Const KEY_SPACE = &H20
Global Const KEY_PRIOR = &H21
Global Const KEY_NEXT = &H22
Global Const KEY_END = &H23
Global Const KEY_HOME = &H24
Global Const KEY_LEFT = &H25
Global Const KEY_UP = &H26
Global Const KEY_RIGHT = &H27
Global Const KEY_DOWN = &H28
Global Const KEY_SELECT = &H29
Global Const KEY_PRINT = &H2A
Global Const KEY_EXECUTE = &H2B
Global Const KEY_SNAPSHOT = &H2C Global Const KEY_INSERT = &H2D
Global Const KEY_DELETE = &H2E
Global Const KEY_HELP = &H2F


' KEY_A thru KEY_Z are the same as their ASCII equivalents: 'A' thru 'Z'
```

```
' KEY_0 thru KEY_9 are the same as their ASCII equivalents: '0' thru '9'

Global Const KEY_NUMPAD0 = &H60
Global Const KEY_NUMPAD1 = &H61
Global Const KEY_NUMPAD2 = &H62
Global Const KEY_NUMPAD3 = &H63
Global Const KEY_NUMPAD4 = &H64
Global Const KEY_NUMPAD5 = &H65
Global Const KEY_NUMPAD6 = &H66
Global Const KEY_NUMPAD7 = &H67
Global Const KEY_NUMPAD8 = &H68
Global Const KEY_NUMPAD9 = &H69
Global Const KEY_MULTIPLY = &H6A
Global Const KEY_ADD = &H6B
Global Const KEY_SEPARATOR = &H6C
Global Const KEY_SUBTRACT = &H6D
Global Const KEY_DECIMAL = &H6E
Global Const KEY_DIVIDE = &H6F
Global Const KEY_F1 = &H70
Global Const KEY_F2 = &H71
Global Const KEY_F3 = &H72
Global Const KEY_F4 = &H73
Global Const KEY_F5 = &H74
Global Const KEY_F6 = &H75
Global Const KEY_F7 = &H76
Global Const KEY_F8 = &H77
Global Const KEY_F9 = &H78
Global Const KEY_F10 = &H79
Global Const KEY_F11 = &H7A
Global Const KEY_F12 = &H7B
Global Const KEY_F13 = &H7C
Global Const KEY_F14 = &H7D
Global Const KEY_F15 = &H7E
Global Const KEY_F16 = &H7F
Global Const KEY_NUMLOCK = &H90

' State (DragOver)
Global Const ENTER = 0
Global Const LEAVE = 1
Global Const OVER = 2

'====================='
' Function parameters '
'====================='
```

```
' MsgBox parameters
Global Const MB_OK = 0                    ' OK button only
Global Const MB_OKCANCEL = 1              ' OK and Cancel buttons
Global Const MB_ABORTRETRYIGNORE = 2      ' Abort, Retry, and Ignore buttons
Global Const MB_YESNOCANCEL = 3           ' Yes, No, and Cancel buttons
Global Const MB_YESNO = 4                 ' Yes and No buttons
Global Const MB_RETRYCANCEL = 5           ' Retry and Cancel buttons

Global Const MB_ICONSTOP = 16             ' Critical message
Global Const MB_ICONQUESTION = 32         ' Warning query
Global Const MB_ICONEXCLAMATION = 48      ' Warning message
Global Const MB_ICONINFORMATION = 64      ' Information message

Global Const MB_DEFBUTTON1 = 0            ' First button is default
Global Const MB_DEFBUTTON2 = 256          ' Second button is default
Global Const MB_DEFBUTTON3 = 512          ' Third button is default


' MsgBox return values
Global Const IDOK = 1                     ' OK button pressed
Global Const IDCANCEL = 2                 ' Cancel button pressed
Global Const IDABORT = 3                  ' Abort button pressed
Global Const IDRETRY = 4                  ' Retry button pressed
Global Const IDIGNORE = 5                 ' Ignore button pressed
Global Const IDYES = 6                    ' Yes button pressed
Global Const IDNO = 7                     ' No button pressed


'===================='
' Method parameters '
'===================='

' Drag (controls)
Global Const CANCEL = 0
Global Const BEGIN_DRAG = 1
Global Const END_DRAG = 2

' GetData, GetFormat, SetData (Clipboard)
Global Const CF_LINK = &HBF00
Global Const CF_TEXT = 1
Global Const CF_BITMAP = 2
Global Const CF_METAFILE = 3
Global Const CF_DIB = 8

' Show (form)
Global Const MODAL = 1
Global Const MODELESS = 0
```

```
'=================='
' Property values '
'=================='

' Alignment (label)
Global Const LEFT_JUSTIFY = 0           ' 0 - Left Justify
Global Const RIGHT_JUSTIFY = 1          ' 1 - Right Justify
Global Const CENTER = 2                 ' 2 - Center

' BackColor, ForeColor, FillColor (standard RGB colors: form, controls)
Global Const BLACK = &H0&
Global Const RED = &HFF&
Global Const GREEN = &HFF00&
Global Const YELLOW = &HFFFF&
Global Const BLUE = &HFF0000
Global Const MAGENTA = &HFF00FF
Global Const CYAN = &HFFFF00
Global Const WHITE = &HFFFFFF

' BackColor, ForeColor, FillColor (system colors: form, controls)
Global Const SCROLL_BARS = &H80000000             ' Scroll-bars gray area.
Global Const DESKTOP = &H80000001                 ' Desktop.
Global Const ACTIVE_TITLE_BAR = &H80000002        ' Active window caption.
Global Const INACTIVE_TITLE_BAR = &H80000003      ' Inactive window caption.
Global Const MENU_BAR = &H80000004                ' Menu background.
Global Const WINDOW_BACKGROUND = &H80000005       ' Window background.
Global Const WINDOW_FRAME = &H80000006            ' Window frame.
Global Const MENU_TEXT = &H80000007               ' Text in menus.
Global Const WINDOW_TEXT = &H80000008             ' Text in windows.
Global Const TITLE_BAR_TEXT = &H80000009          ' Text in caption, size
                                                  ' box, scroll-bar arrow box..
Global Const ACTIVE_BORDER = &H8000000A           ' Active window border.
Global Const INACTIVE_BORDER = &H8000000B         ' Inactive window border.
Global Const APPLICATION_WORKSPACE = &H8000000C   ' Background color of
                                                  ' multiple document
                                                  ' interface (MDI)
                                                  ' applications.
Global Const HIGHLIGHT = &H8000000D               ' Items selected item in a
                                                  ' control.
Global Const HIGHLIGHT_TEXT = &H8000000E          ' Text of item selected in
                                                  ' a control.
Global Const BUTTON_FACE = &H8000000F             ' Face shading on command
                                                  ' buttons.
```

```
Global Const BUTTON_SHADOW = &H80000010        ' Edge shading on command
                                                         'buttons.
Global Const GRAY_TEXT = &H80000011            ' Grayed (disabled) text.
'This color is set to 0 if the current display driver does not support a
'solid gray color.
Global Const BUTTON_TEXT = &H80000012          ' Text on push buttons.

' BorderStyle (form, label, picture box, text box)
Global Const NONE = 0              ' 0 - None
Global Const FIXED_SINGLE = 1      ' 1 - Fixed Single
Global Const SIZABLE = 2           ' 2 - Sizable (Forms only)
Global Const FIXED_DOUBLE = 3      ' 3 - Fixed Double (Forms only)
 ' DragMode (controls)
Global Const MANUAL = 0            ' 0 - Manual
Global Const AUTOMATIC = 1         ' 1 - Automatic

' DrawMode (form, picture box, Printer)
Global Const BLACKNESS = 1         ' 1 - Blackness
Global Const NOT_MERGE_PEN = 2     ' 2 - Not Merge Pen
Global Const MASK_NOT_PEN = 3      ' 3 - Mask Not Pen
Global Const NOT_COPY_PEN = 4      ' 4 - Not Copy Pen
Global Const MASK_PEN_NOT = 5      ' 5 - Mask Pen Not
Global Const INVERT = 6            ' 6 - Invert
Global Const XOR_PEN = 7           ' 7 - Xor Pen
Global Const NOT_MASK_PEN = 8      ' 8 - Not Mask Pen
Global Const MASK_PEN = 9          ' 9 - Mask Pen
Global Const NOT_XOR_PEN = 10      ' 10 - Not Xor Pen
Global Const NOP = 11              ' 11 - Nop
Global Const MERGE_NOT_PEN = 12    ' 12 - Merge Not Pen
Global Const COPY_PEN = 13         ' 13 - Copy Pen
Global Const MERGE_PEN_NOT = 14    ' 14 - Merge Pen Not
Global Const MERGE_PEN = 15        ' 15 - Merge Pen
Global Const WHITENESS = 16        ' 16 - Whiteness

' DrawStyle (form, picture box, Printer)
Global Const SOLID = 0             ' 0 - Solid
Global Const DASH = 1              ' 1 - Dash
Global Const DOT = 2               ' 2 - Dot Global Const
DASH_DOT = 3                       ' 3 - Dash-Dot
Global Const DASH_DOT_DOT = 4      ' 4 - Dash-Dot-Dot
Global Const INVISIBLE = 5         ' 5 - Invisible
Global Const INSIDE_SOLID = 6      ' 6 - Inside Solid

' FillStyle (form, picture box, Printer)
' Global Const SOLID = 0            ' 0 - Solid
```

```
Global Const TRANSPARENT = 1           ' 1 - Transparent
Global Const HORIZONTAL_LINE = 2       ' 2 - Horizontal Line
Global Const VERTICAL_LINE = 3         ' 3 - Vertical Line
Global Const UPWARD_DIAGONAL = 4       ' 4 - Upward Diagonal
Global Const DOWNWARD_DIAGONAL = 5     ' 5 - Downward Diagonal
Global Const CROSS = 6                 ' 6 - Cross
Global Const DIAGONAL_CROSS = 7        ' 7 - Diagonal Cross

' LinkMode (controls)
' Global Const NONE = 0                ' 0 - None
Global Const HOT = 1                   ' 1 - Hot
Global Const COLD = 2                  ' 2 - Cold

' LinkMode (form)
' Global Const NONE = 0                ' 0 - None
Global Const SERVER = 1                ' 1 - Server

' MousePointer (form, controls)
Global Const DEFAULT = 0               ' 0 - Default Global
Const ARROW = 1                        ' 1 - Arrow
Global Const CROSSHAIR = 2             ' 2 - Cross
Global Const IBEAM = 3                 ' 3 - I-Beam
Global Const ICON_POINTER = 4          ' 4 - Icon
Global Const SIZE_POINTER = 5          ' 5 - Size
Global Const SIZE_NE_SW = 6            ' 6 - Size NE SW
Global Const SIZE_N_S = 7              ' 7 - Size N S
Global Const SIZE_NW_SE = 8            ' 8 - Size NW SE
Global Const SIZE_W_E = 9              ' 9 - Size W E
Global Const UP_ARROW = 10             ' 10 - Up Arrow
Global Const HOURGLASS = 11            ' 11 - Hourglass
Global Const NO_DROP = 12              ' 12 - No drop

' ScaleMode (form, picture box, Printer)
Global Const USER = 0                  ' 0 - User
Global Const TWIPS = 1                 ' 1 - Twip
Global Const POINTS = 2                ' 2 - Point
Global Const PIXELS = 3                ' 3 - Pixel
Global Const CHARACTERS = 4            ' 4 - Character
Global Const INCHES = 5                ' 5 - Inch
Global Const MILLIMETERS = 6           ' 6 - Millimeter
Global Const CENTIMETERS = 7           ' 7 - Centimeter

' ScrollBar (text box)
' Global Const NONE = 0                ' 0 - None
Global Const HORIZONTAL = 1            ' 1 - Horizontal
```

```
Global Const VERTICAL = 2          ' 2 - Vertical
Global Const BOTH = 3              ' 3 - Both

' Value (check box)
Global Const UNCHECKED = 0         ' 0 - Unchecked
Global Const CHECKED = 1           ' 1 - Checked
Global Const GRAYED = 2            ' 2 - Grayed

' WindowState (form)
Global Const NORMAL = 0            ' 0 - Normal
Global Const MINIMIZED = 1         ' 1 - Minimized
Global Const MAXIMIZED = 2         ' 2 - Maximized
```

When you load this file, be aware that you might have some replication of constants. There will probably be some redundancy between the global constants in this file and the constants you may have already declared in an application's global module. However, you won't get any error messages if the same constants are declared more than once.

Creating an .EXE File

Before you can begin any data exchange at runtime, you have to compile the application into an executable (.EXE) file that can run outside of Visual Basic. To create an executable file, follow these steps:

1. Open the Wealth project.

2. Select the Make EXE File command from the File menu. A dialog box will appear, as shown in Figure 11.3. (If you have any runtime errors or other bugs, you will have to correct them *before* you can create an executable file.)

3. Enter the name **Wealth** in the File Name text box. The executable file will be saved in the Visual Basic directory unless you specify a different directory.

4. Click the OK button.

The code for the application will be compiled into an executable file. Only applications with executable files can establish a conversation. Otherwise, you will probably get an error message telling you that the Visual Basic application tried to establish a conversation but couldn't find an .EXE file in the directory's path.

FIGURE 11.3:

The Make EXE File dialog box, in which you compile the application to run outside of Visual Basic

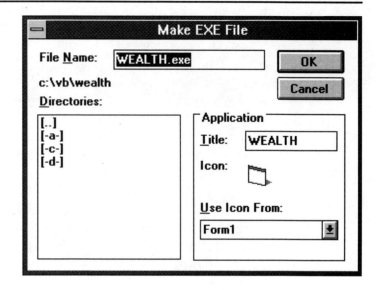

Summary

In this chapter, you learned how you can enable a Visual Basic application to exchange data with another application by using the Windows Dynamic Data Exchange (DDE) feature. It's relatively easy to set up data links between applications as long as they support DDE. You can establish links during design time or at runtime. Several topics were discussed that will help you to use DDE:

- To activate a link between applications, you need to set a form's LinkMode property. The LinkMode property has three settings: Hot (1), Cold (2), and None (0). The default setting for LinkMode is None, which means that nothing will happen until the setting is changed to either Hot or Cold. When a hot link is established, Visual Basic immediately tries to begin a conversation that is specified by the LinkTopic property. This link enables the server to pass data to the client continuously.

- To specify the application that is engaged in the dynamic data exchange, you need to set the LinkTopic property. In other words, the statement that sets the property must contain the name of the server application and the topic of the conversation.

- To specify the particular data item that is involved in the exchange between the applications, you must set the LinkItem property. All Windows applications that support DDE use different conventions for naming data items.

- To establish a conversation between applications that can only be activated with a specific request, you must set the form's LinkMode property to Cold. When you use a cold link, a control does not automatically receive data from another application until a request is made. The LinkRequest method handles this task. Each time an event procedure is invoked by an event, the control can request new data.

- Many important DDE constants are defined and contained in the CONSTANT.TXT file. Therefore, you have to copy this file into an application's global module to make sure these constants are present before you start any data exchange. Otherwise, when you run an application, Visual Basic will respond with error messages telling you that specific constants have not been defined in the particular procedure.

- Before you can initiate any DDE at runtime, you have to compile a Visual Basic application into an executable file that can run as a stand-alone program. To make an executable file, open a project and then choose the Make EXE File command from the File menu. Enter the name of the executable file in the File Name text box. Click the OK button to confirm.

Formatting Output to a Printer

- Using the PrintForm Method

- Modifying a Form's Menu

- Creating a Dynamic Array

- Setting Column Widths with the Tab Function

12

Sending output to the printer requires that (1) you have a printer and (2) you format the output so that it's legible. The task of printing is actually very easy to accomplish.

Using the PrintForm Method

You simply include the following statement in an event procedure to print an entire form:

Form.PrintForm

The statement performs the action of printing *everything* that appears on the form. By using the PrintForm method, you can print a bit-for-bit image of the form. This method sends pixels on the form directly to the printer. A *pixel* is simply the smallest unit of resolution on a monitor. For example, all the figures in this book have been captured on a VGA monitor with 600×480 resolution.

The result of using this method is similar to sending a Print Screen command to the printer, except that **PrintMethod** prints the *entire* form, even if only a portion of the form appears on the screen. For example, to print the Personal Financial Statement form, I only need to include the statement **Form2.PrintForm** in an event procedure. The output looks like that in Figure 12.1. All the information that appears on the form is output; this information includes all the controls and any input you enter on the form. You precede **PrintForm** in the statement with the name of the form you want to print, which in this example is *Form2.* However, if you don't include the form name, Visual Basic assumes that it is the form currently displayed on the screen.

The drawback to using the PrintForm method is that you may not get the highest-quality resolution. If your monitor has better resolution than your printer, then the ouput may not look as good. For example, if you're using a VGA monitor and printing to a dot-matrix printer, any text that you send to the printer will not have the same high clarity. However, if your printer has higher resolution than your monitor, the output will look better than the way it appears on the screen. If you use a monochrome monitor and send the output to a laser printer, any text will have a higher clarity.

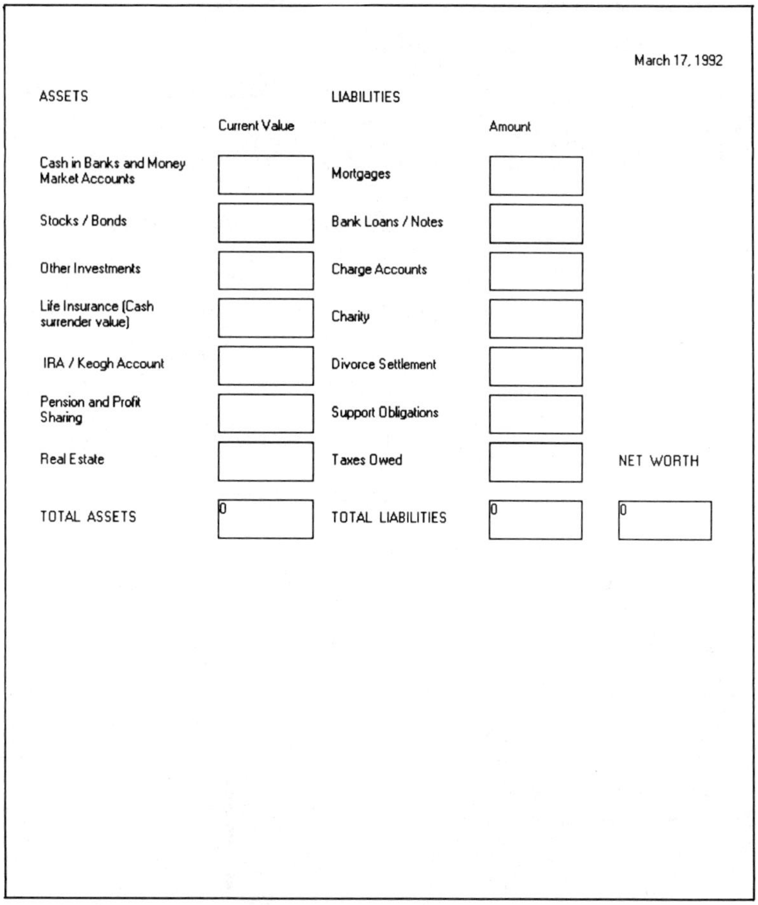

FIGURE 12.1:

The entire Personal Financial Statement form has been outputted to a printer using the PrintForm method

```
                                                              March 17, 1992

ASSETS                          LIABILITIES

              Current Value                      Amount

Cash in Banks and Money         Mortgages
Market Accounts    [      ]                    [      ]

Stocks / Bonds     [      ]     Bank Loans / Notes  [      ]

Other Investments  [      ]     Charge Accounts     [      ]

Life Insurance (Cash            Charity
surrender value)   [      ]                    [      ]

  IRA / Keogh Account [      ]  Divorce Settlement  [      ]

Pension and Profit              Support Obligations
Sharing            [      ]                    [      ]

Real Estate        [      ]     Taxes Owed     [      ]     NET WORTH

TOTAL ASSETS   [0     ]         TOTAL LIABILITIES  [0     ]    [0     ]
```

Directing Output to a Printer

A better, more consistent way to print a form is to write code that directs specified output to a printer. In this chapter, I will show you how to print the Personal Financial Statment form. Given that the form includes many text box controls in which you input text, the form will serve as a good example of formatting specified output to a printer.

Adding the Print Command to the File Menu

The first task is to add the Print command to the form's File menu. At the moment there isn't a way to invoke an event procedure that directs output to a printer. To add a Print command to the File menu, follow these steps:

1. Display the Personal Financial Statement form.

2. Select the Menu Design Window command from the Window menu to display the menu for the form, as shown in Figure 12.2.

3. Highlight the separator bar below the Save command.

4. Click the Insert button to insert a blank line. As you can see, the line is automatically indented.

5. Type **&Print** in the Caption text box.

6. Enter **PrintRecord** in the CtlName text box.

7. Click the Done button when you are finished.

FIGURE 12.2:

The Menu Design window displays the menu controls for the Personal Financial Statement form's File Menu, to which we're adding the Print command

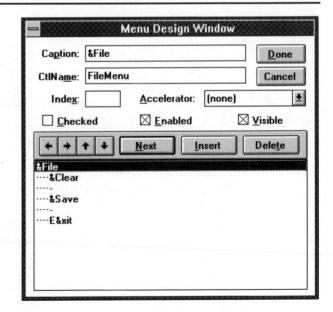

The Print command now appears on the File menu, as shown below. You can now write the code to invoke the event procedure attached to the command.

Attaching the Print Command's Event Procedure

Before you write the Print command's event procedure, you must first declare a dynamic array of Personal Financial Statement records in the declarations section of the form's general procedure. A dynamic array gives you the capability and flexibility of changing the size of the array at runtime; in other words, a dynamic array can be resized at any time.

In this example, the statement allows you to pass any number of records in the array variable to the procedure referencing it; hence the name "dynamic." By declaring the array variable at the form level, you won't have a scope-of-variables problem that you would have if you created a dynamic array that was local to the procedure.

To create the dynamic array, open the Personal Financial Statement form's general procedure in the code window. In the declarations section, add the following two lines under the comment 'The PersonalRecord Structure. This is a logical location for adding the statement, although you can include it anywhere in the declarations section:

```
'Dynamic array of Personal Financial Statement records.

Dim PersonalRecordList () As PersonalRecordType
```

The empty dimension list is indicated by ( ), which allows the application to allocate new space to the array when it needs to.

The long code that follows prints one copy of the Personal Financial Statement at a time:

```
Sub PrintRecord_Click ()

    ' Print a single Personal Financial Statement.

    Dim StatementFileName As String, RecCount As Integer
    Dim Heading As String, DateStr As String, OutFileName As String
    ' Create the complete file name for the time sheet.
```

NOTE The declarations above set the dimensions of the variables StatementFileName, RecCount, Heading, DateStr, and OutFileName.

In the statement **StatementFileName = PathName\$ + "." + ExtName\$** below, the variable StatementFileName is assigned to the path and extension names that were declared in the declarations section of the form's general procedure. The variable *PathName\$* is a constant that was declared in the application's global module. As you can see, the statement adds a period to separate the file name and the extension:

```
    StatementFileName = PathName$ + "." + ExtName$

    ' Open the file and count its records.

    Open StatementFileName For Random As #1 Len = Len(PersonalRecord)
        RecCount = LOF(1) / Len(PersonalRecord)
```

After the procedure assigns the variable **StatementFileName**, the variable is assigned to the **PersonalRecord** random-access file that was declared in the global module. After the file is opened, the records in the database are counted. All the records are actually part of a dynamic array. Using a dynamic array is convenient when you don't declare the size of the array. Therefore, the array can be very large and include many records, or only hold a few records. Declaring an array in this way has its advantages because it helps you manage your system's memory more efficiently. When you're not using the array and don't need the memory, the procedure frees the memory up so that the system can use it. In the statement below, **ReDim PersonalRecordList (RecCount)** redimensions the array. This means that the number of records in the array can always change; each time the ReDim is executed, all the values stored in the array are reset to 0.

> **NOTE**
>
> Remember that the dynamic array PersonalRecordList was declared at the form level. The event procedure Sub PrintRecord_Click () then allocates space for the array because an empty dimension list, ( ), has been included. In the statement **ReDim PersonalRecordList (RecCount)**, the element RecCount has been allocated to the array. You should note that the ReDim statement can only appear in a procedure. Unlike the Dim statement, ReDim is an executable statement; it tells the application to carry out an action at runtime. Each use of ReDim can change the number of elements in the array and the lower and upper bounds of each dimension.

```
' Redimension the array of records accordingly.
ReDim PersonalRecordList (RecCount)

' Read the entire file into the array.

For i% = 1 To RecCount
   Get #1, i%, PersonalRecordList(i%)
Next i%
Close #1
```

The statement **DateStr = Left\$(DayAndTime.Caption, 20)** assigns the variable *DateStr* to the string that appears in the label control DayAndTime, which is the current date. In this example, the Left\$ function returns a string that consists of the leftmost 20 characters of the string. The statement **Heading = "Personal Financial Statement for " + DateStr** assigns the string in quotes to the variable *Heading* and appends the current date that was assigned to DateStr. The statement **OutFileName = PathName\$ + "\" + DateStr + ".TXT"** assigns the variable *OutFileName* to the path name that was declared in the form's general procedure. The statement adds a \ to the path name; in addition, **DateStr** appends the current date to the path name, including the .TXT extension. Finally, the event procedure calls the general procedure **PrintPersonalRecordList,** which takes three parameters, Heading, RecCount, and OutFileName:

```
' Print one Personal Financial Statement file.

DateStr = Left$(DayAndTime.Caption, 20)
Heading = "Personal Financial Statement for " + DateStr
OutFileName = PathName$ + "\" + DateStr + ".TXT"
PrintPersonalRecordList Heading, RecCount, OutFileName
```

```
End Sub   'PrintRecord_Click ()
```

The general procedure **PrintPersonalRecordList** includes all the formatting attributes you need to specify in code so that the printed output is aligned. Otherwise, the output will result in a hodgepodge of illegible data.

Formatting Output to the Printer

You should try to format output to a printer so it looks the same way as it appears on a monitor. Create the following procedure and type the code as it appears:

```
Sub PrintPersonalRecordList (Title As String, NumRecs As Integer, OutFile As String)

    Dim T1 As Double, T2 As Double, RefTot As Double
    Dim ThisRef As String, NextRef As String
    Dim TabForCenter As Integer, Destination As String
    Dim GrandTot As Double
```

The statement **Destination = "Prn"** below assigns the string variable *Destination* to *Prn*, which is a standard device name. Prn is used to communicate to the first connected parallel port, such as LPT1. However, you can use Prn when you don't want to specify (or you don't know) the device name that is attached to your printer. A program doesn't have to know which device is connected to which port. In this example, Prn is referenced and the output is directed to the first connected parallel port, whatever that might be:

```
    Destination = "Prn"

    ' Use the Open statement to open the output file.

    Open Destination For Output As #1
```

The statement **TabForCenter = (75 - Len(Title)) \ 2** below assigns a value to the variable *TabForCenter,* which is used to locate the approximate center of the paper; this value is used by the **Tab** function to print the heading that was declared in the event procedure. The parameter *Heading* was passed by the event procedure to the argument *Title* that was declared as a string. The statement **Print #1** writes data to an open sequential file that is specified by the # (file number) argument, which in this case is 1. Since the variable *Destination* has been assigned to the output device

Prn, Destination is the open file. **Print #** writes an image of the data to the file (the printer), just as the data would be displayed on the monitor if you used the DOS TYPE command. Using commas causes the output to be written in 14-character width columns, or *zones*. Using semicolons causes any item to be written immediately after the previously displayed item. The **Tab** function, when it is used within a Print statement, moves subsequent screen display to the column indicated by the number inside the parentheses (the argument):

> **NOTE** The \ symbol is used for integer division. Do not confuse it with /, which is used for real division.

```
' Print the title and the column headings.

TabForCenter = (75 - Len(Title)) \ 2
Print #1, Tab(TabForCenter); Title
Print #1, Tab(TabForCenter); String$(Len(Title), "=")
Print #1,
Print #1,
Print #1, "ASSETS"; Tab(30); "  Current Value        ";
Print #1, "LIABILITIES            Amount";
Print #1,
Print #1, "------"; Tab(30); "  -------------        ";
Print #1, "-----------            ------";
Print #1,
Print #1,
Print #1, "Cash / Money Market Accounts"; Tab(53); "Mortgages          "
Print #1,
Print #1, "Stocks / Bonds              "; Tab(53); "Bank Loans /Notes  "
Print #1,
Print #1, "Other Investments           "; Tab(53); "Charge Accounts    "
Print #1,
Print #1, "Life Insurance              "; Tab(53); "Charity            "
Print #1,
Print #1, "IRA /Keogh Account          "; Tab(53); "Divorce Settlement "
Print #1,
Print #1, "Pension and Profit Sharing  "; Tab(53); "Support Obligations "
Print #1,
```

```
Print #1, "Real Estate                    "; Tab(53); "Taxes Owed           "
Print #1,
Print #1,
Print #1,
Print #1, "TOTAL ASSETS                   "; Tab(53); "TOTAL LIABILITIES   "

' Print the entire array of records.

For i% = 1 To NumRecs
```

The next two **Print #** statements print the values that are displayed in the *Value* and *Amount* control arrays. Both variables have been defined as fields in the database for the *PersonalRecord* record. The statements for printing the values in the *Total-Assets, Total Liabilities,* and *NetTotal* are also given:

NOTE The Str$ function returns a string representation of the value of a numeric expression, as in the statements below. Here, the statements print the values of T1 and T2.

```
    ' Print a detail line.

    Print #1, PersonalRecordList(i%).ValueField; Tab(32); "    ";
    Print #1, PersonalRecordList(i%).AmountField; Tab(75); "    ";
    T1 = TotalAssets.Caption
    T2 = TotalLiabilities.Caption
    Print #1,
    Print #1,
    Print #1,
    Print #1, Str$(T1); Tab(32); "    ";
    Print #1, Str$(T2); Tab(75); "    ";

Next i%

' Print Net Worth line for the entire report.

GrandTot = GrandTot + (T1 - T2)

Print #1,
Print #1,
Print #1,
Print #1, Tab(53); "NET WORTH";
```

```
Print #1, Str$(GrandTot); Tab(75); "    "

Close #1

End Sub   ' PrintPersonalRecordList
```

Now when you choose the Print command from the File menu, the result will look like that in Figure 12.3. You might have to fiddle with the Tab function to align information in columns. (Please note that the actual numbers won't appear on the statement form when you print it.)

FIGURE 12.3:
This printed form was outputted to a printer by writing code that specified the output and how it should be formatted

```
              Personal Financial Statement for March 17, 1992
              =================================================

ASSETS                        Current Value        LIABILITIES           Amount
------                        -------------        -----------           ------

Cash / Money Market Accounts                       Mortgages

Stocks / Bonds                                     Bank Loans /Notes

Other Investments                                  Charge Accounts

Life Insurance                                     Charity

IRA /Keogh Account                                 Divorce Settlement

Pension and Profit Sharing                         Support Obligations

Real Estate                                        Taxes Owed


TOTAL ASSETS                                       TOTAL LIABILITIES


                                                   NET WORTH
```

Summary

In this chapter, you learned how to format and send output to a printer. There are two ways to print a form, depending on your needs:

- To print an entire form, use the **PrintForm** method. This method is similar to sending a Print Screen command to a printer. You can send any form output to a printer, including all of the controls and text that appears on the form, by using this method.

- If you don't want to specify a printer device, you can use the standard device name *Prn* in a statement to send output to a printer.

Debugging an Application

- **Correcting Compile-Time and Runtime Errors**

- **Using the Immediate Window to Test Code**

- **Examining Visual Basic's Context-Sensitive Help Feature**

- **Single and Procedure Stepping**

- **Writing Error Handlers**

13

One of the marvelous aspects of Visual Basic is how it finds those pesky syntax errors that somehow sneak their way into your application as you write code. You've probably noticed that Visual Basic will tell you immediately when you've entered a line of code incorrectly in a procedure or forgotten to declare a variable. If you select the Syntax Checking command from the Code menu, this handy feature will always be available to assist you during design time.

As any Windows programmer can tell you, syntax errors can also occur during run-time that weren't detected during design time. No matter how hard you strive to write perfect code, you will unavoidably run into compile-time and runtime errors. However, by using Visual Basic's context-sensitive help and other error-handling features, you can shorten debugging time significantly.

Using the Immediate Window to Test Code

While you are writing code, you will sometimes get syntax errors that aren't easily corrected. One way to look at problematic code is to display statements in the Immediate window during runtime; if you get an error message, the program will stop execution. You have a choice of correcting the error and choosing either the Restart command or Break command from the Run menu. While you're in break mode, you can execute the new code in the Immediate window. For example, Figure 13.1 shows a statement as it appears in the Immediate window while in break mode. This statement generated a syntax error.

> **TIP**
>
> While you're working in the Immediate Window, you should first edit the statement to change its effect and then press the Enter key. Don't press Enter unless you want to execute a statement. To move around in the window, use the mouse or the arrow keys. You can press the Home and End keys to move to the beginning and end of the current line, respectively.

FIGURE 13.1:

The Immediate window displays a statement that generated an error message. In this example, the statement is from the Daily Stock Record form.

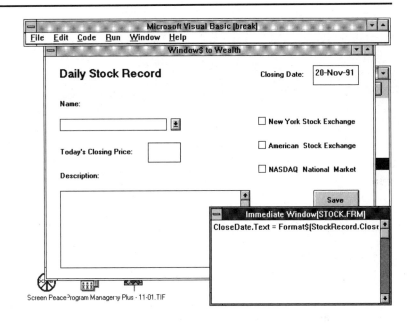

To use the window, follow these steps:

1. Enter the statement in the Immediate window. The form's name will appear in the Immediate window's title bar.

2. Press the Enter key to execute the statement.

3. If you need help with understanding code syntax for a statement, press F1.

4. When you have corrected the syntax, you can copy, cut, or paste the statement into the code window, replacing the incorrect statement.

NOTE Any statement that you write in the Immediate window is *not* saved with a project. To replace the incorrect statement in your application with the new statement, you *must* copy the code to the code window.

Correcting a Compile-Time Error

Compile-time errors always occur when you select the Start command from the Run menu. Sometimes an error won't be detected in your code as you write it during design time. But when you try to run the program, an error message is suddenly displayed on the screen. Another way Visual Basic can generate an error is when you try to compile the program. When you choose the Make EXE File command from the File Menu, Visual Basic automatically checks your code. If you've used the wrong syntax in a statement, Visual Basic will display an error message at this time.

To correct a compile-time error during runtime, follow these steps:

1. Press F1 to display context-sensitive help information about any syntax or debugging feature that you don't understand. Visual Basic will display a topic with all the possible causes for the particular error. For example, Figure 13.2 shows a topic for an error. Visual Basic will also display suggestions for correcting the error.

2. Click the OK button to clear the error message from the screen.

3. Correct the error.

4. Restart the program or select the Make EXE File command.

SHORTCUT To restart the program from the beginning, press Shift-F5.

Correcting a Runtime Error

A runtime error occurs while an application is actually running. If Visual Basic finds an error in the code, it will stop program execution and the code window will appear, displaying the specific error message. For example, Figure 13.3 shows an example of a

FIGURE 13.2:

Pressing F1 displays context-sensitive help for understanding Visual Basic features and conventions, and for correcting error messages generated during runtime

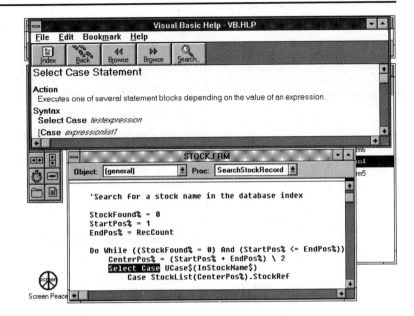

runtime error. The line of code in which the error occurs appears highlighted and displays a blinking insertion point. To correct the error, follow these steps:

1. Press F1 to use the context-sensitve help that is available for the particular topic.

2. When you've discovered the cause of the error, click the OK button to clear the message on the screen.

3. Type the correct syntax.

4. Press F5 to start the program from where it stopped or press Shift-F5 to start the program from the beginning.

Designating Breakpoints in Code

Sometimes you'll want to set a breakpoint in code to help you debug a program. A *breakpoint* is simply a statement that you set in a program so that the program will

FIGURE 13.3:

A runtime error will appear highlighted in an application's code window during execution. In this example, the Format$ function is missing the dollar sign ($).

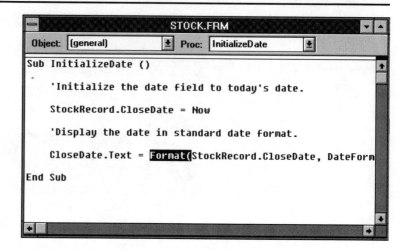

```
STOCK.FRM

Object: [general]          Proc: InitializeDate

Sub InitializeDate ()

    'Initialize the date field to today's date.

    StockRecord.CloseDate = Now

    'Display the date in standard date format.

    CloseDate.Text = Format(StockRecord.CloseDate, DateForm

End Sub
```

automatically stop. When you set a breakpoint, you're actually entering break mode, which enables you to stop program execution and look at a line of problematic code or try new code. The idea is to set breakpoints in code where you know an error is likely to occur. This will tell Visual Basic to stop program execution just before it reaches the specific line of code.

You can also enter break mode during runtime when you choose the Break command from the Run menu or press Ctrl-Break. To set a breakpoint in code during break mode or design time, follow these steps:

1. Open the code window.

2. Position the blinking insertion bar next to any line of code where you want to have a designated breakpoint.

3. Select the Toggle Breakpoint command from the Run menu. The selected line of code will appear in bold, as shown in Figure 13.4.

SHORTCUT   Press F9 to select the Toggle Breakpoint command from the Run menu.

FIGURE 13.4:

A line of of code that has been designated as a breakpoint will appear in bold

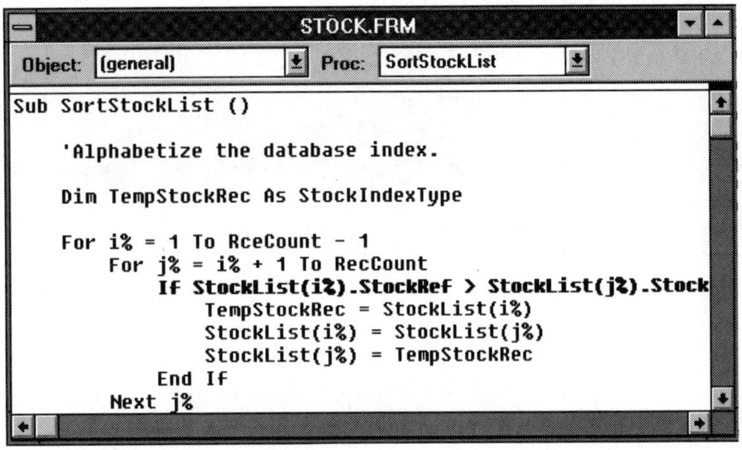

```
┌─────────────────────────────────────────────────────────────┐
│  ─                         STOCK.FRM                    ▼ ▲  │
├─────────────────────────────────────────────────────────────┤
│  Object: [general]         ▼   Proc:  SortStockList     ▼    │
├─────────────────────────────────────────────────────────────┤
│  Sub SortStockList ()                                      ▲ │
│                                                              │
│      'Alphabetize the database index.                        │
│                                                              │
│      Dim TempStockRec As StockIndexType                      │
│                                                              │
│      For i% = 1 To RceCount - 1                              │
│          For j% = i% + 1 To RecCount                         │
│              If StockList(i%).StockRef > StockList(j%).Stock │
│                  TempStockRec = StockList(i%)                │
│                  StockList(i%) = StockList(j%)               │
│                  StockList(j%) = TempStockRec                │
│              End If                                        ▼ │
│          Next j%                                             │
│  ◄                                                        ► │
└─────────────────────────────────────────────────────────────┘
```

To clear a designated breakpoint, follow these steps:

1. With the code window open, position the insertion bar next to the line of code that has the breakpoint; the line will appear in bold.

2. Press F9 or choose the Toggle Breakpoint command from the Run menu. The selected line of code will appear in the regular font.

Stepping through Code Statements

Another way to use breakpoints is to run a specific line of code or procedure that you know causes an error. You can accomplish this by *single stepping* or *procedure stepping*. Sometimes you'll discover that errors exist in a particular section of code, but don't want to correct the errors at that moment. In that case, you can skip over a section of code that contains errors in order to work on other parts of an application. Obviously, the errors won't go away by themselves; you're just putting off the task of correcting them until later. Fortunately, Visual Basic understands this and provides you with a way to put off the inevitable—at least for a little while.

Single Stepping

The action of single stepping is simply the process of executing one line of code at a time. After you set a breakpoint, you can single-step through each statement until you reach the breakpoint. In this way, you can see firsthand the effect of running each statement in your application. When you choose the Single Step command, Visual Basic will run your application temporarily in order to execute the current line of code.

To use single stepping, follow these steps:

1. Open the code window.

2. Select the Single Step command from the Run menu or press F8.

That's all there is to single-stepping!

Procedure Stepping

Procedure stepping is similar to single stepping except that it executes the procedure being called and then steps through each of the statements in the procedure. To execute procedure stepping, choose the Procedure Stepping command from the Run menu or press Shift-F8.

While you're stepping through a procedure, you can skip over any section of code within the procedure that you know is causing errors. You simply set the next statement that you want executed. To accomplish this, follow these steps:

1. Open the code window.

2. Position the insertion bar next to the line of code where you want program execution to begin.

3. Select the Set Next Statement command from the Run menu.

4. Select the Continue command if you want program execution to resume.

Testing for Command-Line Arguments

One of the most intriguing features of Visual Basic is how it enables you to test for command-line arguments established by any statement that includes the **Command$** function. Sometimes you may want to create an application that provides users with a way to specify command-line arguments at runtime. For example, you probably have the experience of using the Windows Program Manager's Run command found on the File menu. When the dialog box is displayed, you can enter an argument in the text box such as **C:VB.EXE**, which starts Visual Basic. The Command$ function returns all arguments entered after the application name. Any command-line argument simply provides an application with important data at startup.

Trapping Errors with Error Handlers

A powerful way to debug a program is to write a customized *error handler* that traps any runtime errors that you anticipate will occur. An error handler is a routine that you include in code that traps possible errors during runtime. For example, when a user runs a program, you don't want the program to terminate when it finds an error in code. This would confuse the user. Furthermore, you don't want the user to start fiddling with the code in an attempt to correct the problem. Therefore, the advantage to using an error handler is that a program won't terminate when it finds an error.

Trappable errors can occur while an application is running, either within the Visual Basic environment or as a stand-alone, executable file. Some of these can also occur during design time or compile time. You can test and respond to trappable errors using the On Error statement and the Err function. Remember, while developing in Visual Basic you can get help on any message you encounter by pressing F1. Table 13.1 includes all the possible trappable errors that you can catch by writing an error handler.

TABLE 13.1: Trappable Errors Found in Visual Basic

Code	Message
3	Return without GoSub
5	Illegal function call
6	Overflow
7	Out of memory
9	Subscript out of range
10	Duplicate definition
11	Division by zero
13	Type mismatch
14	Out of string space
16	String formula too complex
17	Can't continue
19	No Resume
20	Resume without error
28	Out of stack space
35	Sub or Function not defined
48	Error in loading DLL
51	Internal error
52	Bad file name or number
53	File not found
54	Bad file mode
55	File already open
57	Device I/O error
58	File already exists
59	Bad record length
61	Disk full
62	Input past end of file
63	Bad record number
64	Bad file name
67	Too many files
68	Device unavailable
70	Permission denied

TABLE 13.1:   Trappable Errors Found in Visual Basic (continued)

Code	Message
71	Disk not ready
74	Can't rename with different drive
75	Path/File access error
76	Path not found
260	No timer available
280	DDE channel not fully closed; awaiting response from foreign application
281	No More DDE channels
282	No foreign application responded to a DDE initiate
283	Multiple applications responded to a DDE initiate
284	DDE channel locked
285	Foreign application won't perform DDE method or operator
286	Timeout while waiting for DDE response
287	User pressed Alt Key during DDE operation
288	Destination is busy
289	Data not provided in DDE operation
290	Data in wrong format
291	Foreign application quit
292	DDE conversation closed or changed
293	DDE method invoked with no channel open
294	Invalid DDE Link format
295	Message queue filled; DDE message lost
296	PasteLink already performed on this control
297	Can't set LinkMode; Invalid LinkTopic
320	Can't use character device names in file names: " item"
321	Invalid file format
340	Control array element " item" does not exist
341	Invalid object array index
342	Not enough room to allocate control array " item"
343	Object not an array
344	Must specify index for object array
345	Reached limit: cannot create any more controls for thisform

TABLE 13.1: Trappable Errors Found in Visual Basic (continued)

Code	Message
360	Object already loaded
361	Can't load or unload this object
362	Can't unload controls created at design time
363	Custom control " item" not found
364	Object was unloaded
365	Unable to unload within this context
380	Invalid property value
381	Invalid property array index
382	" Item" property can't be set at runtime
383	" Item" property is read-only
384	" Item" property can't be modified when form isminimized or maximized
385	Must specify index when using property array
386	" Item" property not available at runtime
387	" Item" property can't be set on this control
388	Can't set Visible property from a parent menu
400	Form already displayed; can't show form modally
401	Can't show nonmodal form when a modal form is being displayed
402	Must close or hide topmost modal form first
420	Invalid object reference
421	Method not applicable for this object
422	Property " item" not found
423	Property or control " item" not found
424	Object required
425	Invalid object use
430	No currently active control
431	No currently active form
460	Invalid Clipboard format
461	Specified format does not match format of data
480	Can't create AutoRedraw image
481	Invalid picture
482	Printer error

TABLE 13.1: Trappable Errors Found in Visual Basic (continued)

Code	Message
520	Can't empty Clipboard
521	Can't open Clipboard

Note: 280–295 are trappable Dynamic Data Exchange (DDE) errors.

In the following example, an error handler has been written for one of the check boxes on the Daily Stock Record form. The error handler traps a specific error that might occur during a DDE exchange. When a DDE conversation cannot be established, a dialog box displays the error message number 282. If the particular error isn't the culprit, then the error handler displays the number for the error that *did* occur, as shown below.

Here a dialog box displays the DDE error 293 when the New York Stock Exchange check box is clicked on the Daily Stock Record form. This error means that a DDE method was invoked with no channel open. However, the program won't be terminated, which enables the user to continue entering data on the form.

The following code was written for the check box control NewYork:

```
Sub NewYork_Click ()

    On Error GoTo ErrorHandler
```

In the example below, the value **None** is assigned to the LinkMode property. The statement assumes that you have loaded the CONSTANT.TXT file in the application's global module. The constant **None** is declared in the file (as well as other constants).

```
ClosePrice.LinkMode = None
ClosePrice.LinkTopic = "Excel¦Sheet1"
ClosePrice.LinkItem = "R3C3"
ClosePrice.LinkExecute
"[Open(""D:\Excel\Sheet1.Xls"")][Beep][File.Close()][Quit()]"
```

Error 282 can be found in Table 13.1, which lists all trappable errors found in Visual Basic.

```
ErrorHandler:

    'No foreign application responded to a DDE initiate

    If Err = 282 Then
        Temp = Shell("D:\Excel\Excel.Exe")
        Resume
    Else
        MsgBox "Error Number" + Str$(Err)
        Exit Sub
    End If End Sub
```

When the **On Error GoTo** statement is executed, Visual Basic generates a trappable error by passing control to a specific label, which in this case is ErrorHandler. The **GoTo** statement simply transfers control to a different location in the application. The **Err** function is used to determine which error occurred. In this example, the function returns an error number. All error numbers are predefined in Visual Basic.

If the user attempts to correct the problem, the **Resume** statement will enable the user to retry the operation that caused the error. If a different error is encountered, the **MsgBox** statement will display a dialog box with the error number that is specified by Str$(Err).

Summary

In this chapter, you learned how to debug compile-time and runtime errors. A powerful way to debug a program is to write a customized error handler that traps any runtime errors that you anticipate will occur. An error handler is a routine that you include in code that traps possible errors during runtime. The advantage to using an error handler is that a program won't terminate when errors are encountered.

Other topics that were covered include the following:

- To use the Immediate window, enter a statement in the window. Edit the statement to change its effect and then press the Enter key.

- To display context-sensitve help for any Visual Basic convention, press F1. The statement, command, or text must first be highlighted.

- To replace the incorrect statement in your code with the corrected syntax, copy, cut, or paste the statement from the Immediate window into the code window. Remember: a statement that you write in the Immediate window is *not* saved with the project.

- To set a breakpoint, open the code window and position the blinking insertion bar next to any line of code that you want to designate with a breakpoint. Select the Toggle Breakpoint command from the Run menu. The selected line of code will appear in bold.

FOURTEEN

Drawing Bitmaps and Adding Dynamic Graphical Effects

- Using a Timer Control

- Drawing in Microsoft Windows Paintbrush

- Calling a Dynamic Link Library Function in a Procedure

- Creating Custom Icons with Visual Basic's IconWorks

The function of any Windows application is to provide a dynamic interface for performing tasks. By presenting information graphically, Windows creates a visually robust environment in which to work. For example, if you look at the design of the Program Manager, you can see that the colors, patterns, and objects all contribute to the vitality of the environment. Windows uses all sorts of fancy graphics to help draw your attention to the specific task at hand. Even performing the most mundane task can appear more interesting when it is presented in Windows.

The underlying functional aspect of the environment helps you to control all applications that use the same interface. It is the user interface that establishes a familiar way to perform tasks in all Windows applications. It achieves this by using the same kinds of recognizable objects and metaphors. In this way, the behavior of any Windows application is always consistent and predictable.

Having everything predictable, however, doesn't mean you can't also include a surprise or two in your application. A shock of color, of sound, of movement when you least expect it can have a positive effect. This is where Visual Basic can help you. By using various controls, setting properties, and writing event procedures, you can produce unique visual effects that will give your application a dynamic quality.

Using a Timer Event to Create Dynamic Graphical Effects

A Timer is a control that you can program to run code at a regular time interval you set in milliseconds. It runs independently of a user. A Timer control only appears at design time. At runtime, it becomes invisible and processes code in the background. By writing a Timer event procedure that performs an action at a specified interval of time, you can create an interesting visual effect.

The simplest use of a Timer event is displaying a digital clock on a form. Sometimes you may want an application to display the current time. For example, create a label and timer control on a form, set the timer's Interval property to 1000, and write the following event procedure:

```
Sub Timer1_Timer ()
    Label1.Caption = Timer$ End Sub
```

When the application is run, a digital clock will appear. The following code illustrates how the Timer event procedure is first invoked when the form is loaded:

```
Sub Form_Load ()
    Timer1_Timer
End Sub
```

A more interesting use of a Timer control is automatically moving an object across a form when it is loaded. When the following code is executed, a small blue circle moves at a regular interval across a form (you should set the Interval property at 1000):

```
Sub Timer1_Timer ()
    FillStyle = 0
    FillColor = RGB(255, 255, 0)
    DrawMode = 7
    Circle (CurrentX, CurrentY), 500
    CurrentX = CurrentX + 220
    CurrentY = CurrentY + 220        Circle (CurrentX, CurrentY),
500
End Sub
```

To stop program execution, choose the End command from the Run menu.

Creating the Startup Form

A Windows application always opens with a startup window when it is launched. The window can be a small dialog box that simply displays the name of the application, the manufacturer's trademark, and the product's copyright date, or it can be a maximized window that fills the screen with objects that move and colors that change before your eyes. All Windows applications open in similar manner. Regardless of a startup window's design and size, it conveys to the user important information about the product.

A startup window should strive to pique the user's interest and leave the user with a favorable impression of the application. Obviously, you want people to use your application. You want people to perceive your product as the best thing to happen since the fax machine. Here is an opportunity for you to really put your creativity and programming skills to work when you're creating a form. In essence, you're creating a *reason* for a person to use the application. One way to accomplish this is by adding dynamic graphical effects to the opening form.

The advantage of programming in Visual Basic is that it enables you to add dynamic graphical effects to your Windows applications with relative ease. If you don't exploit this potential in your Visual Basic applications, you're really missing out on the opportunity to create exciting and interesting visual effects. For example, by simply changing an application's default background and foreground colors from white and black to two different colors, you will greatly improve the application's appearance. You don't even have to write any code to invoke these changes unless you want the colors to change at runtime; you can set a control's Backcolor and Forecolor properties at design time. It can be that easy.

Adding the Startup Form to the Project

As you plan each of the forms and controls that comprise an application, you probably won't work in a linear fashion. Most of us simply don't work that way. Despite all the preliminary planning that you put into designing an application, it will evolve over time. Developing an application is always a learning process. Depending on how you work, you'll refine the design and modify the functional code as you go along. In the process, you'll gain an appreciation of how a user works and understand more about how the application should be accessed. As you learn more about the application, the overall functionality of the application should greatly improve.

By using controls, a user will navigate each form in the particular sequence you've established. However, you won't always create every form in the same order that the user will follow. When you've run the Window$ to Wealth application up to now, the form named Main has been the startup form because it was the first one you created. By default, the first form you create in any project is the form that is launched when you run the application. However, you can always change the startup form by designating another form you want launched first.

When you choose the Startup Form command from the Run menu, a list box will appear. This list box displays all the names of the forms that comprise the application. You simply select the name of the form that you want launched first and confirm your choice.

The new startup form we're creating here will display the logo *Window$ to Wealth*. To create the logo, you will draw it in Microsoft Windows Paintbrush. It is an easy-to-use paint program that is bundled with Windows. It's a good program to use when you want to create simple bitmap graphics to import into Visual Basic applications. I've also used the Paintbrush Shrink and Grow command to increase the size of the logo.

When the user launches the application, the logo will appear in a window. The window will then begin to spontaneously generate a specified number of smaller windows that display the same logo. This dynamic effect is achieved by placing a timer control on the form. You set the timer's interval property in milliseconds at design time. It will never appear on a form at runtime.

The control's event procedure is invoked when the form is loaded. The procedure uses a simple If…Then control structure to determine the number of iterations. In this example, I've chosen to generate five smaller windows. However, you can change the number of iterations to any value. The result is an opening startup window that is visually dynamic.

To create the new startup form, follow these steps:

1. Open the Wealth project. All the form names will appear in the Project window.

2. Select New Form from the File menu. A new form will appear. The default name will be **Form***x*, where *x* is a consecutive number given to each form in the order that is created.

3. Choose Set Startup Form from the Run menu. A dialog box will appear.

4. Choose the name of the new form from the list box that is displayed.

5. Confirm your choice by clicking OK.

6. Set the following properties for the form:

Left	195
Top	600
Height	5970
Width	9195

Caption   Window$ to Wealth

ScaleMode   3

BackColor   &HFF00 (or Green from the Color Palette)

7. Save the form.

Drawing a Graphic in Microsoft Windows Paintbrush

You don't have to exit Visual Basic before you open Paintbrush. Just click on the minimize button to reduce the Visual Basic window, then double-click on the Paintbrush icon from the Accessories group in the Program Manager. As a precaution, however, remember to save your Visual Basic work before opening Paintbrush.

To create the logo, follow these steps:

1. Open Paintbrush.

2. Choose the Text tool (the button with *abc* on it).

3. Set the Foreground color to Green. (Point to the color and click the *left* mouse button.)

4. Select the Roman typeface from the Font menu.

NOTE If you are running a different version of Paintbrush that shows a Text menu instead of a Font menu, click on the Text menu and select the Font command. A dialog box will appear. Select Roman from the Font list box, Bold from the Font Style list box, and 72 from the Size list box. (72 point is the biggest font available in this version.)

5. Select Bold from the Style menu.

6. Select 84 point from the Size menu and click on OK.

7. Position the I-beam cursor in the center of the work area and click. This places the insertion point for the text.

8. Type the following text exactly as it appears, pressing Enter after each word and pressing the spacebar to center the text (be sure to use a $ instead of the letter *s*):

```
Window$
   to
Wealth
```

To increase the size of the graphic, you use the Shrink and Grow command from the Pick menu. This command enables you to increase or decrease the size of any selected area. You can also create many interesting visual effects with this command.

You can only enable the Pick menu after you select a cutout area. The menu will always appear dimmed until you have selected an area. First, click on the Pick tool (the scissors above the Text tool). To select the rectangular cutout area to be enlarged, follow these steps:

1. Position the cross hair at the upper-left corner of the first word.

2. Hold down the left mouse button and drag the crosshair downward diagonally to the right until the entire text appears in a rectangular box.

3. Release the button. The dotted box indicates the cutout area.

4. Select the Shrink and Grow command from the Pick menu.

To create the effect of larger text, you will need to draw a box that approximates the size you want the words to appear in the logo. You don't have to be exact because you can always resize a form after you paste the logo on it from the Clipboard. (Don't worry about making a mistake; you can always start over.) You want to make the new box larger than the current box; if you don't, the size of the text won't appear larger:

1. Position the cross hair in the upper-left corner of the work area, hold the mouse button down, and drag the cross hair downward *over the dotted box* to the lower-right corner. The text will appear in a dotted box.

> **TIP**
>
> Select the Clear command from the Pick menu. When the Clear setting is on, the original cutout area will be erased when the newly sized copy is created. Otherwise, the original area will remain intact.

   2. Release the mouse button. The enlarged text will appear in its new box.

If the text doesn't appear larger than before, repeat the two steps as many times as you want until you are satisfied with the results. You can't make a mistake.

When you are satisfied with size of the text and the appearance of the logo, you can copy it to the Clipboard so you can paste it on the new startup form. As this point, the Pick menu is still enabled; if you select a cutout area and release the mouse button, a new box will appear. Therefore, before you select an area to cut or copy to the Clipboard, click on the Pick tool to disable the Pick menu. It will appear dimmed. Then:

   1. Select the area you want to copy to the Clipboard.

   2. Choose the Copy command from the Edit menu.

   3. If you want to save the logo, choose Save from the File menu.

   4. Choose the Exit command to close Paintbrush.

   5. Return to Visual Basic.

If you reduced Visual Basic to an icon, double-click on the icon to maximize it. Otherwise, just load Visual Basic again. When you've opened the project, display the new startup form.

Pasting a Bitmap from the Clipboard

There are two ways to display a bitmapped graphic that you're pasting on a form from the Clipboard: you can either paste the graphic directly on the form or you can paste it in a picture box control. The first method has one big disadvantage. Once you paste a bitmap directly on a form, you can't manipulate it; you can't select it, move it, copy it, or resize it. You can only make those types of changes to the form itself. Since you won't have any flexibility, I wouldn't recommend you use this method.

Using the second method is preferable because it gives you the flexibility you associate with any control. After you create a picture box control, you select it and paste the bitmap on it. You can then manipulate it like you would any control. The picture box and bitmap are treated as a single entity. This is particularly important, as you will want to be able to move and size the picture box.

After saying all that, there will be occasions when you'll want to paste a bitmap directly on a form. In this example, you will use both methods. You will paste the logo on the form and then create a picture box on top of the graphic. The dynamic effect is achieved by generating a consecutive number of smaller picture boxes that display the same graphic.

First you have to display the form. Next you have to select the Paste command from the Edit menu. The graphic will appear on the form. If the Paste command is still dimmed, you'll have to copy the graphic again in Paintbrush by following the steps in the previous sections.

Resizing a Form

When the graphic appears on the form, you'll probably have to size the form to accommodate the graphic. Carefully position the pointer on any edge of the form's frame so that it changes to the two-headed pointer. When you are in the right position, the color or intensity of the window's edge will change to indicate that you are resizing the window. Hold the mouse button down and drag the edge to the desired position. Release the mouse button when you are satisfied with the results. You can continue to repeat the process if you want to increase or decrease the form's size.

SHORTCUT The easiest way to resize a form is to drag one of the corners.

Once the form is sized, you can center it on the screen by dragging its title bar. The default form always appears centered on the screen. However, once you resize the form, it will appear where you've positioned it on the screen. If it isn't centered, it will look awkward.

Creating a Picture Box Control

Now you'll create the picture box control that displays the copy of the bitmap. This control decreases in size as it creates the picture-in-picture effect when the Window$ to Wealth application is launched. After the control is drawn, you can resize and position it either by dragging the sizing handles to the desired size and repositioning it on the form, or by setting the Left, Top, Height, and Width properties. The second method is more precise, which in this case is important. You want the control to appear in a specific location on the form:

1. Double-click on the Picture Box tool. The control will appear on the form.

2. Set the following properties for the control:

Left	3600
Top	1320
Height	2895
Width	5055
ScaleMode	3

Creating the Timer Control

To draw the Timer control, simply double-click on the Timer tool. You can then move the control to any location on the form—any blank area or corner will do. The Timer control only appears at design time. At runtime, it becomes invisible.

The only property you need to set for the Timer control is the Interval property. This property determines the number of milliseconds in the timer's countdown interval. In this example, you should set the interval to **1000.** The number of milliseconds will determine when the application calls the Timer event procedure that is associated with the control.

Creating the Label

As you can see in Figure 14.1, there appears on the form a label with the words "Your First Steps to Financial Planning." To create the label, double-click on the Label tool. The following properties and values should be set:

Left	24
Top	128
Height	105
Width	129
Caption	Your First Steps to Financial Planning
FontSize	13.5
FontItalic	True
Alignment	Center
ForeColor	&H00800000& (or Blue from the Color Palette)

FIGURE 14.1:
The Startup Form displays the blank picture box control in which "Window$ to Wealth" will appear dynamically at runtime

Creating the Form's Menu Bar

The form displays two menus: Program and Help. The Program menu offers two commands, Open and Exit. When the user clicks the Open command, the **Sub OpenCommand_Click** event procedure is invoked. This procedure closes the Startup form and displays the Menu form.

When the user clicks the Exit command, the **Sub ExitCommand_Click** event procedure is invoked. This procedure calls the **Sub ExitApplication** general procedure, which displays a dialog box that gives the user the choice of exiting the program or canceling the request.

The Help menu offers the About Window$ to Wealth… command. When the user clicks this command, the **Sub AboutCommand_Click** event procedure is invoked. This procedure displays the dialog box shown below, which gives information about the Window$ to Wealth application.

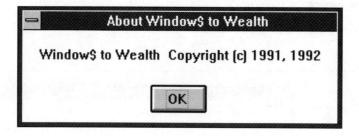

Writing the Functional Code

Now that you've built the form, you need to write the functional code that generates the graphical "picture-in-picture" effect. In this example, you will write an event procedure that calls a Dynamic Link Library (DLL) from the Windows Application Programming Interface (API). Using the Windows API extends the flexibility and power of Visual Basic by giving you added capabilities. The API contains 550 messages and 200 functions, with a huge number of parameters.

This application demonstrates how an API function is called. DLL functions must be declared so that Visual Basic can locate the appropriate library and check the data types being passed. A function is called once, and then it can be called any number of times. The simple Windows API function that you will use is called *StretchBlt*; the event procedure that calls this API has only a few lines of code.

StretchBlt copies bitmaps from one rectangular region to another, stretching or compressing the bitmap to fit the new dimensions. Our application copies the entire area of the opening form into a picture box control on that form, giving you a dynamic picture-in-picture effect.

StretchBlt takes eleven arguments. Since StretchBlt returns a value (a copy of the form), it is declared as a function. In the application, the function is declared as follows:

```
Declare Function StretchBlt Lib "GDI" (ByVal DestDC%, ByVal
     DestX%, ByVal DestY%, ByVal DestWd%, ByVal DestHt%, ByVal
     SrcDC%, ByVal SrcX%, ByVal SrcY%, ByVal SrcWd%, ByVal SrcHt%,
     ByVal Rop&) As Integer
```

```
Const SRCCOPY = &HCC0020
```

The Lib *libname* clause in the Declare statement tells Visual Basic where to find the DLL that contains the StretchBlt function. In this case, it is one of the operating environment DLLs, "GDI."

By default, Visual Basic passes arguments by reference. You need to use the *ByVal* keyword in front of the argument declarations in the Declare statement to pass them by value. Unless a function specifically requires a long pointer, the parameters should be declared by ByVal. This ensures that each time the application calls the procedure, the arguments are passed by value. Otherwise, the procedure will get bad data and probably not work.

Understanding the Scope of Variables

You do have some flexibility where you declare the function. You can place the code in the application's global module; if you do, then you'll have to precede the constant statement with the word "Global." However, since no other form or control needs to recognize this information, it's more logical to place the code for both the function and constant in the declarations section of the particular form that needs the information.

When the application is launched from Windows, the startup form will display the bitmap and generate the graphical effects automatically. You don't want the user to take any action to invoke the event procedure. That would destroy the overall effect. You want to load the form in order to invoke the event procedure for the Timer control, which in turn calls the StretchBlt routine. Therefore, you want to change the default event for the form from Click to Load so that the declarations and procedure are automatically "loaded" when the application is launched:

1. Double-click on the form. The code window will appear.

2. Click on the Procedures box. A combo box will appear.

3. Select the Load event from the list.

4. Type the following call to the Timer1_Timer event procedure:

   ```
   Timer1_Timer
   ```

5. Click on the Object box.

6. Select **[general]** from the list. The code window will clear and the Procedures box will display **[declarations]**.

> **NOTE**
>
> I've indented the code for the function declaration below to indicate that it is all on one line. You must type the entire function on one line. Otherwise, you will get an error message if you press Enter or the ↓ key to move to the next line. Visual Basic allows you to enter a maximum of 255 characters on a line.

7. Type the code for the function and constant:

   ```
   '     StretchBlt DLL Function from Windows API
   Declare Function StretchBlt Lib "GDI" (ByVal DestDC%, ByVal
       DestX%, ByVal DestY%, ByVal DestWd%, ByVal DestHt%, ByVal
       SrcDC%, ByVal SrcX%, ByVal SrcY%, ByVal SrcWd%, ByVal
       SrcHt%, ByVal Rop&) As Integer

   '     Constant to represent size of bitmap copy
   Const SRCCOPY = &HCC0020
   ```

8. Add the following line; it declares a local variable that will be referenced in the Timer1_Timer event procedure:

   ```
   '     Variable referenced in Timer1_Timer event procedure
   Dim I As Integer
   ```

9. Close the code window.

The Timer1_Timer control invokes an event procedure that uses a simple If...Then control structure. This control structure is used to generate a specified number of iterations, which in this case is five. A local variable named *I* has been declared to test the condition.

NOTE The term *control structure* has nothing to do with controls on a form.

To write the event procedure for the Timer control, follow these steps:

1. Open the code window for the Timer control.

2. Type the following code within the Sub Timer1_Timer ()...End Sub template:

```
If I < 5 Then
        I = I + 1
        temp% = StretchBlt(picture1.hdc, 0, 0, picture1.scalewidth,
                picture1.scaleheight, hdc, 0, 0, scalewidth,
                scaleheight, SRCCOPY)
End If
```

3. Close the code window.

4. Save the file.

5. Save the project.

NOTE Indenting the statements in a control structure makes it easier to read the block of code.

Running the Application

To run the application, follow these steps:

1. Select Set Startup Form from the Run menu.

2. Choose Form6 from the list in the dialog box.

3. Click the OK button.

4. Select Start to run the program.

When you run the program, the Startup form will display the dynamic graphical effect of producing five shrinking boxes, each one smaller than the last. The results are shown in Figure 14.2.

FIGURE 14.2:
Using an API function can produce dynamic graphical effects that would otherwise be difficult to create

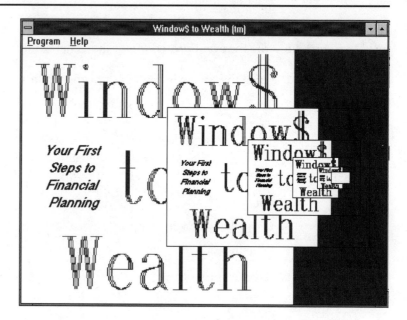

Using IconWorks to Create Your Own Icons

In addition to the Calculator and Cardfile applications that are provided with Visual Basic is an application called the IconWorks Editor. The advantage to using this tool is that you can create your own icon (and display it along with the application name in the Program Manager), rather than choose an icon from Visual Basic's icon library—even though the selection is extensive.

To create an icon, follow these steps:

1. Select Open Project from the File menu. The Open File dialog box will appear.

2. Double-click on the Samples directory.

3. Double-click on the Iconwrks directory.

4. Double-click on ICONWRKS.MAK. The IconWorks project will appear in the project window.

To start the program, press F5. The IconWorks Editor will appear. To create an icon, you first have to prepare the editing area:

1. Open the View menu and select the Grid command. A grid appears over the editing area, as shown in Figure 14.3.

2. Select the Paint command from the Tools menu. This action selects the Paint tool from the tool palette. The Paint tool paints one pixel at a time in the editing area.

FIGURE 14.3:
Using a grid makes it easy to create an icon, especially if you're drawing straight and diagonal lines

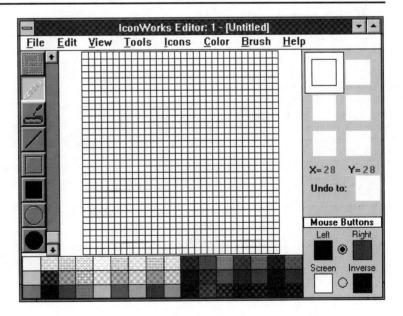

3. Click on green in the color palette with the *left* mouse button. This action designates one currently selected foreground color (also called the *left mouse color*).

> **TIP**
>
> When using the Paint tool, it's a good idea to make one of the icon's mouse colors the same color as the icon's background color. That way, if you make a mistake, you can paint over it.

4. Click on white with the *right* mouse button. This designates the other foreground color (also called the *right mouse color*). You can switch between the two foreground colors simply by clicking either the left or right mouse button.

Now that you've prepared the editing area, you can begin creating the icon. For the Window\$ to Wealth application, you are going to create a dollar sign (\$), as shown in Figure 14.4. As you can see, the drawing occupies a series of squares on the grid. Since the Paint tool allows you to draw the dollar sign one pixel at a time, all you have to do is count the grid's squares to make sure each line is the same length. This approach may seem a little crude, but it will serve our purpose. The completed icon won't appear as jagged as it does in the editing area; it will have a smoother appearance when it is reduced to its actual size.

To draw the icon, follow these steps:

1. Position the Paint tool in the upper-left corner of the grid. As you can see in the status area to the right of the editing area, the x and y coordinates display the current mouse location, which in this case is (0,0).

2. Using Figure 14.4 as a guide, click each square on the grid with the left mouse button. This action will paint each pixel green.

3. Select the Save command from the File menu when you are finished. The Save dialog box will appear.

4. Double-click on the directory in which you want to save the file.

5. Type **wealth** in the FileName text box.

FIGURE 14.4:

The completed icon appears jagged because the squares on the grid are enlarged to make it easier to draw each pixel at a time

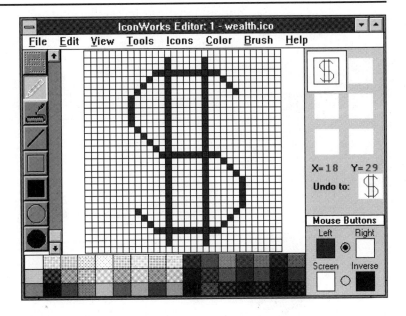

6. Click the Save button. The .ICO extension will be appended to the icon's file name automatically.

When you save an icon, it is attached to the current startup form. Since you selected **Form6** as the new startup form, this icon will appear once you add Window$ to Wealth to the Program Manager.

Adding an Application to the Program Manager

Visual Basic allows you to add any Windows application to the Program Manager after you've compiled it into an executable file. Once you create the .EXE file, the application can run as a stand-alone program outside of Visual Basic as long as the VBRUN100.DLL file is located in the same directory. To launch the program, you simply click the icon that accompanies the program.

To add a program to the Program Manager, follow these steps:

1. Open the Program Manager.

2. Select the Visual Basic window.

3. Select the New command from the File menu. A dialog box appears.

4. Choose Program Item if it isn't selected.

5. Click the OK button. The Program Item Properties dialog box appears, as shown below.

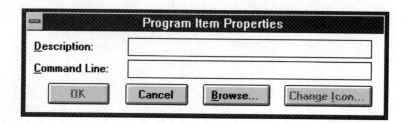

6. Click the Browse button.

7. Double-click on the root [..] directory.

8. Double-click on the Visual Basic directory.

9. Double-click on the Wealth directory.

10. Double-click on WEALTH.EXE. The Program Item Properties dialog box reappears, displaying the current path in the Command Line text box.

11. Click on the Change Icon button. A dialog box will appear, displaying the dollar sign icon.

12. Click the OK button to display the Program Item Properties dialog box again.

13. Click the OK button again. The Window$ to Wealth program name (and icon) will appear in the Visual Basic window, as shown in Figure 14.5.

FIGURE 14.5:

The Window$ to Wealth application now appears in the Visual Basic group window. It can be launched from the Program Manager by double-clicking the icon.

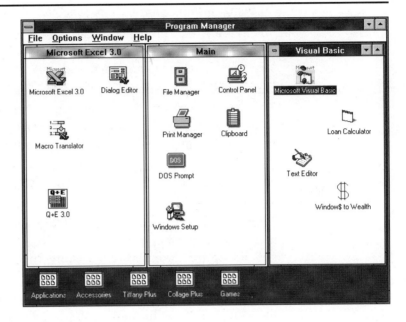

Summary

In this chapter, you learned how to add a dynamic graphical effect to an application by using a Windows API (Application Programming Interface) function. Using the Windows API extends the flexibility and power of Visual Basic by giving you added capabilities. The API contains 550 messages and 200 functions, with a huge number of parameters.

The simple Windows API function that was used in this chapter is called **StretchBlt**. This function copies bitmaps from one rectangular region to another, stretching or compressing the bitmap to fit the new dimensions. A dynamic picture-in-picture effect was thus achieved.

The following topics were also discussed in this chapter:

- To call a Dynamic Link Library (DLL) function from the Windows API, it must be declared so that Visual Basic can locate the appropriate library and check the data types being passed. Once a function is called, it can be called any number of times.

- To change a startup form, choose Set Startup Form from the Run menu.

- To create a bitmap graphic, you can draw it in Microsoft Windows Paintbrush. This is an easy-to-use paint program that is bundled with Windows. It's a good program to use when you want to create simple bitmap graphics to import into Visual Basic applications.

- There are two ways to display a bitmapped graphic that you're pasting on a form from the Clipboard: you can either paste the graphic directly on the form, or you can paste it in a picture box control.

- Once you paste a bitmap directly on a form, you can't manipulate it; you can't select it, move it, copy it, or resize it. You can only make those types of changes to the form itself.

- After you create a picture box control, you select it and paste the bitmap on it. You can then manipulate it like you would any control. The picture box and bitmap are treated as a single entity. This is particularly important when you want to move and size the picture box.

- After a control is drawn, you can resize and position it either by dragging the sizing handles to the desired size and repositioning it on the form, or by setting the Left, Top, Height, and Width properties.

- To create a custom icon that will appear in the Program Manager with your Windows application, use the IconWorks program that is provided with Visual Basic. IconWorks is found in the Samples directory.

P A R T IV

A Reference Guide to Visual Basic Statements, Functions, Methods, Events, Objects, and Properties

Part IV provides a summary of all the Visual Basic statements, functions, methods, events, controls, and properties. All the entries are listed alphabetically to help you find information quickly and easily.

Each entry contains the syntax of the item and a brief description to help you understand what the item is and how it works.

Abs

Type

Function

Syntax

Abs(*numeric-expression*)

Description

The Abs function returns the absolute value of a numeric expression. (The absolute value is the unsigned magnitude of its argument.) The argument *numeric-expression* can be any numeric data type. For example, Abs(−1) and Abs(1) are both 1.

ActiveControl, ActiveForm

Type

Properties

Syntax

Screen.ActiveControl
Screen.ActiveForm

Description

The ActiveControl and ActiveForm properties apply to a screen object. Active-Control displays the control that has the focus. It is invalid if all controls on the form are invisible or disabled; is read-only at runtime; and is not available at design time. ActiveForm displays the form that has the focus. It is invalid if no forms are loaded; is read-only at runtime; and is not available at design time.

AddItem

Type

Method

Syntax

`control.AddItem item$[, index%]`

Description

The AddItem method adds an item to a list box or combo box at runtime. The *item$* argument is a string expression that is added to the list. The index% argument is optional.

Alignment

Type

Property

Syntax

`[form.][label.]Alignment[= setting%]`

Description

The Alignment property applies to label. It sets or returns the alignment of text in a label. The *form and label* control names and *setting%* argument are optional.

AppActivate

Type

Statement

Syntax

`AppActivate titletext$`

Description

The AppActivate statement activates an application window.

Archive, Hidden, Normal, ReadOnly, System

Type

Properties

Syntax

```
[form.]filelistbox.Archive[= boolean%]
[form.]filelistbox.Hidden[= boolean%]
[form.]filelistbox.Normal[= boolean%]
[form.]filelistbox.ReadOnly[= boolean%]
[form.]filelistbox.System[= boolean%]
```

Description

These properties apply to the file list box. They determine whether a file list box contains files with Archive, Hidden, Normal, ReadOnly, or System attributes. The *form* and *filelistbox* control names and *boolean%* argument are optional.

Asc

Type

Function

Syntax

```
Asc(stringexpression$)
```

Description

The Asc function returns a numeric value that is equivalent to the ASCII or ANSI code for the first character in a string expression. If the argument *stringexpression$* is null, Visual Basic generates a runtime error message.

Atn

Type

Function

Syntax

```
Atn(numeric-expression)
```

Description

The Atn function returns the arctangent of a numeric expression that indicates a ratio. The arctangent is the inverse of the tangent. The argument *numeric-expression* can be any numeric data type. Atn evaluates the ratio of two sides of a right triangle and returns the corresponding angle in radians.

AutoRedraw

Type

Property

Syntax

```
[form.][picturebox.]AutoRedraw[= boolean%]
```

Description

The AutoRedraw property applies to a form and picture box. It sets or returns output from a graphics method to a persistent bitmap. The *form* and *picturebox* control names and the *boolean%* argument are optional.

AutoSize

Type

Property

Syntax

```
[form.]{label.|picturebox.}AutoSize[= boolean%]
```

Description

The AutoSize property applies to a label and picture box. It determines whether a control is resized automatically to fit its contents.

BackColor, ForeColor

Type

Properties

Syntax

```
[form.][control.]BackColor[= color&]
[form.][control.]ForeColor[= color&]
```

Description

These properties apply to the form, check box, combo box, command button (Back-Color only), directory list box, drive list box, file list box, frame, label, list box, option button, picture box, Printer object (ForeColor only), and text box. The BackColor property sets or returns the background color of an object. The Fore-Color property sets or returns the foreground color used to display text and graphics in an object. The *color&* argument is optional.

Beep

Type

Statement

Syntax

```
Beep
```

Description

The Beep statement sounds a tone through the computer's speaker.

BorderStyle

Type

Property

Syntax

```
[form.][control.]BorderStyle
```

Description

The BorderStyle property applies to the form, label, picture box, and text box. It sets the border style for an object; for forms and text boxes, the property determines the border style at runtime only.

Call

Type

Statement

Syntax

Call *name* [(*argumentlist*)]

or

name [*argumentlist*]

Description

The Call statement transfers program control to a procedure in a dynamic-link library (DLL) or a Visual Basic Sub procedure. If you use the Call keyword to call a procedure that requires arguments, *argumentlist* must be enclosed in parentheses. If you omit the Call keyword, you must also omit the parentheses around *argumentlist*. Generally, arguments are passed to procedures by reference. This means that the called procedure can alter the passed argument, which in turn reflects the change back to the calling procedure.

Cancel

Type

Property

Syntax

commandbutton.Cancel[= *boolean%*]

Description

The Cancel property applies to the command button. It determines if a command button is the Cancel button on a form. The *boolean%* argument is optional.

Caption

Type
Property

Syntax
[*form.*][*control.*]Caption[= *stringexpression$*]

Description
The Caption property applies to the form, check box, command button, frame, label, menu, and option button. The *stringexpression$* argument determines the text in the caption. A form specifies the text displayed in the form's title bar. When the form is minimized, this text is displayed below the form's icon. A control specifies the text displayed in or next to a control.

CCur

Type
Function

Syntax
CCur(*numeric-expression*)

Description
The CCur function converts a numeric expression to a currency value. The argument *numeric-expression* can be of any numeric data type. The CCur function has the same effect as assigning *numeric-expression* to a currency variable. The CCur function explicitly controls the data type of a numeric expression.

CDbl

Type
Function

Syntax

CDbl(*numeric-expression*)

Description

The CDbl function converts a numeric expression to a double-precision value. The argument *numeric-expression* can be of any numeric data type. The CDbl function has the same effect as assigning *numeric-expression* to a double-precision variable. The results of CDbl are no more accurate than the original expression. The added digits of precision are not significant unless the expression is calculated with double-precision accuracy.

Change

Type

Event

Syntax

Sub *ctlname*_Change (Index as Integer)

Description

The Change event applies to the combo box, directory list box, drive list box, horizontal scroll bar, label, picture box, text box, and vertical scroll bar. The event indicates that the contents of a control have changed. The argument *Index* uniquely identifies a control in a control array. A Change event procedure can synchronize or coordinate data display between controls. For example, you can use a scroll bar's Change procedure to update the scroll bar's Value property setting in a text box. Or you might use a Change procedure to display data and formulas in a work area and the results in another area.

ChDir

Type

Statement

Syntax

ChDir *path$*

Description

The ChDir statement changes the current default directory for the specified drive. The argument *path$* is a string expression that identifies which directory is to become the new default directory. The *path$* must have fewer than 128 characters. It has to be of the following syntax:

[*drive:*][\]*directory*[*directory*]

The argument *drive* is an optional drive specification. If you omit *drive*, ChDir changes the default directory on the current drive. The ChDir statement changes the default directory but not default drive. For example, if the default drive is C, the following statement will change the default directory on drive D, but C will remain the default drive:

ChDir "D:\TMP."

Use CurDir$ to display the current directory and ChDrive, below, to change the default drive.

ChDrive

Type

Statement

Syntax

ChDrive *drive$*

Description

The ChDrive statement changes the current drive. The argument *drive$* is a string expression that specifies a new default drive. It must correspond to an existing drive and must be in the range A–X, where X is the maximum drive letter you set in your CONFIG.SYS file.

Check Box

Type
Control

Description
A check box displays an option that can be turned on or off. You can use this control to give the user a true/false or yes/no option. Check boxes can also be used in groups to display multiple choices from which the user can choose one or more options. While check boxes and option buttons may appear to function similarly, there is an important difference: When a user selects an option button, the other option buttons in the same group are automatically cancelled. By contrast, any number of check boxes can be selected. To display text next to the check box, set the Caption property. To determine the state of the box as cleared, selected, or disabled, set the Value property.

Checked

Type
Property

Syntax
menuitem.Checked[= *boolean%*]

Description
The Checked property applies to the menu. It determines whether a check mark is displayed next to a menu command. The *boolean%* argument is optional.

Chr$

Type
Function

Syntax
Chr$(*code%*)

Description

The Chr$ function returns a one-character string whose ANSI code is the argument. The argument *code%* is an integer between 0 and 255, inclusive. ANSI is the character set used by Visual Basic. ANSI character codes in the range 0 to 31, inclusive, are the same as the standard, non-printable ASCII codes. For example, Chr$(13) is a carriage-return character and Chr$(10) is a line-feed character. Together they can be used to force a new line when formatting message strings used with MsgBox or InputBox$.

CInt

Type
Function

Syntax

```
CInt(numeric-expression)
```

Description

The CInt function converts a numeric expression to an integer by rounding the fractional part of the expression. The argument *numeric-expression* can be any numeric data type and must have a value between 32,768 and 32,767, inclusive. If *numeric-expression* is outside the acceptable range, Visual Basic will generate a runtime error message. The CInt function has the same effect as assigning *numeric-expression* to an integer variable. CInt differs from the Fix and Int functions, which *truncate*, rather than round, the fractional part.

Circle

Type
Method

Syntax

```
[object.]Circle [Step](x!, y!), radius![, [color&][, [start!][,
    [end!][, aspect!]]]]
```

Description

The Circle method draws a circle, ellipse, or arc.

Clear

Type

Method

Syntax

```
Clipboard.Clear
```

Description

The Clear method clears the contents of the operating environment Clipboard.

Click

Type

Event

Syntax

```
Sub Form_Click ()
Sub ctlname_Click (Index as Integer)
```

Description

The Click event applies to the form, check box, combo box, command button, directory list box, file list box, label, list box, menu, option button, and picture box. The event occurs when the user presses and then releases a mouse button over an object.

Clipboard

Type

Object

Description

The Clipboard object is accessed with the keyword Clipboard, and is used to manipulate text and graphics in the Clipboard. You can use this object to enable a user to copy, cut, and paste text or graphics into your application.

CLng

Type
Function

Syntax
`CLng(numeric-expression)`

Description
The CLng function converts a numeric expression to a long (4-byte) integer by rounding the fractional part of the expression.

Close

Type
Statement

Syntax
`Close [[#] filenumber%][, [#] filenumber%]...`

Description
The Close statement concludes input/output to a file.

Cls

Type
Method

Syntax

`[object.]Cls`

Description

The Cls method clears runtime-generated graphics and text output from a form or picture box. The object can be a form or a picture box. If *object* is omitted, Cls clears text and graphics from the current form. Cls clears text and graphics generated at runtime with graphics and printing statements.

Combo Box

Type

Control

Description

A combo box combines the features of a text box and list box. Use this control to enable the user to make a selection by typing text into a text box or by selecting an item from the list below it.

Command Button

Type

Control

Description

A command button performs a task when chosen by the user, who either clicks the button or presses a key. When chosen, a command button appears pushed in, and it is thus sometimes called a "push button."

Command$

Type

Function

Syntax

Command$

Description

The Command$ function returns a string containing the argument portion of the command line used to launch Visual Basic or an application developed with Visual Basic.

Const

Type

Statement

Syntax

[Global] Const *constantname* = *expression*[, *constantname* = *expression*]...

Description

The Const statement declares symbolic constants for use in place of values.

ControlBox

Type

Property

Syntax

[*form*.]ControlBox

Description

The ControlBox property applies to a form. It determines whether a control box appears on a form at runtime. It is read-only at runtime.

Cos

Type
Function

Syntax
Cos(*numeric-expression*)

Description
The Cos function returns the cosine of an angle given in radians.

CSng

Type
Function

Syntax
CSng(*numeric-expression*)

Description
The Csng function converts the *numeric-expression* argument to a single-precision value.

CtlName

Type
Property

Syntax
ctlname

Description
The CtlName property applies to a check box, combo box, command button, directory list box, drive list box, file list box, frame, horizontal scroll bar, label, list box,

menu, option button, picture box, text box, timer, and vertical scroll bar. Every control must have a control name. The property sets the unique identifier that is used to access the control in code and is not available at runtime. By default, the name for this property includes the control name and an integer, yielding a unique name such as "Option1" or "Check3." A CtlName must start with a letter and can be a maximum of 40 characters, including alphanumeric or underscore characters. A CtlName cannot be a reserved word. You should note that CtlName is distinct from other properties that label or display a control's contents at runtime, such as the Caption, Text, or Value properties.

CurDir$

Type
Function

Syntax
```
CurDir$[(drive$)]
```

Description
The CurDur$ function returns the path currently in use for the specified drive.

CurrentX, CurrentY

Type
Properties

Syntax
```
{[form.][picturebox.]Printer.}CurrentX[= x!]
{[form.][picturebox.]Printer.}CurrentY[= y!]
```

Description
The CurrentX and CurrentY properties apply to a form, picture box, and printer object. It sets or returns the current horizontal (x) and vertical (y) screen or page coordinates for output from graphics methods. It is not available at design time.

Date$

Type
Function

Syntax
```
Date$
```

Description
The Date$ function returns the current system date as a ten-character string. The form of the string is *mm-dd-yyyy,* where *mm* is the month (01–12), *dd* is the day (01–31), and *yyyy* is the year (1980–2099). The output of the Date$ function is equivalent to

```
Format$(Now,"mm-dd-yyyy")
```

To set the system date, use the Date$ statement below.

Date$

Type
Statement

Syntax
```
Date$ = stringexpression$
```

Description
The Date$ statement sets the current system date.

DateSerial

Type
Function

Syntax
```
DateSerial(year%,month%,day%)
```

Description

The DateSerial function returns a serial number that represents the date of the integer arguments.

DateValue

Type

Function

Syntax

DateValue(*date$*)

Description

The DateValue function returns a serial number that represents the date of the string argument.

Day

Type

Function

Syntax

Day(*serial#*)

Description

The Day function returns an integer between 1 and 31, inclusive, that represents the day of the month corresponding to the serial argument.

DblClick

Type

Event

Syntax

```
Sub Form_DblClick ()
Sub ctlname_DblClick (Index as Integer)
```

Description

The DblClick event applies to a form, combo box, directory list box, file list box, label, list box, option button, and picture box. In general, the event occurs when the user presses and releases a mouse button, then presses it again over an object.

Debug

Type

Object

Description

The Debug object is accessed with the keyword Debug and is used to send output to the Immediate window at runtime.

Declare

Type

Statement

Syntax

```
Declare Sub globalname Lib libname$ [Alias aliasname$]
     [([argumentlist])]
```

or

```
Declare Function globalname [Lib libname$ [Alias aliasname$]]
     [([argumentlist])] [As type]
```

Description

The Declare statement declares references to external procedures in dynamic-linked libraries (DLLs).

Def*type*

Type
Statement

Syntax

```
DefInt letterrange[, letterrange]...
DefLng letterrange[, letterrange]...
DefSng letterrange[, letterrange]...
DefDbl letterrange[, letterrange]...
DefCur letterrange[, letterrange]...
DefStr letterrange[, letterrange]...
```

Description

The Def*type* statement is used in the declarations section of forms and modules to set the default data type for variables and function procedures. A Deftype statement only affects the module in which it is used. For example, a DefInt statement in the global module only affects the default data type of variables declared in the global module; the default data type for forms and other modules is unaffected.

Default

Type
Property

Syntax

`[form.]commandbutton.Default[= boolean%]`

Description

The Default property applies to a command button. It determines which command button is the default button on a form.

Dim

Type
Statement

Syntax

```
Dim [Shared] variablename [([subscripts])] [As type]
    [, variablename [([subscripts])] [As type]]...
```

Description

The Dim statement is used at module level and procedure level to declare variables and allocate storage space.

Dir$

Type

Function

Syntax

```
Dir$[(filespec$)]
```

Description

The Dir$ function returns a file name that matches the specified pattern. The argument *filespec$* is a string expression that specifies a path or file name, which can include a drive specification and any valid wildcard characters (? and *). Visual Basic generates an error if you don't specify *filespec$* when you first call Dir$. Dir$ returns the first file name that matches *filespec$*. Dir$ is not case-sensitive.

Directory List Box

Type

Control

Description

A directory list box displays directories and paths at runtime. You can use this control to display a hierarchical list of directories. This is useful if you want to create dialog boxes in your application that, for example, enable the user to open a file from a list of available files in all the available directories.

Do...Loop

Type

Statement

Syntax

```
Do [{While|Until} condition]
    [statementblock]
    [Exit Do]
    [statementblock]
Loop
```

or

```
Do
    [statementblock]
    [Exit Do]
    [statementblock]
Loop [{While|Until} condition]
```

Description

The Do...Loop statement repeats a block of statements while a condition is true or until a condition becomes true. The argument condition is a numeric expression that Visual Basic evaluates as true (nonzero) or false (zero). The program lines between the Do and Loop statements will be repeated as long as condition is true. An infinite loop can be created by using no arguments with Do...Loop. With this method, the only way to exit the control structure is to use an Exit Do statement after some desired condition has been met. An Exit Do statement, which may be used only inside a Do...Loop, provides an alternate way to exit a Do...Loop control structure.

DoEvents

Type

Function

Syntax

```
DoEvents( )
```

Description

The DoEvents Function causes Visual Basic to yield execution temporarily so that the operating environment can process events. DoEvents returns the number of Visual Basic forms that are loaded, which is determined by the set of parentheses. No arguments are specified. DoEvents passes control to the operating environment until it has finished processing the events in its queue and all keys in the SendKeys queue have been sent.

Drag

Type

Method

Syntax

```
[control.]Drag [action%]
```

Description

The Drag method begins, ends, or cancels dragging controls. Use of the Drag method to control dragging and dropping is required only when the DragMode property of the control to drag is set to 0 (Manual). However, you may still use Drag on a control whose DragMode property is 1 (Automatic).

DragDrop

Type

Event

Syntax

```
Sub Form_DragDrop (Source As Control, X As Single, Y As Single)
Sub ctlname_DragDrop ([Index as Integer] Source As Control, X As
    Single, Y As Single)
```

Description

The DragDrop event applies to a form, check box, combo box, command button, directory list box, drive list box, file list box, frame, horizontal scroll bar, label, list box, option button, picture box, text box, and vertical scroll bar. The event occurs when a drag-and-drop operation is completed as a result of dragging a control over a form or control and releasing the mouse button, or using the Drag method with the action% argument = 2.

DragIcon

Type
Property

Syntax
[*form.*]*control*.DragIcon[= *icon*]

Description
The DragIcon property applies to a check box, combo box, command button, directory list box, drive list box, file list box, frame, horizontal scroll bar, label, list box, option button, picture box, text box, and vertical scroll bar. The property sets or returns the icon to be displayed as the pointer in a drag-and-drop operation. It is write-only at design time.

DragMode

Type
Property

Syntax
[*form.*]*control*.DragMode[= *mode%*]

Description
The DragMode property applies to a check box, combo box, command button, directory list box, drive list box, file list box, frame, horizontal scroll bar, label, list box, option button, picture box, text box, and vertical scroll bar. The property sets manual or automatic dragging mode for a drag-and-drop operation.

DragOver

Type

Event

Syntax

```
Sub Form_DragOver (Source As Control, X As Single, Y As Single,
    State As Integer)
Sub ctlname_DragOver ([Index as Integer] Source As Control, X As
    Single, Y As Single, State As Integer)
```

Description

The DragOver event applies to a form, check box, combo box, command button, directory list box, drive list box, file list box, frame, horizontal scroll bar, label, list box, option button, picture box, text box, and vertical scroll bar. The event occurs when a drag-and-drop operation is in progress. You can use this event to monitor when the mouse pointer enters, leaves, or is directly over a valid target. The mouse pointer position determines which target object receives this event.

DrawMode

Type

Property

Syntax

```
{[form.][picturebox.]Printer.}DrawMode[= mode%]
```

Description

The DrawMode property applies to a form, picture box, and printer object. The property sets or returns the appearance of output from graphics methods. You can use this property to produce visual effects when drawing with the PSet, Line, and Circle methods. Visual Basic compares each pixel in the draw pattern to the corresponding pixel in the existing background then it applies bitwise operations.

DrawStyle

Type
Property

Syntax
{[*form.*][*picturebox.*]|Printer.}DrawStyle[= *style%*]

Description
The DrawStyle property applies to a form, picture box, and printer object. It sets the line style for output from graphics methods.

DrawWidth

Type
Property

Syntax
{[*form.*][*picturebox.*]|Printer.}DrawWidth[= *size%*]

Description
The DrawWidth property applies to a form, picture box, and printer object. The property sets the line width for output from graphics methods. By default, this property is set to 1, for one pixel. You can produce thicker line widths by increasing this value. For example, a setting of 10 produces a thick line while using the Line method and a heavy, brush-like effect while using the PSet method.

Drive List Box

Type
Control

Description
A drive list box finds and switches between valid disk drives at runtime. You can use this control to display a list of all the valid drives in the user's system. This is

useful if you want to create dialog boxes in your application that, for example, enable the user to open a file from a list of available files on a disk in a different drive.

Drive

Type
Property

Syntax
`drivelistbox.Drive[= drivespec$]`

Description
The Drive property applies to a drive list box. The property sets or returns the selected drive at runtime; it is not available at design time.

DropDown

Type
Event

Syntax
`Sub ctlname_DropDown (Index as Integer)`

Description
The DropDown event applies to a combo box. It occurs when the list portion of a combo box is about to drop down; this event does not occur for combo boxes with Style = 1 (Simple Combo). Use a DropDown procedure to make final updates to a combo box list before the user makes a selection. This allows you to add or remove items from the list, using the AddItem or RemoveItem methods.

Enabled

Type
Property

Syntax

```
[form.][control.]Enabled[= boolean%]
```

Description

The Enabled property applies to a form, check box, combo box, command button, directory list box, drive list box, file list box, frame, horizontal scroll bar, label, list box, menu, option button, picture box, text box, timer, and vertical scroll bar. The property determines whether the form or control can respond to user-generated events such as keypresses and mouse events. This property permits forms and controls to be enabled or disabled at runtime.

End

Type

Statement

Syntax

```
End [{Function|Select|Sub|Type}]
```

Description

The End statement ends a Visual Basic program, procedure, or block. By itself, the End statement stops program execution, closes all files, clears the value of all variables, and destroys all forms. If End is encountered in a stand-alone Visual Basic application, the program terminates. Termination that occurs when End is executed is equivalent to selecting the End command from the Run menu.

EndDoc

Type

Method

Syntax

```
Printer.EndDoc
```

Description

The EndDoc method terminates a document sent to the printer, releasing it to the print device or spooler. If EndDoc is invoked immediately after NewPage, no additional blank page is printed.

Environ$

Type

Function

Syntax

Environ$(*environmentstring$*)

or

Environ$(*n%*)

Description

The Environ$ function returns an operating system environment string. If you specify an environment variable name that cannot be found in the environment-string table, Environ$ returns a null string. Otherwise, Environ$ displays the text assigned to the environment variable; that is, the function displays the text following the equal sign in the environment-string table for that environment variable. If you specify a numeric argument (*n%*), the *n*th string in the environment-string table is displayed. In this case, the returned string includes all of the text, including *environmentstring$*. If the *n*th string does not exist, Environ$ returns a null string. The argument *n%* can be any numeric expression, but it is rounded to an integer before it is used by Environ$.

EOF

Type

Function

Syntax

EOF(*filenumber%*)

Description

The EOF function returns a value during file input that indicates whether or not the end of a file has been reached. Use the EOF function with sequential files to test for the end of a file. This helps you avoid the error that occurs when you attempt to get input past the end of a file. When used with random-access or binary files, EOF returns a value of True if the last executed Get statement was unable to read an entire record.

Erase

Type

Statement

Syntax

`Erase arrayname[, arrayname]...`

Description

The Erase statement reinitializes the elements of static arrays and deallocates dynamic arrays. The argument *arrayname* is the name of the array to erase. It is important to know whether an array is static or dynamic because Erase behaves differently depending on the type of array. For static arrays, no memory is recovered. For dynamic arrays, Erase frees the memory used by the array. Before your program can refer to the dynamic array again, it must redeclare the array variable's dimensions with a Dim or ReDim statement. If you redeclare the array's dimensions with a Dim statement without first erasing it, Visual Basic generates the runtime error message `Array already dimensioned`. The Erase statement is not required when dimensions are redeclared with a ReDim statement.

Erl, Err

Type

Functions

Syntax

`Erl`
`Err`

Description

Both functions return an error status. After an error, the Erl function returns an integer that is the line number where the error occurred, or the closest line number before the line where the error occurred. The Err function returns an integer that is the runtime error code for the error that occurred. Because Erl and Err return meaningful values only after an error has occurred, they are usually used in error-handling routines to determine the error and the corrective action. If you set up an error handler using On Error GoTo, and that error handler calls another procedure, the value of Erl and Err may be reset to zero.

Err

Type

Statement

Syntax

```
Err = n%
```

Description

The Err statement sets Err to a specific value. The argument $n\%$ is either an integer expression with a value between 1 and 32,767, inclusive, that specifies a runtime error code, or 0, which means no runtime error has occurred. When running an application, Visual Basic uses Err to record whether or not a runtime error has occurred and what the error was. When a program starts running, Err is 0; when and if a runtime error occurs, Visual Basic sets Err to the error code for that error. Use the Err statement to set Err to a nonzero value to communicate error information between procedures.

Error

Type

Statement

Syntax

```
Error errorcode%
```

Description

The Error statement simulates the occurrence of a Visual Basic or user-defined error. The argument *errorcode%* represents the error code. It must be an integer between 1 and 32,767, inclusive. If *errorcode%* is an error code already used by Visual Basic, the Error statement simulates the occurrence of that error. To define your own error code, use a value that is greater than any used by the standard Visual Basic error codes. (Start at error code 32,767 and work down.) If an Error statement is executed when no error-handling routine is enabled, Visual Basic generates an error message and stops program execution. If the Error statement specified an error code that is not used by Visual Basic, the message User-defined error is displayed.

Error$

Type

Function

Syntax

```
Error$[(errorcode%)]
```

Description

The Error$ function returns the error message that corresponds to a given error code. The argument *errorcode%* represents an error code. It must be an integer between 1 and 32,767, inclusive. If *errorcode%* is omitted, Error$ returns the message string corresponding to the most recent runtime error. Some of the error messages use internal variables that give specific information about an error. When an error occurs, Visual Basic substitutes the appropriate words in the error message string, depending on the context of the error.

Exit

Type

Statement

Syntax

```
Exit {Do|For|Function|Sub}
```

Description

The Exit statement exits a Do...Loop, a For...Next loop, a Function procedure, or a Sub procedure.

Exp

Type

Function

Syntax

Exp(x)

Description

The Exp function returns e (the base of natural logarithms) to the power of x. The exponent x must not exceed 88.02969 for single-precision values or 709.782712893 for double-precision values. If you use a value of x that is outside those limits, Visual Basic generates an error message. Exp is calculated in single precision if x is an integer or single-precision value. If you use any other numeric data type, Exp is calculated in double precision. The Exp function complements the action of the Log function.

File List Box

Type

Control

Description

A file list box finds and specifies files to be opened, saved, or otherwise manipulated at runtime. You can use this control to display a list of file names selected according to their attributes. This is useful if you want to create dialog boxes in your application that, for example, enable the user to open a file from a list of available files in the current directory.

FileAttr

Type
Function

Syntax
`FileAttr(filenumber%, attribute%)`

Description
The FileAttr function returns file mode or operating system file handle information about an open file.

FileName

Type
Property

Syntax
`[form.][filelistbox.]FileName[= filename$]`

Description
The FileName property applies to a file list box. It sets or returns the selected file from the list portion of a file list box. You can also set drive, path, or pattern using the FileName property. It is not available at design time. The FileName property is set to an empty string (" ") for no currently selected file, when the control is created at runtime. Reading this property returns the currently selected file name from the list.

FillColor

Type
Property

Syntax
`{[form.][picturebox.]Printer.}FillColor[= color&]`

Description

The FillColor property applies to a form, picture box, and printer object. It sets the color used to fill in circles and boxes created with the Circle and Line graphics methods. By default, FillColor is set to 0 (black). You should note that when the FillStyle property setting is set at its default, 1 (Transparent), it can't be used with FillColor. All other FillStyle settings can be used.

FillStyle

Type
Property

Syntax

`{[form.][picturebox.]|Printer.}FillStyle[= style%]`

Description

The FillStyle property applies to a form, picture box, and printer object. The property sets or returns the pattern used to fill in circles and boxes created with the Circle and Line graphics methods.

Fix

Type
Function

Syntax

`Fix(numeric-expression)`

Description

The Fix function removes the fractional part of *numeric-expression* and returns the resulting integer.

FontBold, FontItalic, FontStrikethru, FontTransparent, FontUnderline

Type

Properties

Syntax

```
{[form.][control.]|Printer.}FontBold[= boolean%]
{[form.][control.]|Printer.}FontItalic[= boolean%]
{[form.][control.]|Printer.}FontStrikethru[= boolean%]
{[form.][picturebox.]|Printer.}FontTransparent[= boolean%]
{[form.][control.]|Printer.}FontUnderline[= boolean%]
```

Description

These properties apply to a form, check box, combo box, command button, directory list box, drive list box, file list box, frame, label, list box, option button, picture
box, text box, and printer object. They determine font styles in the following formats: FontBold, FontItalic, FontStrikethru, and FontUnderline. FontTransparent
determines whether background text or graphics are included along with the characters in a particular font; this property applies only to forms, picture boxes, and the
printer object. Use these font properties to format text displayed within controls,
either at design time through the Properties bar or by code at runtime. For forms,
picture boxes, and the printer object, setting these properties does not affect
graphics or print output already drawn to a form, picture box, or printer object. For
all other controls, font changes take effect on the screen immediately.

FontCount

Type

Property

Syntax

```
{Printer|Screen}.FontCount
```

Description

The FontCount property applies to a printer object and screen object. The property returns the number of fonts available for the current display device or currently active printer. It is not available at design time and read-only at runtime. You can use this property with the Fonts property to see a list of available screen or printer fonts. Fonts available in Visual Basic vary according to your system configuration, display devices, and printing devices.

FontName

Type

Property

Syntax

{[*form.*][*control.*]¦Printer.}FontName[= *font$*]

Description

The FontName property applies to a form, check box, combo box, command button, directory list box, drive list box, file list box, frame, label, list box, option button, picture box, text box, and printer object. The property sets or returns the font used to display text in a control, or in a runtime drawing or printing operation. Fonts available with Visual Basic vary according to your system configuration, display devices, and printing devices. Font-related properties can be set only to values for which real fonts exist. In general, you should change FontName before setting size and style attributes with the FontSize, FontBold, FontItalic, FontStrikethru, Font-Transparent, and FontUnderline properties.

Fonts

Type

Property

Syntax

{Printer¦Screen}.Fonts(*index%*)

Description

The Fonts property applies to a printer object or screen object. The property returns all font names available for the current display device or active printer, when enumerated from 0 to FontCount –1. The property is not available at design time and is read-only at runtime. This property works in conjunction with the Font-Count property, which returns the number of font names available for the object. Fonts available in Visual Basic vary according to your system configuration, display devices, and printing devices. Use both the Fonts and the FontCount properties to get information about available screen or printer fonts.

FontSize

Type
Property

Syntax
{[*form.*][*control.*]|Printer.}FontSize[= *points%*]

Description

The FontSize property applies to a form, check box, command button, combo box, directory list box, drive list box, file list box, frame, label, list box, option button, picture box, text box, and printer object. The property sets or returns the size of the font to be used for text displayed in a control or in a runtime drawing or printing operation. Use this property to format text in the font size you want. The default is determined by the operating environment. To change the default, specify the size of the font in number of points.

For...Next

Type
Statement

Syntax
```
For counter = start To end [Step increment ]
    [statementblock]
    [Exit For]
```

```
     [statementblock]
Next [counter[, counter]]
```

Description

This statement repeats a group of instructions a specified number of times. A For...Next loop executes only if *start* and *end* are consistent with *increment*. If *end* is greater than *start*, *increment* must be positive. If *end* is less than *start*, *increment* must be negative. Visual Basic checks this at runtime by comparing the sign of (*end* − *start*) with the sign of *step*. If both have the same sign, and *end* does not equal *start*, the For...Next loop is entered. If not, the entire loop is skipped. With a For...Next loop, the program lines following the For statement are executed until the Next statement is encountered.

ForeColor

See *BackColor*...

Form

Type

Control

Description

A form is a window or dialog box that makes up the background of your application's interface. You can draw up to 255 controls on each form to create an application that responds in a way you specify. Forms have a set of properties that define how they look (for example, position, size, or color) and how they work (for example, whether the user can size it). Forms also respond to events for which procedures have been written. These events can either be activated by the user or triggered by the system. In addition to properties and events, some Visual Basic keywords can be used for displaying forms and drawing graphics or text. These keywords are called *methods*. Forms also can be set up as server links in a DDE conversation, with a label, picture box, or text box control furnishing the data. To do this, set the LinkTopic property to establish a link, the LinkItem property to specify an item for the conversation, and the LinkMode property to activate the link. When these have been set, Visual Basic attempts to initiate the conversation, and displays a message if it's unable to do so.

Format$

Type
Function

Syntax
`Format$(numeric-expression[, fmt$])`

Description
The Format$ function converts a number to a string and formats it according to instructions contained in a format expression. If *fmt$* is omitted or is a null string, Format$ provides the same functionality as the Str$ function; that is, it simply converts numeric values to strings. Note that positive numbers converted to strings using Format$ do not have the leading space reserved to display the sign of the value, whereas those converted using Str$ retain the leading space. When no display formatting is required, use the Str$ function to convert numbers to strings.

FormName

Type
Property

Syntax
`Form_Event Name`

Description
The FormName property applies to a form. It sets the identifier used to access a form in code and is not available at runtime. By default, this property assigns a name to a form that includes "Form" with a unique integer, starting at 1. The numbers assigned are cumulative: Form1, Form2, Form3, and so on. To change the default, specify a unique name for the form. A FormName must start with a letter and can have a maximum of 40 characters, including alphanumeric or underscore characters. A FormName cannot be a reserved word. Note that FormName is distinct from the Caption property, which appears in the title bar if the window has one.

Frame

Type

Control

Description

A frame provides a graphical and functional grouping for controls. You can also use this control to subdivide a form graphically, for example, to separate a group of option buttons from other groups of option buttons or controls. To group controls, draw the frame first, then draw controls inside the frame. This enables you to move the frame and the controls together instead of having to move each one separately.

FreeFile

Type

Function

Syntax

```
FreeFile
```

Description

The FreeFile function returns the next valid unused file number. Use FreeFile when you need to supply a file number and you want to ensure that the file number is not already in use.

Function

Type

Statement

Syntax

```
[Static]
```

Description

The Function statement declares the name, arguments, and code that form the body of a Function procedure. All executable code in a Visual Basic application must be in Function or Sub procedures. You cannot define a Function procedure inside another Function or Sub procedure.

Get

Type

Statement

Syntax

```
Get [#] filenumber%,[recordnumber&,] recordvariable
```

Description

The Get statement reads from a disk file into a record variable. For files opened in random-access mode, it reads the number of the record to be read. For files opened in binary mode, it reads the byte position where reading starts. The first byte in a file is at position 1; the second byte is at position 2, and so on. If you omit *recordnumber&*, the next record or byte (the one after the last Get or Put statement, or the one pointed to by the last Seek) is read from. The largest possible record number is $2^{31} - 1$, or 2,147,483,647. For random-access files, you can use any variable as long as the length of the variable is less than or equal to the length of the record—that is, the length specified in the Len clause of the Open statement. Usually a record variable defined to match the fields in a data record is used. Multiple element record variables are defined using the Type statement. For files opened in binary mode, you can use any variable. The Get statement reads as many bytes as there are in the variable.

GetData

Type

Method

Syntax

```
Clipboard.GetData ([format%])
```

Description

The GetData method returns a picture from the operating environment Clipboard object.

GetFormat

Type
Method

Syntax
`Clipboard.GetFormat (format%)`

Description

The GetFormat method returns an integer indicating whether there is an item in the operating environment Clipboard that matches a specified format.

GetText

Type
Method

Syntax
`Clipboard.GetText ([format%])`

Description

The GetText method returns a text string from the Windows operating environment Clipboard.

Global

Type
Statement

Syntax

```
Global variablename [([subscripts])] [As type] [, variablename
    [([subscripts])] [As type] ]...
```

Description

The Global statement is used in the global module to declare global variables and allocate storage space. The Global statement also provides a way to declare variables to be user-defined types.

GoSub...Return

Type

Statements

Syntax

```
GoSub {linelabel│linenumber}
    .
    .
    .
Return
```

Description

The GoSub...Return statements branch to, and return from, a subroutine within a procedure. The arguments *linelabel* and *linenumber* are labels that mark the first line of the subroutine. The argument *linelabel* must begin with an alphabetic character and must end with a colon. Each line label must be unique within its form or module. That is, within a form or module, you cannot have a line label in one procedure that has the same name as the line label in another procedure. The length of *linelabel* is limited to no more than 40 characters. The use of Visual Basic keywords as labels is not permitted, either. Line labels are not case-sensitive. They may also begin in any column as long as they are the first nonblank characters on the line. The argument *linenumber* is an alternative way of labeling program lines. If used, *linenumber*, like *linelabel*, must be unique in the form or module where it is used. Do not end a line number with a colon. A subroutine can contain more than one Return statement A Return statement causes Visual Basic to branch back to the statement immediately following the most recent GoSub statement.

GotFocus

Type

Event

Syntax

```
Sub Form_GotFocus ()
Sub ctlname_GotFocus (Index as Integer)
```

Description

The GotFocus event applies to a form, check box, combo box, command button, directory list box, drive list box, file list box, horizontal scroll bar, list box, option button, picture box, text box, and vertical scroll bar. The event occurs when the object receives the focus after the user clicks or tabs to the object or by changing the focus in code through the SetFocus method. You should note that a form receives the focus only when all visible controls are disabled.

GoTo

Type

Statement

Syntax

```
GoTo {linelabel| linenumber}
```

Description

The GoTo statement branches unconditionally to the specified line within a procedure. GoTo can only branch to lines within the procedure where the GoTo occurs. You cannot use a GoTo statement to enter or exit another Sub or Function procedure. It is generally considered good programming practice to use structured control statements (Do...Loop, For...Next, If...Then...Else, Select Case) instead of GoTo statements, because programs with many GoTo statements can be difficult to read and debug.

hDC

Type
Property

Syntax
{[*form.*][*picturebox.*]¦Printer.}hDC

Description
The hDC property applies to a form, picture box, and printer object. The property returns a handle provided by the operating environment to the device context of an object. It is not available at design time and is read-only at runtime. This property is a Microsoft Windows device-context handle. The operating environment manages the system display by assigning a device context for the printer object and for each form and picture box in your application. You can refer to the handle for an object's device context with the hDC property, which provides a value to pass to Windows API calls.

Height, Width

Type
Properties

Syntax
{[*form.*][*control.*]¦Printer.¦Screen.}Height[= *height!*]
{[*form.*][*control.*]¦Printer.¦Screen.}Width[= *width!*]

Description
The Height and Width properties apply to a form, check box, combo box, command button, directory list box, drive list box, file list box, frame, horizontal scroll bar, label, list box, option button, picture box, printer object, text box, screen object, and vertical scroll bar. Both properties set or return the dimensions of an object. By default, the values of the Height and Width properties are equivalent to the height and width of the object at design time. To set either property for a form or control, specify a single-precision integer greater than 0. Maximum limits for these properties for all objects are system-dependent. Use Height and Width—and their related

properties, Left and Top—for operations or calculations based on an object's total area, such as sizing or moving the object.

Hex$

Type
Function

Syntax
Hex$(*numeric-expression*)

Description
The Hex$ function returns a string that represents the hexadecimal value of the decimal argument. The argument *numeric-expression* is rounded to the nearest whole number before the Hex$ function evaluates it. If the argument is an integer, Hex$ returns a string of up to four hexadecimal characters; if the argument is a long integer, Hex$ returns a string of up to eight hexadecimal characters. You can represent hexadecimal numbers directly by preceding numbers in the proper range with &H. For example, &H10 represents decimal 16 in hexadecimal notation.

Hidden

See *Archive...*

Hide

Type
Method

Syntax
[*form.*]Hide

Description
The Hide method hides a form, but does not unload it. The argument *form* is the name of the form to hide. When a form is hidden, it is removed from the screen and

its Visible property is set to False (0). A hidden form's controls are not accessible to the user, but they are available to the running Visual Basic program, to other processes that may be communicating with the application through DDE, and to timer events. When a form is hidden, control does not return to the user until all code in the event procedure that caused the form to be hidden has finished executing. If the form is not loaded when the Hide method is invoked, it is loaded, but not shown.

Horizontal and Vertical Scroll Bars

Type
Controls

Description
Both types of scroll bars are graphical tools for quickly navigating through a long list of items or a large amount of information, and for indicating the current position on a scale. A scroll bar can also be used as an input device or an indicator of speed or quantity; for example, to control the sound volume of a computer game or to view the time elapsed in a timed process. When you're using a scroll bar as an indicator of quantity or speed or as an input device, use the Max and Min properties to set the range appropriate to the use of the control. To specify the amount of change to report in a scroll bar, use the LargeChange property for clicking in the bar and the SmallChange property for clicking the arrow at either end of the bar. The scroll bar's Value property increases or decreases by the amounts set for the Large-Change and SmallChange properties. You can position the scroll box at runtime by setting Value to between 0 and 32,767, inclusive.

Hour

Type
Function

Syntax
Hour(*serial#*)

Description

The Hour function returns an integer between 0 (12:00 A.M.) and 23 (11:00 P.M.), inclusive, that represents the hour of the day corresponding to the argument. The argument *serial#* is a serial number that represents a date and/or time between 1 January 1753 and 31 December 2078, inclusive, where 1 January 1900 is 2. Numbers to the left of the decimal point in *serial#* represent the date; numbers to the right represent the time. Negative numbers represent dates prior to 30 December 1899.

hWnd

Type
Property

Syntax
[*form.*]hWnd

Description

The hWnd property applies to a form. It returns a handle to a window, where the handle is provided by the operating environment. It is not available at design time and is read-only at runtime. This property is a Microsoft Windows handle. The operating environment identifies a form in an application by assigning a handle to it. You can access this handle with the hWnd property, which provides values to pass to Windows API calls.

Icon

Type
Property

Syntax
[*form.*]Icon

Description

The Icon property applies to a form. It returns the icon displayed for a form at runtime when the form is minimized. It is write-only at design time. Use this property to specify an icon for any form that the user can minimize at runtime. For example, you can assign a unique icon to a form that indicates the form's function. You can use Visual Basic's Icon Library (in the ICONS subdirectory) as a source for icons. When you create an executable file, you can assign an icon to the application by using the Icon property of any form in that application.

If...Then...Else

Type
Statement

Syntax

If *condition* Then *thenpart* [Else *elsepart*]

or

```
If condition1 Then
    [statementblock-1]
    [ElseIf condition2 Then
    [statementblock-2] ]
    [Else
    [statementblock-n] ]
End If
```

Description

This statement allows conditional execution, based on the evaluation of an expression. The single-line form of the statement is best used for short, straightforward tests where one of two possible actions is taken based on the evaluation of an expression. Any program using single-line If...Then...Else statements can be written using block form. The block form provides several advantages. It provides more structure and flexibility than the single-line form by allowing conditional branches across several lines. With the block form, more complex conditions can be tested. The block form lets you use longer statements and structures within the Then...Else portion of the statement. The block form also allows your program's structure to be guided by logic rather than by how many statements fit on a line.

Image

Type
Property

Syntax
[*form.*][*picturebox.*]Image

Description
The Image property applies to a form and picture box. It returns a handle to a persistent bitmap, where the handle is provided by the operating environment. It is not available at design time and is read-only at runtime. This property is a Microsoft Windows bitmap handle. An object's AutoRedraw property determines whether the repainting of an object occurs with a persistent bitmap or through Paint events. The operating environment identifies an object's persistent bitmap by assigning a handle to it; you can use the Image property to get this handle. An Image value exists regardless of the setting for AutoRedraw. If AutoRedraw is set to True and nothing has been drawn, the image contains only the color set with the BackColor property and the picture. You can assign the value of Image to the Picture property. The Image property also provides a value to pass to Windows API calls. The Image, DragIcon, and Picture properties must be used directly when assigning values to other properties, when saving with the SavePicture statement, or when placing something onto the Clipboard. You cannot assign these to temporary variables and then use the results.

Index

Type
Property

Syntax
[*form.*]*control*[(I%)].Index

Description
The Index property applies to a check box, combo box, command button, directory list box, drive list box, file list box, frame, horizontal scroll bar, label, list box, menu,

option button, picture box, text box, timer, and vertical scroll bar. It sets or returns the number that uniquely identifies a control in a control array, and is only available if the control is part of a control array. It is read-only at runtime. Since control array elements share the same CtlName, use of the Index property in code is necessary to refer to a particular control in the array. The Index must appear as a number in parentheses next to the control array name—for example, Amount(3). When a control in the array recognizes that an event has occurred, Visual Basic calls the array's event procedure and passes the applicable Index as an additional argument. This property is also used when you are creating controls dynamically at runtime with the Load statement or removing them with the Unload statement.

Input

Type
Statement

Syntax
Input # `filenumber%, variablelist`

Description
The Input # statement reads data from a sequential file and assigns the data to variables. The argument *filenumber%* is the number used in the Open statement to open the file. The argument *variablelist* is a comma-delimited list of the variables that are assigned values read from the file. All data items in a file must appear in the same order as the variables in the variable list. Be sure you match data in the file with the proper variable types; that is, string data into string variables and numeric data into numeric variables. Leading spaces on a line are ignored.

With numeric variables, the first character encountered that is not a space is assumed to be the start of a number. The number terminates when a space, comma, or the end of a line is encountered. Blank lines are input as zero.

With string variables, the first character encountered that is not a space is assumed to be the start of the string. The string terminates when a comma or the end of a line is encountered. Blank lines are input as null strings. If the end-of-file is reached when a numeric or string item is being inputted, the input is terminated.

Input$

Type
Function

Syntax
Input$(*n%*, [#] *filenumber%*)

Description
The Input$ function returns a string of characters read from a file. If the file is opened for random access, the argument *n%* must be less than or equal to the record length set by the Len clause in the Open statement. (If the record length is not set, *n%* must be less than or equal to 128.) If the given file is opened for binary or sequential access, *n%* must be less than or equal to 32,767. Unlike the Input# statement, Input$ returns all characters it reads including carriage returns, line feeds, and leading spaces.

InputBox$

Type
Function

Syntax
InputBox$(*prompt$*[, *title$*[, *default$*[, *xpos%*, *ypos%*]]])

Description
The InputBox$ function displays a prompt in a dialog box, waits for the user to input some text or choose a button, and returns the contents of the edit box. The length of *prompt$* is restricted to approximately 255 characters, depending on the width of the characters. If *prompt$* is to consist of more than one line, be sure to include a carriage return (Chr$(13)) and a line-feed character (Chr$(10)) between each line. If the argument *title$* is omitted, nothing is placed in the title bar. If *default$* is omitted, the edit box is displayed empty. If you omit *xpos%*, you must also omit *ypos%*. In that case, the dialog box is horizontally centered and vertically positioned

approximately one third the way down the screen. If the user chooses the OK button or presses Enter, InputBox$ returns whatever is in the edit box. If the user chooses the Cancel button, InputBox$ returns an empty string (" ").

InStr

Type
Function

Syntax
Instr([start&,] strexpr1$, strexpr2$)

Description
The InStr function returns the character position of the first occurrence of a string within another string. Use the Len function to find the length of *strexpr1$*.

Int

Type
Function

Syntax
Int(numeric-expression)

Description
The Int function converts a numeric expression to the largest integer less than or equal to the expression. The argument *numeric-expression* is a single- or double-precision numeric expression. The Int function removes the fractional part of the expression and returns the resulting integer. The difference between Int and Fix is that for a negative numeric expression, Int returns the first negative integer less than *numeric-expression*, while Fix returns the first negative integer greater than *numeric-expression*. For example, Int converts –8.4 to –9, while Fix converts –8.4 to –8.

Interval

Type

Property

Syntax

[*form.*]*timer*.Interval[= *milliseconds&*]

Description

The Interval property applies to a timer. It sets or returns the number of milliseconds in a timer's countdown interval to determine when to call a timer control's associated Timer event procedure. You can set a timer control's Interval property at design time or runtime. When using the Interval property, remember that the timer control's Enabled property determines whether the timer control responds to the passage of time. Set Enabled to False (0) to turn the timer off, and to True (–1) to turn it on. Write a Timer event procedure to tell Visual Basic what to do each time the Interval has passed.

KeyDown, KeyUp

Type

Events

Syntax

```
Sub Form_KeyDown
Sub Form_KeyUp
Sub ctlname_KeyDown
Sub ctlname_KeyUp
```

Description

These events apply to a form, check box, combo box, command button, directory list box, drive list box, file list box, horizontal scroll bar, list box, option button, picture box, text box, and vertical scroll bar. They occur when the user presses (KeyDown) or releases (KeyUp) a key while an object has the focus. These events detect all keys on the keyboard, though they are generally used for extended character keys. For either event, the object with the focus receives all keystrokes. A form can have the focus only if it has no visible and enabled controls.

KeyPress

Type
Event

Syntax
```
Sub Form_KeyPress (KeyAscii As Integer)
Sub ctlname_KeyPress ([Index as Integer] KeyAscii As Integer)
```

Description
The Keypress event applies to a form, check box, combo box, command button, directory list box, drive list box, file list box, horizontal scroll bar, list box, option button, picture box, text box, and vertical scroll bar. It occurs when the user presses and releases an ASCII key. The object with the focus receives the event. A form can receive the event only if it has no visible and enabled controls. A KeyPress event can involve any printable keyboard character, the Ctrl key combined with a character from the standard alphabet or one of a few special characters, and the Enter or Backspace key.

KeyUp

See *KeyDown*...

Kill

Type
Statement

Syntax
```
Kill filespec$
```

Description
The Kill statement deletes files from a disk. The Kill statement is similar to the DOS commands ERASE or DEL. Kill is used for all types of disk files: program files, random-access data files, and sequential data files. The argument *filespec$* is a string expression that can contain a path and wildcards. Kill deletes files only. To delete

directories, use the DOS command RMDIR or the Visual Basic RmDir statement. Using Kill to delete a file that is currently open produces an error. Be extremely careful when using wildcards with Kill; you can unintentionally delete the wrong files.

Label

Type
Control

Description
A label displays text that the user normally can't change. You can also write code that changes the label in response to events at runtime. For example, if your application takes a few minutes to commit a change, you may want to create a message that displays its processing status. A label can also be used to identify a control, such as a text box, that does not have its own Caption property. You can set only one line of text with the Caption property at design time. To set multiple lines of text, you need to write code that includes carriage returns at line breaks. A label can also be set up as a client link in a DDE conversation. To do this, set the LinkTopic property to establish a link, set the LinkItem property to specify an item for the conversation, and set the LinkMode property to activate the link. When these have been set, Visual Basic attempts to initiate the conversation and displays a message if it's unable to do so.

LargeChange, SmallChange

Type
Properties

Syntax
```
[form.]{hscrollbar|vscrollbar}.LargeChange[= change%]
[form.]{hscrollbar|vscrollbar}.SmallChange[= change%]
```

Description
These properties apply to the horizontal and vertical scroll bars. LargeChange determines the amount of change to report in a scroll bar control when the user clicks the area between the scroll box and scroll arrow. The scroll bar's Value

property increases or decreases by this amount. SmallChange determines the amount of change to report in a scroll bar control when the user clicks a scroll arrow. The scroll bar's Value property increases or decreases by this amount. Typically, you set LargeChange and SmallChange at design time. You can also reset them in code at runtime when the scrolling increment must change dynamically.

LBound

Type
Function

Syntax
`LBound(array[, dimension%])`

Description
The LBound function returns the smallest available subscript for the indicated dimension of *array*. The LBound function is used with the UBound function to determine the size of an array.

LCase$

Type
Function

Syntax
`LCase$(stringexpression$)`

Description
The LCase$ function returns a string where all letters have been converted to lowercase. The LCase$ function takes a string variable, string constant, or string expression as its single argument. Only uppercase letters are converted to lowercase; all lowercase letters and nonletter characters remain unchanged. LCase$ works with both variable- and fixed-length strings. LCase$ and UCase$ are helpful in making string comparisons that are not case-sensitive.

Left, Top

Type
Properties

Syntax

```
[form.][control.]Left[= x!]
[form.][control.]Top[= y!]
```

Description
The Left and Top properties apply to a form, check box, combo box, command button, directory list box, drive list box, file list box, frame, horizontal scroll bar, label, list box, option button, picture box, text box, and vertical scroll bar. Left determines the distance between the internal left edge of an object and the left edge of its container. Top determines the distance between the internal top edge of an object and the top edge of its container. For a form, the Left and Top properties are always expressed in twips; for a control, they are measured in units according to the coordinate system of its container. The values for these properties change as the object is moved by the user or by code.

Left$

Type
Function

Syntax

```
Left$(stringexpression$, n&)
```

Description
The Left$ function returns a string consisting of the leftmost $n\&$ characters of a string. The argument $n\&$ is an integer expression indicating how many characters to return. It must be between 0 and approximately 65.535, inclusive. If $n\&$ is 0, the null string (zero length) is returned. If $n\&$ is greater than or equal to the number of characters in *stringexpression$*, the entire string is returned. To find the number of characters in the string, use Len(*stringexpression$*) below.

Len

Type
Function

Syntax
Len(*stringexpression$*)

or

Len(*variablename*)

Description
The Len function returns the number of characters in a string or the number of storage bytes required by a variable. In the first syntax form, Len returns the number of characters in the argument *stringexpression$*. The second syntax returns the number of bytes required for storage of the variable of a given data type. Because Len works with user-defined data types as well as fundamental Visual Basic data types, this syntax is particularly useful for determining record size for random-access files.

Let

Type
Statement

Syntax
[Let] *variable = expression*

Description
The Let statement assigns the value of an expression to a variable. The keyword Let is optional; any assignment of an expression to a variable can be done without the Let keyword. String expressions may only be assigned to string variables, and numeric expressions to numeric variables. Assigning an expression of one numeric data type to a variable of a different numeric data type causes the value of the expression to be forced into the data type of the variable. Let statements can be used with record variables only when both variables are of the same user-defined type. Use the LSet statement to assign record variables of different user-defined types.

Line Input

Type

Statement

Syntax

```
Line Input #filenumber%, stringvariable$
```

Description

The Line Input # statement is used to read a text file one line at a time. It reads all characters in a sequential file up to a carriage return, then skips over the carriage-return/line-feed sequence.

Line

Type

Method

Syntax

```
[object.]Line [[Step](x1!, y1!)] — [Step](x2!, y2!)[, [color&], B
    [F]]]
```

Description

The Line method draws lines and rectangles on a form, picture box, or printer object. When drawing lines that are connected, they should be drawn so that after the initial line is drawn, subsequent lines begin at the end points of the previous lines. The width of the line drawn depends on the DrawWidth property. The way a line or box is drawn on the background depends on the setting of the DrawMode property. When Line is executed, CurrentX and CurrentY are set to the end point specified by the arguments.

LinkClose

Type

Event

Syntax

```
Sub Form_LinkClose ()
Sub ctlname_LinkClose (Index as Integer)
```

Description

The LinkClose event applies to a form, label, picture box, and text box. It occurs when a DDE conversation terminates or ends. Either application in a DDE conversation may terminate a conversation at any time. Typically, you use a LinkClose procedure to notify the user that a DDE conversation has been terminated. You might also include troubleshooting information on how to reestablish a connection or where to go for assistance. For brief messages, use the MsgBox function and MsgBox statement.

LinkError

Type

Event

Syntax

```
Sub Form_LinkError (LinkErr As Integer)
Sub ctlname_LinkError ([Index as Integer] LinkErr As Integer)
```

Description

The LinkError event applies to a form, label, picture box, and text box. The event occurs when there is an error during a DDE conversation. This event is recognized only as the result of a DDE-related error that occurs when no Visual Basic code is being executed. The error number is passed as an argument. Use a LinkError procedure to notify the user of the particular error that has occurred. You might also include code to fix the problem or troubleshooting information on how to re-establish a connection or where to go for assistance. For brief messages, use the MsgBox function and MsgBox statement.

LinkExecute

Type

Event

Syntax

```
Sub Form_LinkExecute (CmdStr As String, Cancel As Integer)
```

Description

The LinkExecute event applies to a form. It occurs when a command string is sent by a client application in a DDE conversation. The client application expects the server application to perform the operation described by the string. There is no required syntax for CmdStr. How your application responds to different strings is completely up to you. If you have not created a LinkExecute event procedure, Visual Basic will reject command strings from client applications.

LinkExecute

Type

Method

Syntax

```
control.LinkExecute cmdstr$
```

Description

The LinkExecute method sends a command string to the other application in a DDE conversation. The exact contents of the *cmdstr$* argument will vary depending on the server application. For example, Microsoft Excel and Microsoft Word for Windows accept command strings that consist of their macro commands surrounded by square brackets. To see what command strings a server application accepts, consult the documentation for that application.

LinkItem

Type

Property

Syntax

```
[form.]{label|picturebox|textbox}.LinkItem[= stringexpression$]
```

Description

The LinkItem property applies to a label, picture box, and text box. It specifies the data passed to a client control in a DDE conversation with another application; corresponds to the item argument in the standard DDE syntax, with *app, topic,* and *item* as arguments. To set this property, specify a recognizable unit of data in an application as a reference—for example, a cell reference such as "R2C6" in Microsoft Excel. Use LinkItem in combination with the LinkTopic property to specify the complete data link for a client control to a server application. To activate this link, set the Link-Mode property. You set LinkItem only for a control used as a client. When a Visual Basic form is a server in a DDE conversation, the name of any label, picture box, or text box on the form can be the item argument in the *app* | topic!item string used by the client.

LinkMode

Type

Property

Syntax

[*form.*][*control.*]LinkMode[= *mode%*]

Description

The LinkMode property applies to a form, label, picture box, and text box. It determines the type of link used for a DDE conversation.

LinkOpen

Type

Event

Syntax

```
Sub Form_LinkOpen (Cancel As Integer)
Sub ctlname_LinkOpen ([Index as Integer] Cancel As Integer)
```

Description

The LinkOpen event applies to a form, label, picture box, and text box. The event occurs when a DDE conversation is being initiated. This event occurs for forms when a client application is initiating a DDE conversation with the form. It occurs for controls when a control is initiating a DDE conversation with a server application.

LinkPoke

Type
Method

Syntax

control.LinkPoke

Description

The LinkPoke method transfers the contents of a control to the server application in a DDE conversation. The argument *control* is a text box, picture box, or label involved in a DDE conversation as a client. If *control* is a text box, LinkPoke transfers the current contents of the Text property to the server. If *control* is a picture box, LinkPoke transfers the current contents of the Picture property to the server. If *control* is a label, LinkPoke transfers the current contents of the Caption property. Typically, information in a DDE conversation flows from server to client. However, LinkPoke allows a client control to supply data to the server. Not all server applications will accept information supplied in this way; if the server application does not accept the data, an error will occur.

LinkRequest

Type
Method

Syntax

control.LinkRequest

Description

The LinkRequest method asks the server in a DDE conversation to update the contents of a control. The control is a text box, picture box, or label involved in a DDE conversation as a client. LinkRequest causes the server application to provide fresh data to the control, updating the Text property if the control is a text box, the Picture property if the control is a picture box, or the Caption property if the control is a label. If the LinkMode property of the control is set to HOT (1), the server application will automatically update the control and LinkRequest will not be needed. However, if the LinkMode property of the control is set to COLD (2), the server application will only update the control when requested to with the LinkRequest method.

LinkSend

Type

Method

Syntax

`control.LinkSend`

Description

The LinkSend method transfers the contents of a picture control to the client application in a DDE conversation. The control must be a picture box on a form that is acting as a server in a DDE conversation. When other applications establish hot links with a form in your application, Visual Basic automatically notifies them when the contents of text boxes and labels on the form change. However, Visual Basic does not automatically notify DDE clients when the Picture property of a picture on a server form changes. Because the amount of data in a picture can be very large, and because it seldom makes sense to update clients as each pixel in the picture changes, Visual Basic requires that you use the LinkSend method to notify DDE clients explicitly when a picture box has changed.

LinkTimeout

Type

Property

Syntax

[*form*.]{*label*|*picturebox*|*textbox*}.LinkTimeout[= *duration%*]

Description

The LinkTimeout property applies to a label, picture box, and text box. The property determines the amount of time a control waits for a response to a DDE message. By default, the LinkTimeout property is set to 50 (equivalent to 5 seconds). You can specify other settings in tenths of a second. DDE response time from server applications will vary. Use this property to adjust the time a client control waits for a response from a server application. This helps avoid generating an error by Visual Basic, should a given server application take too long to respond. Please note that setting LinkTimeout to −1 tells the control to wait indefinitely for a response in a DDE conversation. The user can force the control to stop waiting by pressing the Alt key.

LinkTopic

Type

Property

Syntax

[*form*.][*control*.]LinkTopic[= *link$*]

Description

The LinkTopic property applies to a form, label, picture box, and text box. As a client control, the property determines the server application and the topic. You use LinkTopic with the LinkItem property to specify the complete data link. As a server form, it determines the topic that the server form responds to in a DDE conversation. The LinkTopic property consists of a string that supplies part of the information necessary to set up either a client link or server link. The string you use depends on whether you're working with a client control or a server form.

List

Type

Property

Syntax

[*form.*]*control*.List(*index%*)[= *stringexpression$*]

Description

The List property applies to a combo box, list box, directory list box, drive list box, and file list box. The property sets or returns the items contained in a control's list portion. The list area is a string array in which each element is a list item. It is not available at design-time; it is read-only at runtime for directory list boxes, drive list boxes, and file list boxes; and it is read-only at runtime for combo boxes and list boxes. Initially, combo boxes and list boxes contain an empty list. For the file-system controls, the list is based on conditions that exist when the control is created at runtime. The List property works in conjunction with the related properties, ListCount and List-Index.

List Box

Type

Control

Description

A list box displays a list of items from which the user can choose one. If the number of items exceeds what can be displayed, a scroll bar is automatically added to the list box so the user can scroll up and down through the list. You can add code that enables the user to add or remove an item from the list at runtime. If you want to add or delete items in the list, use the AddItem or RemoveItem method. Set the List, ListCount, and ListIndex properties to enable a user to access items in the list.

ListCount

Type

Property

Syntax

[*form.*]*control*.ListCount

Description

The ListCount property applies to a combo box, directory list box, drive list box, file list box, and list box. It returns the number of items in the list portion of the control. It is not available at design time and is read-only at runtime.

ListIndex

Type

Property

Syntax

[*form.*]*control*.ListIndex[= *index%*]

Description

The ListIndex applies to a combo box, directory list box, drive list box, file list box, and list box. The property sets or returns the index of the currently selected item in the control. It also tracks the selected entry. The property is not available at design time. The ListIndex property works in conjunction with two related properties, List and ListCount. The expression List(ListIndex) returns the string for the currently selected item. For all controls except directory list boxes, ListIndex returns –1 if no item is selected. For combo boxes, ListIndex also returns –1 if the user enters a choice in a combo box instead of selecting from predefined choices.

Load

Type

Event

Syntax

Sub Form_Load ()

Description

The Load event applies to a form. It occurs when a form is loaded. The Load event occurs when an application starts, as the result of a Load statement, or as the result of an "implicit load" (caused by a reference to an unloaded form's properties or controls). Typically, you use a Load procedure to include initialization code for a form—for example, specifying default settings for controls, indicating contents to be loaded into combo boxes or list boxes, and initializing form-level variables. Whenever a form is shown, Visual Basic also calls the related events in this order: Load, Resize, Paint, and GotFocus. When you are attaching procedures for these related events, be sure that their actions don't conflict.

Load

Type
Statement

Syntax
```
Load object
```

Description
The Load statement loads a form or control into memory. The argument *object* is a form or control array element to load. It is not necessary to use the Load statement with forms unless you want to load a form without displaying it. Any reference to a form automatically loads it if it is not already loaded. For example, the Show method loads an unloaded form before displaying it. Once the form is loaded, all properties for the form and its controls can be altered by the program, whether or not the form is actually visible. Under some circumstances, you may want to load all your forms during intitialization and display them later as they are needed. When Visual Basic loads a form, it sets form properties to their initial values, then performs the Load event procedure. When an application starts, Visual Basic automatically loads and displays the application's start-up form.

LoadPicture

Type
Function

Syntax
```
LoadPicture([stringexpression$])
```

Description

The LoadPicture function loads a picture into a form or picture box. The argument *stringexpression$* is the name of a picture file to be loaded. Pictures are cleared from forms and picture boxes by assigning LoadPicture with no argument. Picture files recognized by Visual Basic include bitmaps (.BMP), icons (.ICO), and Windows Metafile (.WMF) files. To load pictures for display in a picture box or as the background of a form, the return value of LoadPicture must be assigned to the Picture property of the object on which the picture is displayed.

Loc

Type
Function

Syntax

```
Loc(filenumber%)
```

Description

The Loc function returns the current position within an open file. The argument *filenumber%* is the number used in the Open statement to open the file. For random-access files, the Loc function returns the number of the last record read from or written to the file. For sequential files, Loc returns the current byte position in the file, divided by 128. For binary mode files, Loc returns the position of the last byte read or written.

Lock...Unlock

Type
Statements

Syntax

```
Lock [#] filenumber%[, {record&|[start&] To end&}]
    .
    .
    .
Unlock [#] filenumber%[, {record&|[start&] To end&}]
```

Description

These statements control access by other processes to all or part of an opened file. These statements are used in networked environments where several processes might need access to the same file. For binary-mode files, *record&*, *start&*, and *end&* represent the number of a byte relative to the beginning of the file. The first byte in a file is byte 1. For random-access files, *record&*, *start&*, and *end&* represent the number of a record relative to the beginning of the file. The first record is record 1. If the file has been opened for sequential input or output, Lock and Unlock affect the entire file, regardless of the range specified by *start&* and *end&*. The Lock and Unlock statements are always used in pairs. The arguments to Lock and Unlock must match exactly. If you specify just one record, then only that record will be locked or unlocked. If you specify a range of records and omit a starting record (*start&*), then all records from the first record to the end of the range (*end&*) will be locked or unlocked. Lock without the *record&* argument locks the entire file, while Unlock with no *record&* argument unlocks the whole file.

LOF

Type

Function

Syntax

LOF(*filenumber%*)

Description

The LOF function returns the size of an open file in bytes. The argument *filenumber%* is the number used in the Open statement to open the file. LOF can be used only on disk files.

Log

Type

Function

Syntax

Log(*numeric-expression*)

Description

The Log function returns the natural logarithm of a numeric expression. The argument *numeric-expression* must be greater than zero. The natural logarithm is the logarithm to the base *e*. (The constant *e* is approximately equal to 2.718282.) Log is calculated in single precision if *numeric-expression* is an integer or single-precision value. If you use any other numeric type, Log is calculated in double precision. You can calculate base-*n* logarithms for any number *x* by dividing the natural logarithm of *x* by the natural logarithm of *n*.

LostFocus

Type
Event

Syntax

```
Sub Form_LostFocus ()
Sub ctlname_LostFocus (Index As Integer)
```

Description

The LostFocus event applies to a form, check box, combo box, command button, directory list box, drive list box, file list box, horizontal scroll bar, list box, option button, picture box, text box, and vertical scroll bar. The event occurs when an object loses the focus either by user action, or as a result of changing the focus in code through the SetFocus method.

LSet

Type
Statement

Syntax

```
LSet stringvariable$ = stringexpression$
```
or
```
LSet recordvariable1 = recordvariable2
```

Description

The LSet statement left-justifies the value of a string expression within a fixed-length string variable, or copies one record variable to another.

LTrim$

Type

Function

Syntax

LTrim$(*stringexpression$*)

Description

The LTrim$ function returns a copy of a string with its leftmost spaces removed. The argument *stringexpression$* can be any string expression. The LTrim$ function works with both fixed- and variable-length string variables.

Max, Min

Type

Properties

Syntax

```
[form.]{hscrollbar|vscrollbar}.Max[= limit%]
[form.]{hscrollbar|vscrollbar}.Min[= limit%]
```

Description

The Min and Max properties apply to a horizontal scroll bar and vertical scroll bar. Max determines a scroll bar position's maximum value, or Value property setting, which occurs when the scroll box is in its bottommost position (vertical scroll bar) or rightmost position (horizontal scroll bar). Min determines a scroll bar position's minimum value, or Value property setting, which occurs when the scroll box is in its topmost position (vertical scroll bar) or leftmost position (horizontal scroll bar). For each property, you can specify an integer between –32,768 to 32,767, inclusive. The operating environment automatically sets ranges for scroll bars proportional to the contents of forms, combo boxes, and list boxes. For a scroll bar control, however, you must specify these ranges. Use Max and Min to set a range appropriate to how the scroll bar control is used—for example, as an input device or as an indicator of speed or quantity. Typically, you set Max and Min at design time. You can also set them in code at runtime if the scrolling range must change dynamically—for example, when adding records to a database that can be browsed with a scroll bar. You set the maximum and minimum scrolling increments for a scroll bar control with the LargeChange and SmallChange properties.

MaxButton

Type
Property

Syntax
[*form.*]MaxButton

Description
The MaxButton property applies to a form. The property determines whether a form has a maximize button in the upper-right corner and it is read-only at runtime. A maximize button enables users to enlarge a form window to full-screen size. To display a maximize button, you must also set the form's BorderStyle property to either 1 (Fixed Single) or 2 (Sizable). A maximize button automatically becomes a restore button when a window is maximized. Minimizing or restoring a window automatically changes the restore button back to a maximize button. The settings you specify for MaxButton, MinButton, BorderStyle, and ControlBox are not reflected in the form's appearance until runtime.

Menu

Type
Control

Description
A menu displays a customized menu for your application. Items on a menu can include commands the user can choose to carry out an action, submenu names, and separator bars. You can create up to six levels of menus. Set the Caption property

to display text. To create a separator bar, enter a single hyphen (–) in the Menu Design window's Caption box. To display a check mark to the left of a menu item when it is selected, check the Menu Design window's Checked box, or set the Checked property to True.

Mid$

Type
Function

Syntax

```
Mid$(stringexpression$, start&[, length&])
```

Description

The Mid$ function returns a string that is part of another string. The arguments *start&* and *length&* must be between 1 and approximately 65,535, inclusive. If *length&* is omitted or if there are fewer than *length&* characters in the string (including the *start&* character), the Mid$ function returns all characters from the position *start&* to the end of the string. If *start&* is greater than the number of characters in *stringexpression$*, Mid$ returns a null string. Use the Len function to find the number of characters in *stringexpression$*.

Mid$

Type
Statement

Syntax

```
Mid$(stringvariable$, start&[, length&]) = stringexpression$
```

Description

The Mid$ statement replaces part of a string with another string. The arguments *start&* and *length&* must be between 1 and approximately 65,535, inclusive. The argument *stringvariable$* is a string variable, but *stringexpression$* can be a string variable, a string constant, or a string expression. The optional *length&* argument refers to the number of characters from the argument *stringexpression$* that are used in the replacement. If *length&* is omitted, all of *stringexpression$* is used. The replacement of characters never goes beyond the original length of *stringvariable$*, whether or not *length&* is included.

Min

See *Max...*

MinButton

Type
Property

Syntax
`[form.]MinButton`

Description
The MinButton property applies to a form. The property determines whether or not a form has a minimize button in the upper-right corner at runtime, and it is read-only at runtime. A minimize button enables users to shrink a form window to an icon. To display a minimize button, you must also set the form's BorderStyle property to either 1 (Fixed Single) or 2 (Sizable). The settings you specify for Max-Button, MinButton, BorderStyle, and ControlBox are not reflected in the form's appearance until runtime.

Minute

Type
Function

Syntax
`Minute(serial#)`

Description

The Minute function returns an integer between 0 and 59, inclusive, that represents the minute of the hour corresponding to the serial argument. The argument *serial#* is a serial number that represents a date and/or time between 1 January 1753 and 31 December 2078, inclusive, where 1 January 1900 equals 2. Numbers to the left of the decimal point in *serial#* represent the date; numbers to the right represent the time. Negative numbers represent dates prior to 30 December 1899.

MkDir

Type

Statement

Syntax

`MkDir pathname$`

Description

The MkDir statement creates a new directory. The argument *pathname$* is a string expression that specifies the name of the new directory to create. The *pathname$* argument must have fewer than 128 characters. The MkDir statement works like the DOS command MKDIR. However, the syntax in Visual Basic cannot be shortened to MD, as it can in DOS. You can use MkDir to create a directory with a name that contains an embedded space. Although you may be able access that directory with some applications, you will be unable to remove it with standard operating system commands. You can remove it using RmDir from within Visual Basic or a Visual Basic application.

Month

Type

Function

Syntax

`Month(serial#)`

Description

The Month function returns an integer between 1 and 12, inclusive, that represents the month of the year corresponding to the serial argument. The argument *serial#* is a serial number that represents a date and/or time between 1 January 1753 and 31 December 2078, inclusive, where 1 January 1900 equals 2. Numbers to the left of the decimal point in *serial#* represent the date; numbers to the right represent the time. Negative numbers represent dates prior to 30 December 1899.

MouseDown, MouseUp

Type

Events

Syntax

```
Sub Form_MouseDown (Button As Integer, Shift As Integer, X As
    Single, Y As Single)
Sub ctlname_MouseDown ([Index as Integer] Button As Integer, Shift
    As Integer, X As Single, Y As Single)
Sub Form_MouseUp (Button As Integer, Shift As Integer, X As
    single, Y As Single)
Sub ctlname_MouseUp ([Index as Integer] Button As Integer, Shift
    As Integer, X As Single, Y As Single)
```

Description

The MouseDown and MouseUp events apply to a form, file list box, label, list box, and picture box. They occur when the user presses a mouse button (MouseDown) or releases a mouse button (MouseUp). Use a MouseDown or MouseUp procedure to prescribe actions to occur when a given mouse button is pressed or released. Unlike the Click and DblClick events, MouseDown and MouseUp events allow you to distinguish between the left, right, and middle mouse buttons. You can also code for mouse-keyboard combinations that use the Shift, Ctrl, and Alt keyboard modifiers. You can use a MouseMove procedure to respond to an event caused by moving the mouse. The *Button* argument for MouseDown and MouseUp differs from the *Button* argument used for MouseMove. For MouseDown or MouseUp, the *Button* argument indicates exactly one button per event; for MouseMove, it indicates the current state of all buttons.

MouseMove

Type
Event

Syntax

```
Sub Form_MouseMove (Button As Integer, Shift As Integer, X As
    Single, Y As Single)
Sub ctlname_MouseMove ([Index as Integer] Button As Integer, Shift
    As Integer, X As Single, Y As Single)
```

Description

The MouseMove event applies to a form, file list box, label, list box, and picture box. It occurs continually as the mouse pointer moves across objects. Unless another object has captured the mouse, an object recognizes a MouseMove event whenever the mouse position is within its borders. If you need to test for the *Button* or *Shift* arguments, you can declare constants that define the bits within the argument by loading the CONSTANT.TXT file into the global module.

MousePointer

Type
Property

Syntax

{[*form*.][*control*.]¦Screen.}MousePointer[= *setting%*]

Description

The MousePointer property applies to a form, check box, combo box, command button, directory list box, drive list box, file list box, frame, horizontal scroll bar, label, list box, option button, picture box, screen object, text box, and vertical scroll bar. It sets or returns the type of mouse pointer displayed when the mouse is over a particular part of a form or control at runtime. The MousePointer property controls the shape of the mouse pointer. This property is useful when you want to cue the user to changes in functionality as the mouse passes over various controls on a form or dialog box. The Wait pointer setting (11) is useful for indicating that the user should wait for a process or operation to finish. When set for the screen object,

MousePointer changes across the entire screen; that is, it overrides all MousePointer settings for other objects and other applications. Setting MousePointer to 0 restores the previous behavior.

MouseUp

See *MouseDown…*

Move

Type
Method

Syntax

[*object*.]Move *left!*[, *top!*[, *width!*[, *height!*]]]

Description

The Move method moves a form or control. Only the *left!* argument is required. However, to specify any other arguments, you must specify all arguments that appear in the syntax before the argument you want to specify. For example, you cannot specify *width!* without specifying *left!* and *top!*. Any trailing arguments that are unspecified remain unchanged. For forms and controls within frames, the coordinate system is always in twips. Moving a form on the screen or moving a control within a frame is always relative to the origin (0,0), which is the upper-left corner. When moving controls on a form or in a picture control, the coordinate system of the object is used. The coordinate system is set using the ScaleHeight, ScaleWidth, ScaleLeft, and ScaleRight properties.

MsgBox

Type
Function

Syntax

MsgBox(*msg$*[, *type%*[, *title$*]])

Description

The MsgBox function displays a message in a dialog box, waits for the user to choose a button, and returns a value indicating which button the user chose. If the message box has a Cancel button, pressing the Esc key is the same as pressing the Cancel button.

MsgBox

Type

Statement

Syntax

MsgBox *msg$*[, *type%*[, *title$*]]

Description

The MsgBox statement displays a message in a dialog box. MsgBox displays a maximum of 1024 characters. If your message is longer than that, it is truncated after the 1024th character. Message strings longer than 255 characters with no intervening spaces are truncated after the 255th character. MsgBox breaks lines automatically at the right of the dialog box. If you want to set line breaks yourself, use Chr$(13) (carriage return) and Chr$(10) (line-feed character) before the text that is to begin each new line. The argument *type%* is the sum of values that describe the number and type of buttons to display, the icon style, and the identification of the default button. If you omit *type%*, MsgBox displays a single OK button in the dialog box and makes it the default button. No icon is displayed.

MultiLine

Type

Property

Syntax

[*form.*]*textbox*.MultiLine

Description

The MultiLine property applies to a text box. The property determines whether a text box can accept and display multiple lines of text, and is read-only at runtime. A multiline text box wraps text as the user types text extending beyond the display area. You can also add scroll bars to larger text boxes, using the ScrollBars property. If no horizontal scroll bar is specified, the text in a multiline text box automatically wraps. On a form with no default button, pressing Enter in a multiline text box moves the focus to the next line. If a default button exists, you must press Ctrl-Enter to move to the next line.

Name

Type

Statement

Syntax

```
Name oldfilespec$ As newfilespec$
```

Description

The Name statement changes the name of a disk file or directory, and is similar to the DOS command RENAME. Name also can move a file from one directory to another but cannot move a directory. The arguments *oldfilespec$* and *newfilespec$* are string expressions, each of which contains a file name and an optional path. If the path in *newfilespec$* is different from the path in *oldfilespec$,* and the path exists, the Name statement moves the file to the new directory and renames the file if necessary. If only the path is different, the file is moved and the file name remains unchanged. The file *oldfilespec$* must exist and *newfilespec$* cannot already exist. Both *newfilespec$* and *oldfilespec$* must be on the same drive. If you use Name with different drive designations in the old and new filenames, Visual Basic generates an error message.

NewPage

Type

Method

Syntax

```
Printer.NewPage
```

Description

The NewPage method advances to the next printer page and resets the print position to the upper-left corner of the new page. When invoked, NewPage increments the printer object's Page property by 1.

Normal

See *Archive...*

Now

Type

Function

Syntax

```
Now
```

Description

The Now function returns a serial number that represents the current date and time according to the setting of the computer's system date and time. The returned double-precision serial number represents a date and time. Numbers to the left of the decimal point represent the date; numbers to the right represent the time.

Oct$

Type

Function

Syntax

```
Oct$(numeric-expression)
```

Description

The Oct$ function returns a string that represents the octal value of the decimal argument. The argument *numeric-expression* is rounded to the nearest whole number before the Oct$ function evaluates it. If the argument is an integer, Oct$ returns a string of up to four octal characters; if the argument is a long integer, Oct$ returns a string of up to 11 octal characters. You can directly represent octal numbers by preceding numbers in the proper range with &O. For example, &O10 is the octal notation for decimal 8.

On Error

Type

Statement

Syntax

```
On [Local] Error {GoTo line|Resume Next|GoTo 0}
```

Description

The On Error statement enables an error-handling routine and specifies the location of that routine within a procedure. It can also be used to disable an error-handling routine. If no On Error statement is used, any runtime error that occurs is fatal; that is, Visual Basic generates an error message and stops program execution. An error handler is enabled when it is referred to by an On Error GoTo line statement. Once an error handler is enabled, a runtime error causes program control to jump to the enabled error-handling routine and makes the error handler "active." An error handler is active from the time a runtime error has been trapped until a Resume statement is executed in the error handler.

On...GoSub, On...GoTo

Type

Statements

Syntax

```
On expression GoSub line-label-list
```

or

```
On expression GoTo line-label-list
```

Description

These statements branch to one of several specified lines, depending on the value of an expression. The argument *expression* can be any numeric expression that evaluates to a value between 0 and 255, inclusive. (The expression is rounded to an integer value before the On...GoSub or On...GoTo statement is evaluated.) The argument *line-label-list* consists of a list of line numbers or line labels, separated by commas. The value of the expression determines the line to which the program branches.

Open

Type

Statement

Syntax

```
Open file$ [For mode] [Access access] [lock] As [#] filenumber%
    [Len = reclen%]
```

Description

The Open statement enables input/output (I/O) to a file. You must open a file before any I/O operation can be performed on it. Open allocates a buffer for I/O to the file and determines the mode of access used with the buffer. In input, random-access, and binary modes, you can open a file under a different file number without first closing the file. In Output or Append mode, you must close a file before opening it with a different file number.

Option Base

Type

Statement

Syntax

```
Option Base n%
```

Description

The Option Base statement declares the default lower bound for array subscripts. The value of $n\%$ must be either 0 or 1. The default base is 0. The Option Base statement can be used only once in a form or module and can appear only in the declarations section. If you choose to use an Option Base statement, it must be used before you declare the dimensions for any arrays.

Option Button

Type

Control

Description

An option button, sometimes called a "radio button," displays an option that can be turned on or off. Usually, option buttons are used as part of an option group to display multiple choices from which the user can choose only one. While option buttons and check boxes may appear to function similarly, there is an important difference: When a user selects an option button, the other option buttons in the same group are automatically cancelled. By contrast, any number of check boxes can be selected.

Page

Type

Property

Syntax

```
Printer.Page
```

Description

The Page property applies to a printer object. The property specifies which page receives graphics and print output. It is not available at design time and is read-only at runtime. Output that does not fit on one page is not sent to a new page; it is simply clipped to fit the printable area of the paper. Visual Basic keeps a count of pages printed since your application started or since the last Printer.EndDoc statement was executed. This count starts at one and increases by one if you use the NewPage method, or you use the Print method and the text you wish to print does not fit on the page.

Paint

Type

Event

Syntax

```
Sub Form_Paint ()
Sub ctlname_Paint ([Index as Integer])
```

Description

The Paint event applies to a form and picture box. It occurs when part or all of a form or control is exposed after it has been moved or enlarged, or a window previously covering it has been moved. Your application may need to redraw data in the newly uncovered area. Note that this applies only when a related property, AutoRedraw, is set to False (0), the default setting. When AutoRedraw is set to True (−1), repainting or redrawing is done automatically, so no Paint events are necessary. The Paint event is also invoked when the Refresh method is used. The argument *Index* uniquely identifies a control in a control array. A Paint procedure is useful if you have output from graphics methods such as Circle, Line, PSet, or Print in your code. With a Paint procedure, you can ensure that such output is repainted when necessary.

Parent

Type

Property

Syntax

control.Parent

Description

The Parent property applies to a check box, combo box, command button, directory list box, drive list box, file list box, frame, horizontal scroll bar, label, list box, menu, option button, picture box, text box, timer, and vertical scroll bar. It returns the form on which a control is located. It is not available at design time and is read-only at runtime. Use the Parent property to access properties, methods, or controls of a control's parent form—for example, MyButton.Parent.MousePointer = 4. The Parent property is useful in an application in which you pass controls as arguments. For example, you might pass a control variable to a general procedure in a module, and use the Parent property to access its parent form.

Path

Type

Property

Syntax

[*form*.]{*dirlistbox*.|*filelistbox*.}Path[= *spec$*]

Description

The Path property applies to a directory list box and file list box. It sets or returns the current path; it also returns the complete, absolute path (no relative paths), including the drive name. It is not available at design time. By default, this property is set to the current path when the control is created at runtime. Use this property when building an application's file-browsing and manipulation capabilities. Setting the Path property has effects on the control similar to the DOS CHDIR command—relative paths are allowed with or without a drive. Setting only a drive (with colon) selects the current directory on that drive.

PathChange

Type

Event

Syntax

Sub *ctlname*_PathChange ([Index as Integer])

Description

The PathChange event applies to a file list box. It occurs when the selected path changes by setting the FileName or Path properties from code. The argument *Index* uniquely identifies a control in a control array. You can use a PathChange procedure to respond to path changes in a file list box. When you assign a string containing a new path to the FileName property, the file list box control invokes the PathChange event.

Pattern

Type

Property

Syntax

[*form.*]*filelistbox*.Pattern[= *display$*]

Description

The Pattern property applies to a file list box. It determines which file names are displayed in a file list box at runtime; it may include wildcards. By default, the Pattern property is set to all files (*.*). This property plays a key role in designing an application's file-browsing and manipulation capabilities. Use Pattern in combination with other file-control properties to provide the user with various ways to explore files or groups of similar files in an application. For example, in an application dedicated to launching other programs, you might designate that only .EXE files be displayed in the file list box (*.EXE). Other key file-control properties include Drive, FileName, and Path. Changing the value of Pattern generates a PatternChange event.

PatternChange

Type
Event

Syntax
```
Sub ctlname_PatternChange (Index as Integer)
```

Description
The PatternChange event applies to a file list box. It occurs when the file-listing pattern (such as *.*) has changed by setting the FileName or Pattern properties from code. The argument *Index* uniquely identifies a control in a control array. You can use a PatternChange procedure to respond to pattern changes in a file list box. When you assign a string containing a new pattern to the FileName property, the file list box invokes the PathChange event.

Picture Box

Type
Control

Description
A picture box can display a graphic from a bitmap, icon, or metafile. It displays only as much of the graphic as fits into the rectangle you've drawn with the picture box tool. You can also use a picture box to display output from graphics statements and text written with the Print method, and to group option buttons. A picture box can also be set up as a client link in a DDE conversation. To do this, set the LinkTopic property to establish a link, the LinkItem property to specify an item for the conversation, and the LinkMode property to activate the link. When these have been set, Visual Basic attempts to initiate the conversation and displays a message if it's unable to do so.

Picture

Type
Property

Syntax

`[form.][picturebox.]Picture[= picture]`

Description

The Picture property applies to a form and picture box. The property specifies a graphic to be displayed in a form or picture box, and is write-only at design time. At design time, you can transfer a graphic by the Clipboard with the Copy, Cut, and Paste commands on the Edit menu. At runtime, you can use Clipboard methods such as GetData, SetData, and GetFormat with the non-text Clipboard formats CF_BITMAP, CF_METAFILE, and CF_DIB, as defined in CONSTANT.TXT, a Visual Basic file that specifies system defaults. When setting the Picture property at design time, the graphic is saved and loaded with the form. If you create an executable file, the file will contain the image. When you load a graphic at runtime, the graphic is not saved with the application. Use the SavePicture statement to save a graphic from a form or picture box into a file.

Point

Type
Method

Syntax

`[object.]Point (x!, y!)`

Description
The Point method returns the RGB color of the specified point on a form or picture box.

Print

Type
Statement

Syntax

`Print # filenumber%, expressionlist [{:|,}]`

Description

The Print # statement writes data to a sequential file. Print # writes an image of the data to the file, just as the data would be displayed if they were displayed on the terminal screen using the DOS command TYPE. For this reason, be careful to delimit the data so they are printed correctly. If you use commas as delimiters, the blanks between print fields will also be written to the file.

Printer Object

Type
Control

Description

The printer object is accessed with the keyword Printer. The keyword is used to control text and graphics printed on a page and to send output directly to the default system printer. For example, you can use this object to manipulate the appearance of your printed output by changing fonts. You may need to check and revise the layout of your forms if you want to print them. When you use the Print method to print, graphical images are clipped at the bottom of the page and text is carried over to the next page.

PrintForm

Type
Method

Syntax

[*form.*]PrintForm

Description

The PrintForm method sends a bit-for-bit image of a form to the printer. The argument *form* is the form to print. If omitted, the current form is printed. PrintForm prints all visible controls and bitmaps on the form. PrintForm also prints graphics added to the form or picture controls on the form at runtime if AutoRedraw is True (–1) when the graphics are drawn. The printer used by PrintForm is determined by the operating environment control panel.

PSet

Type
Method

Syntax
`[object.]PSet [Step](x!, y!)[, color&]`

Description
The PSet nethod sets a point on a form, picture box, or printer to a specified color. The size of the point drawn depends on the DrawWidth property. When Draw-Width is 1, PSet sets a single pixel to the specified color. When DrawWidth is greater than 1, the point is centered on the specified coordinates. The way the point is drawn depends on the setting of the DrawMode property. When PSet is executed, CurrentX and CurrentY are set to the point specified by the arguments. Clear a single pixel with the PSet method by specifying the coordinates of the pixel and using BackColor as the *color&* argument.

Put

Type
Statement

Syntax
`Put [#] filenumber%, [recordnumber&,] recordvariable`

Description
The Put statement writes from a record variable to a disk file. For random-access files, you can use any variable as long as the length of the variable is less than or equal to the length of the record—that is, the length specified in the Len clause of the Open statement. Usually, *recordvariable* is a user-defined type that matches the fields in a data record in the file. When a variable-length string is outputted to a random-access file using Put, a two-byte descriptor is always added to the length of *recordvariable.* For this reason, a variable-length string must be at least two characters shorter than the record length specified in the Len clause of the Open statement. For files opened in binary mode, you can use any variable. The Put statement writes

as many bytes as there are in the variable. When you use a variable-length string variable, the statement writes as many bytes as there are in the characters in the string's value.

QBColor

Type
Function

Syntax
QBColor(*qbcolor%*)

Description
The QBColor function returns the RGB color code corresponding to a color number. The *qbcolor%* argument is an integer in the range 0–15, inclusive, that corresponds to the color values used by other versions of BASIC (such as Microsoft QuickBasic and BASIC Compiler). Starting with the least-significant byte, the returned value specifies the red, green, and blue values used to set the appropriate color in the RGB system used by Visual Basic.

Randomize

Type
Statement

Syntax
Randomize [*numeric-expression%*]

Description
The Randomize statement initializes (reseeds) the random-number generator. The argument *numeric-expression%* is an integer expression. If you omit *numeric-expression%*, Visual Basic uses the value returned by the Timer function as the initial seed.

When you use the argument, Visual Basic uses this value to initialize the random-number generator instead. If the random-number generator is not reseeded, the Rnd function returns the same sequence of random numbers each time the program is run. To change the sequence of random numbers every time the program is run, place a Randomize statement with no argument at the beginning of the program.

ReadOnly

See *Archive...*

ReDim

Type
Statement

Syntax
```
ReDim [Shared] variablename (subscripts) [As type][,variablename
    (subscripts) [As type]]...
```

Description
The ReDim statement is used at the procedure level to declare dynamic-array variables and allocate or reallocate storage space. The ReDim statement initializes all elements of numeric arrays to zero and all elements of string arrays to null strings. The fields of record variables are initialized to zero, including fixed-length string elements. The ReDim statement is normally used to size or resize a dynamic array that has already been formally declared using a Global or Dim statement with empty parentheses (no dimension subscripts.)

Refresh

Type
Method

Syntax
```
[object.]Refresh
```

Description

The Refresh method forces an immediate refresh of a form or control. The *object* is the form or control to refresh. Generally, refreshing a form or control is handled automatically when the idle loop is reached. However, there may be situations where you want the form or control refreshed before such an event takes place. For example, if you use a file list box, a directory list box, or a drive list box, to show the current status of the file system, you can use Refresh to update the status anytime a change is made.

Rem

Type
Statement

Syntax

```
Rem remark
```

or

```
' remark
```

Description

The Rem statement allows explanatory remarks in a program. The argument *remark* is the text of any comments you want to include with your program. Spaces and punctuation are permitted. Rem statements are ignored when you create an executable file; they appear exactly as entered when the program is listed. Comments are useful to document how your code works or provide any other information you may want to include with your code. You can branch from a GoTo or GoSub statement to a Rem statement. Execution continues with the first executable statement after the Rem statement. As shown in the syntax, a single quotation mark (apostrophe) can be used instead of the Rem keyword. If the Rem keyword follows other statements on a line, it must be separated from the statements by a colon. The colon is not required when you use a single quotation mark after other statements.

RemoveItem

Type
Method

Syntax
`control.RemoveItem index%`

Description
The RemoveItem method removes an item from a list box or combo box at runtime.

Resize

Type
Event

Syntax
`Sub Form_Resize ()`

Description
The Resize event applies to a form. It occurs when the size of the form changes. This event also occurs when the form is first displayed. Use a Resize procedure when you need to move or resize controls when the parent form itself is resized. A Resize procedure can also be used to recalculate variables or properties (such as Scale-Height and ScaleWidth) that may depend on the size of the form. To invoke the Paint event every time a form is resized, use the Refresh method in a Resize event if you want graphics to maintain sizes proportional to the form when the form is resized. Whenever the AutoRedraw property is set to False (0) and the form is re-sized, Visual Basic also calls the related events in this order: Resize, Paint. When you are attaching procedures for these related events, be sure that their actions don't conflict.

Resume

Type
Statement

Syntax
```
Resume {[0]|Next|line}
```

Description
The Resume statement resumes program execution after an error-handling routine is finished. If you use a Resume statement outside an error-handling routine, Visual Basic generates an error message. When an error-handling routine is active and the end of the program is encountered before executing a Resume statement, Visual Basic generates an error message. This also is true if an End statement (or an End Sub or End Function statement for an error handler) is executed before a Resume statement. If the error handler that contains the Resume statement is in a procedure other than the one in which the error occurred, then the last statement executed in that procedure is the last call out of that procedure.

Return

Type
Statement

Syntax
```
Return
```

Description
The Return statement causes an unconditional return from a subroutine. Return is used along with GoSub. After a GoSub causes program execution to branch to a subroutine, Return continues execution beginning with the statement following the GoSub statement. GoSub and Return can be used anywhere in a procedure but the GoSub and corresponding Return must be within the same procedure. A Return statement cannot be used to return control to a calling procedure from another procedure defined by a Sub statement; use Exit Sub for this purpose.

RGB

Type
Function

Syntax
RGB(*red%, green%, blue%*)

Description
The RGB function returns a long integer representing an RGB color value. Visual Basic methods and properties that accept a color specification expect that specification to be a long integer representing an RGB color value. An RGB color value specifies the relative intensity of red, green, and blue, which, when taken together, cause a specific color to be displayed. If the value for any argument to RGB exceeds 255, it is assumed to be 255.

Right$

Type
Function

Syntax
Right$(*stringexpression$, n&*)

Description
The Right$ function returns a string consisting of the rightmost *n&* characters of a string. The argument *stringexpression$* can be any string variable, string constant, or string expression. The argument *n&* is a long integer expression indicating how many characters to return. It must be between 0 and approximately 65,535, inclusive. If *n&* is 0, the null string (zero-length) is returned. If *n&* is greater than or equal to the number of characters in *stringexpression$*, the entire string is returned. To find the number of characters in *stringexpression$*, use Len(stringexpression$).

RmDir

Type
Statement

Syntax
RmDir *pathname$*

Description
The RmDir statement removes an existing directory. The argument *pathname$* is a string expression that specifies the name of the directory to be removed; it must have fewer than 128 characters. The RmDir statement works like the DOS command RMDIR. However, the syntax in Visual Basic cannot be shortened to RD, as it can in DOS.

Rnd

Type
Function

Syntax
Rnd[(*number#*)]

Description
The Rnd function returns a single-precision random number between 0 and 1. The value of *number#* determines how Rnd generates the next random number.

RSet

Type
Statement

Syntax
RSet *stringvariable$* = *stringexpression$*

Description

The RSet statement right-justifies the value of a string expression within a fixed-length string variable. If *stringexpression$* is shorter than *stringvariable$*, RSet right-justifies *stringexpression$* within *stringvariable$*. RSet replaces any unchanged characters in stringvariable$ with spaces, back to its beginning. If *stringexpression$* is longer than *stringvariable$*, only the leftmost characters, up to the length of *stringvariable$*, are placed in *stringvariable$*. Characters beyond the length of *stringvariable$* are truncated from the right. RSet cannot be used to assign values from one user-defined type to another.

RTrim$

Type

Function

Syntax

```
RTrim$(stringexpression$)
```

Description

The RTrim$ function returns a copy of a string with rightmost spaces removed. The *stringexpression$* can be any string expression. The RTrim$ function works with both fixed- and variable-length string variables.

SavePicture

Type

Statement

Syntax

```
SavePicture picture, stringexpression$
```

Description

The SavePicture statement saves a picture from a form or picture box into a file. If a picture was loaded from a file to the Picture property, either at design time or at runtime, it will be saved using the same format as the original file. Pictures from the Image property are always saved as bitmap (.BMP) files.

Scale

Type
Method

Syntax

`[object.]Scale [(x1!, y1!) - (x2!, y2!)]`

Description
The Scale method defines the coordinate system for a form, picture box, and printer object. It allows you to reset the coordinate system to any scale you choose. Scale with no arguments resets the coordinate system to twips. Scale affects the coordinate system for the both the runtime graphics statements and the placement of controls.

ScaleHeight, ScaleWidth

Type
Properties

Syntax

`{[form.][picturebox.]¦Printer.}ScaleHeight[ = scale!]`
`{[form.][picturebox.]¦Printer.}ScaleWidth[ = scale!]`

Description
The ScaleHeight and ScaleWidth properties apply to a form, picture box, and printer object. They set or return the range of the vertical (ScaleHeight) and horizontal (ScaleWidth) axes for an object's internal coordinate system. The coordinate system is used for positioning controls on forms and picture boxes; it is also used by graphics methods for these objects. On a form, the coordinate system includes the form's internal area, not including borders and title bar. For the printer object, it represents the printable area on the paper. The ScaleHeight and ScaleWidth properties define the object's coordinate system by defining units of measurement in terms of

the current width and height of the internal area. In this way, you can use them to set up a custom coordinate system. For example, the statement `ScaleHeight = 100` defines the internal height of the form as 100 units, or one vertical unit as $1/100$ of the height. If the form is later resized, the unit of measurement remains the same and the value of ScaleHeight changes.

ScaleLeft, ScaleTop

Type
Properties

Syntax

```
{[form.][picturebox.]¦Printer.}ScaleLeft[= scale!]
{[form.][picturebox.]¦Printer.}ScaleTop[= scale!]
```

Description

The ScaleLeft and ScaleTop properties apply to a form, picture box, and printer object. They set or return the horizontal (ScaleLeft) and vertical (ScaleTop) coordinates that describe the left and top corners of an object's internal area. The coordinate system is used for placing controls on forms and picture boxes. It is also used for graphics output for all objects: for a form or control, this includes its internal area, not including borders and title bar; for the printer object, it represents the printable area on the paper. Use the scale-related properties for calculations and operations based on the internal dimensions of an object. Typically, such operations entail drawing in an object with the graphics methods or moving other objects within an object. By default, these properties are set to 0.

ScaleMode

Type
Property

Syntax

```
{[form.][picturebox.]¦Printer.}ScaleMode[= mode%]
```

Description

The ScaleMode property applies to a form, picture box, and printer object. It sets or returns the units of measurement in an object's coordinate system. The coordinate system is used for positioning controls on forms and picture boxes. It is also used for graphics output for all applicable objects: for a form, this includes its internal area, without borders and title bar; for the printer object, it represents the printable area on the paper. Use the coordinate system set by ScaleMode for calculations and operations based on the internal dimensions of an object. Typically, such operations entail drawing in an object with the graphics methods or moving other objects within an object. Directly setting the dimensional scale properties—ScaleHeight and ScaleWidth, or ScaleLeft and ScaleTop—is a way to define a custom coordinate system.

Screen Object

Type
Control

Description

The screen object is accessed with the keyword Screen and is used to activate a specified form or control at runtime. For example, you could set the screen object properties in a drawing application to automatically activate a certain tool each time the application is started.

ScrollBars

Type
Property

Syntax

`[form.]textlistbox.ScrollBars`

Description

The ScrollBars property applies to a text box. It determines whether a text box has horizontal or vertical scroll bars, and is read-only at runtime. Use this property to add scroll bars to a text box with the Multiline property set to True (−1). At runtime the operating environment automatically puts into effect a standard keyboard interface to allow navigation in text box controls with the direction keys, Home and End keys, and so on. Adding scroll bars to a large multiline text box further facilitates browsing and navigating through the text.

Second

Type

Function

Syntax

Second(*serial#*)

Description

The Second function returns an integer between 0 and 59, inclusive, that represents the second of the minute corresponding to the serial argument. The argument *serial#* is a serial number that represents a date and/or time between 1 January 1753 and 31 December 2078, inclusive, where 1 January 1900 equals 2. Numbers to the left of the decimal point in *serial#* represent the date; numbers to the right represent the time. Negative numbers represent dates prior to 30 December 1899.

Seek

Type

Function

Syntax

Seek(*filenumber%*)

Description

The Seek function returns the current file position. The argument *filenumber%* is the number used in the Open statement to open the file. Seek returns a value between 1 and 2,147,483,647, inclusive (equivalent to $2^{31} - 1$). For files open in random-access mode, Seek returns the number of the next record read or written. For files opened in binary, output, append, or input mode, Seek returns the byte position in the file where the next operation is to take place. The first byte in a file is at position 1; the second byte is at position 2, and so on.

Seek

Type
Statement

Syntax

```
Seek [#] filenumber%, position&
```

Description

The Seek statement sets the position in a file for the next read or write. For files opened in random-access mode, *position&* is the number of a record in the file. For files opened in binary, input, output, or append mode, *position&* is the byte position relative to the beginning of the file. The first byte in a file is at position 1; the second byte is at position 2, and so on. After a Seek operation, the next file input/output operation starts at the specified byte. Performing a file write after doing a Seek operation beyond the end of a file extends the file. If you attempt a Seek operation to a negative or zero position, Visual Basic generates an error message.

Select Case

Type
Statement

Syntax

```
Select Case testexpression
[Case expressionlist1
    [statementblock-1] ]
```

```
[Case expressionlist2
    [statementblock-2] ]
[Case Else
    [statementblock-n] ]
End Select
```

Description

The Select Case statement executes one of several statement blocks depending on the value of an expression. If *testexpression* matches the expression list associated with a Case clause, the statement block following that Case clause is executed up to the next Case clause, or for the last one, up to End Select. Control then passes to the statement following End Select. If you use the To keyword to indicate a range of values, the smaller value must appear first. If Case Else is used, its associated statements are executed only if *testexpression* does not match any of the other Case selections. Although not required, it is a good idea to have a Case Else statement in your Select Case block to handle unforeseen *testexpression* values. If an expression appears in more than one Case clause, only the statements associated with the first appearance of the expression are executed. Select Case statements can be nested. Each Select Case statement must have a matching End Select statement.

SelLength, SelStart, SelText

Type

Properties

Syntax

```
[form.]{combobox¦textbox}.SelLength[= length&]
[form.]{combobox¦textbox}.SelStart[= index&]
[form.]{combobox¦textbox}.SelText[= stringexpression$]
```

Description

The SelLength, SelStart, and SelText properties apply to a combo box and text box. SelLength sets or returns the number of characters selected. SelStart sets or returns the starting point of text selected; it indicates the position of the insertion point if no text is selected. SelText sets or returns the string containing the currently selected text; it consists of an empty string (" ") if no characters are selected. These properties, not available at design time, are useful for working with selected text.

SendKeys

Type
Statement

Syntax
SendKeys *keytext$*[, *wait%*]

Description
The SendKeys statement sends one or more keystrokes to the active window, as if they were typed at the keyboard. SendKeys cannot send keystrokes to a non-Windows application.

SetData

Type
Method

Syntax
ClipBoard.SetData *data%*[, *format%*]

Description
The SetData method puts a picture in the operating environment Clipboard using the specified format. The argument *data%* is the picture (Image or Picture property) to place on the Clipboard.

SetFocus

Type
Method

Syntax
object.SetFocus

Description

The SetFocus method sets the focus to the specified object. The *object* must be a form or control to which the focus is changed. After SetFocus is executed, any user input is directed to the specified form or control.

SetText

Type
Method

Syntax
```
Clipboard.SetText data$[, format%]
```

Description

The SetText method puts a text string in the operating environment Clipboard using the specified Clipboard format. The argument *data$* is the data string to be placed on the Clipboard.

Sgn

Type
Function

Syntax
```
Sgn(numeric-expression)
```

Description

The Sgn function returns a value indicating the sign of a numeric expression.

Shell

Type
Function

Syntax

Shell(*commandstring$*[, *windowstyle%*])

Description

The Shell function runs an executable program. If the Shell function is successful in executing the named program, it returns the task identification (ID) of the started program. The task ID is a unique number that identifies the running program. If Shell is unsuccessful in starting the named program, Visual Basic generates an error message.

Show

Type

Method

Syntax

[*form.*]Show [*style%*]

Description

The Show method displays a form. If the specified form is not loaded when the Show method is invoked, Visual Basic automatically loads it. When a modeless form is displayed, Visual Basic code that occurs after the Show method is executed as it is encountered. When a modal form is displayed, no Visual Basic code after the Show method is executed until the form is hidden or unloaded. When displaying a modal form, it is also important to note that no user input (keyboard or mouse click) can occur in any other form until the modal form is hidden or unloaded. The program must hide or unload a modal form (usually in response to some user action) before further user input can occur. Although other forms in your application are disabled when a modal form is displayed, other applications are not. The startup form of an application is automatically shown after its load event is executed.

Sin

Type

Function

Syntax

`Sin(numeric-expression)`

Description

The Sin function returns the sine of an angle given in radians. The argument *numeric-expression* can be of any numeric data type. The sine of an angle in a right triangle is the ratio between the length of the side opposite the angle and the length of the hypotenuse. Sin is calculated in single precision if *numeric-expression* is an integer or single-precision value. If you use any other numeric data type, Sin is calculated in double precision. To convert degrees to radians, multiply degrees by $\pi/180$ (or 0.0174532925199433). To convert radians to degrees, multiply radians by $180/\pi$ (or 57.2957795130824). In both cases, $\pi = 3.141593$.

SmallChange

See *LargeChange...*

Sorted

Type

Property

Syntax

`[form.]{combobox| listbox}.Sorted`

Description

The Sorted property applies to a a combo box and list box. It determines whether the elements of a combo box or list box are automatically sorted alphabetically. It is read-only at runtime. Once you set this property, Visual Basic normally handles all necessary string processing to maintain alphabetical order, including changing the index numbers for items as required by the addition or removal of items. Using the AddItem method to add an element to a specific location, however, may violate the sort order, and subsequent additions may not be properly sorted.

Space$

Type

Function

Syntax

Space$(*numeric-expression*)

Description

The Space$ function returns a string consisting of a specified number of spaces. The argument *numeric-expression* specifies the number of spaces you want in the string. It can be of any numeric data type (but is rounded to a long integer) and must be between 0 and approximately 65,535, inclusive.

Spc

Type

Function

Syntax

Spc(*number%*)

Description

The Spc function skips a specified number of spaces in a Print # statement or Print method, starting at the current print position. The Spc function can only be used with the Print # statement or the Print method. The argument *number%* is an integer between 0 and 32,767, inclusive, and it determines the number of blank characters to print. A semicolon (;) is assumed to follow the Spc function. Note that the Spc function does more than move the text cursor to a new print position. The *number%* blank or space characters are printed starting at the current print position. For files, the behavior of the Spc function depends on the relationship between three values: *number%*, the output line print position when the Spc function is executed, and the current output-line width.

Sqr

Type

Function

Syntax

Sqr(*numeric-expression*)

Description

The Sqr function returns the square root of a nonnegative numeric expression. The argument *numeric-expression* may be of any numeric data type but must be greater than or equal to 0.

Static

Type

Statement

Syntax

Static *variablename* [([*subscripts*])] [As *type*] [, *variablename* [([*subscripts*])] [As *type*]]...

Description

The Static statement is used at the procedure level to declare a static variable and allocate storage space.

Stop

Type

Statement

Syntax

Stop

Description

The Stop statement suspends execution of the program and opens the code window. You can place Stop statements anywhere in the program to suspend program execution. The Stop statement suspends program execution, but does not close files or clear variables. If Stop is encountered when an executable file is running, the program terminates. To continue a program suspended with the Stop statement, choose the Continue command from the Run menu. Under certain circumstances, you also may be able to restart program execution immediately after the Stop statement by entering a statement in the Immediate window.

Str$

Type

Function

Syntax

Str$(*numeric-expression*)

Description

The Str$ function returns a string representation of the value of a numeric expression. Use the Str$ function to convert simple numeric values to strings. Use the Format$ function to convert numeric values you want formatted as dates, times, currency, or other user-defined format. When numbers are converted to strings, Visual Basic always reserves a leading space for the sign of the numeric expression. If *numeric-expression* is positive, the string returned by the Str$ function contains a leading blank but the plus sign is implied. The Val function complements Str$.

String$

Type

Function

Syntax

String$(*number&, charcode%*)

or

String$(*number&, stringexpression$*)

Description

The String$ function returns a string whose characters all have a given ANSI code or whose characters are all the first character of a string expression. Use the String$ function to create a string of one character repeated over and over.

Style

Type

Property

Syntax

[*form.*]*combo*.Style

Description

The Style property applies to a combo box. The property determines the type of combo box and the behavior of the list box portion of the control. It's read-only at runtime.

Sub

Type

Statement

Syntax

```
[Static] Sub globalname [(argumentlist)]
     [statementblock]
     [Exit Sub]
     [statementblock]
End Sub
```

Description

The Sub statement declares the name, arguments, and code that form the body of a Sub procedure. All executable code in a Visual Basic application must be in a Sub or Function procedure. You cannot define a Sub procedure inside another Sub or Function procedure.

System

See *Archive...*

Tab

Type

Function

Syntax

Tab(*column%*)

Description

The Tab function moves the text cursor to a specified print position when used with the Print # statement or Print method.

The argument *column%* is an integer expression that is the column number of the new print position. The leftmost print position on an output line is always 1. For forms, there is no limit to the rightmost print position. When printing to files (using the Print # statement), the rightmost print position is the current width of the output file, which can be set with the Width statement. The behavior of the Tab function depends on the relationship between three values: *column%*, the output line print position when the Tab function is executed, and the current output line width. However, output line width is only used with files, not forms. When using the Tab function with the Print method, the surface of the form or control is divided into uniform, fixed-width columns. The width of each column is an average of the width of all characters in the point size for the chosen font. The Tab function uses the average column width to move the cursor to the next print position as specified by the *column%* argument.

TabIndex

Type

Property

Syntax

[*form.*]*control*.TabIndex[= *index%*]

Description

The TabIndex property applies to a check box, combo box, command button, directory list box, drive list box, file list box, frame, horizontal scroll bar, label, list box, option button, picture box, text box, and vertical scroll bar. The property sets or returns a control's position in the tab order within its parent form.

TabStop

Type

Property

Syntax

[*form.*]*control*.TabStop[= *boolean%*]

Description

The TabStop property applies to a check box, combo box, command button, directory list box, drive list box, file list box, horizontal scroll bar, list box, option button, picture box, text box, and vertical scroll bar. The property determines if tabbing stops at the control. It allows you to add or remove a control from the tab order on a form. For example, instead of having the Tab key move through each button in an option button group, you can designate that the whole group be treated as one tab location. To do this, set TabStop to True (–1) for the first option button in the group and set TabStop to False (0) for the other option buttons in the group.

Tag

Type

Property

Syntax

{[*form.*][*control.*]}Tag[= *stringexpression$*]

Description

The Tag property applies to a form, check box, combo box, command button, directory list box, drive list box, file list box, frame, horizontal scroll bar, label, list box, menu, option button, picture box, text box, timer, and vertical scroll bar. The property stores unique data with an object and is used only for identification and data-storage purposes. By default, the Tag property is set to an empty string (" "). Use this property to assign an identification string to an object without affecting any of its other property settings or causing side effects. The Tag property is useful when you need to identify a specific control that is passed as a variable to a procedure.

Tan

Type

Function

Syntax

Tan(*numeric-expression*)

Description

The Tan function returns the tangent of an angle given in radians. The argument *numeric-expression* can be of any numeric data type. The tangent of an angle (the value returned by the Tan function) in a right triangle is the ratio between the length of the side opposite the angle and the length of the side adjacent to it. Tan is calculated in single precision if *numeric-expression* is an integer or single-precision value. If you use any other numeric data type, Tan is calculated in double precision. To convert degrees to radians, multiply degrees by $\pi/180$ (or 0.0174532925199433). To convert radians to degrees, multiply radians by $180/\pi$ (or 57.2957795130824). In both cases, $\pi = 3.141593$.

Text Box

Type

Control

Description

A text box control, sometimes called an "edit field" or "edit control," can display either information that you specify or that the user enters. To display multiple lines of text in a text box at runtime, set the MultiLine property to True. To display numeric input in a text box, use the Val function. A text box can also be set up as a client link in a DDE conversation. To do this, set the LinkTopic property to establish a link, the LinkItem property to specify an item for the conversation, and the Link-Mode property to activate the link. When these have been set, Visual Basic attempts to initiate the conversation and displays a message if it's unable to do so.

TextHeight

Type

Method

Syntax

[*object.*]TextHeight (*stringexpression$*)

Description

The TextHeight method returns the height of a text string as it would be printed in the current font of a form, picture box, or printer object. The height is expressed in terms of the Scale coordinate system in effect for object. Use TextHeight to determine the amount of vertical space required to display the text. The height returned includes the normal leading above and below the string, so you can use the height to calculate and position multiple lines of text within a form, picture box, or printer object. If *stringexpression$* contains embedded carriage returns, TextHeight returns the cumulative height of the lines, including the leading above and below each line.

Text

Type
Property

Syntax
[*form.*]{*combobox¦listbox¦textbox*}.Text[= *stringexpression$*]

Description
The Text property applies to a combo box, list box, and text box. Setting this property allows you to input a text string into any of the aforementioned controls.

TextWidth

Type
Method

Syntax
[*object.*]TextWidth (*stringexpression$*)

Description
The TextWidth method returns the width of a text string as it would be printed in the current font of a form, picture box, or printer object. The width is expressed in terms of the coordinate system of object. Use TextWidth to determine the amount of horizontal space required to display the text. If *stringexpression$* contains embedded carriage returns, TextWidth returns the width of the longest line.

Time$

Type
Function

Syntax
Time$

Description

The Time$ function returns the current system time as an eight-character string. The form of the string is *hh:mm:ss,* where *hh* is the hour (00–23), *mm* is minutes (00–59), and *ss* is seconds (00–59). A 24-hour clock is used; therefore, 8:00 P.M. is shown as 20:00:00. The output of the Time$ function is equivalent to Format$ (Now,"hh:mm:ss"). To set the system time, use the Time$ statement below.

Time$

Type

Statement

Syntax

Time$ = *stringexpression$*

Description

The Time$ statement sets the system time. The argument *stringexpression$* must have one of the following forms, where *hh* is the hour (00–23), *mm* is the minute (00–59), and *ss* is the second (00–59). The Time$ statement complements the Time$ function above, which returns the current time. The Time$ statement changes the system time, which stays changed until you change it again or turn off your computer. Many computers have battery-powered CMOS RAM that retains date and time information when the computer is turned off. To change the date in the CMOS RAM permanently, you may have to use your Setup disk or some equivalent action. Refer to the documentation for your particular system.

Timer

Type

Control

Description

A timer is a control that you can program to run code at a regular time interval you specify. It works independently of the user, so it's useful for background processing. This control is invisible to the user.

Timer

Type
Event

Syntax
`Sub ctlname_Timer ([Index as Integer])`

Description
The Timer event applies to a timer control. It occurs when a preset interval for a timer control has elapsed. The interval's frequency is stored in the control's Interval property, which specifies the length of time in milliseconds. The argument *Index* uniquely identifies a control in a control array. Use this procedure to tell Visual Basic what to do at every timer interval.

Timer

Type
Function

Syntax
`Timer`

Description
The Timer function returns the number of seconds elapsed since midnight. The Timer function can be used with the Randomize statement to generate a random number. It also can be used to time programs or parts of programs.

TimeSerial

Type
Function

Syntax
`TimeSerial(hour%,minute%,second%)`

Description

The TimeSerial function returns a serial number that represents the time of the integer arguments. When expressing specific times, such as 11:59:59, the range of numbers for each TimeSerial argument should conform to the accepted range of values for the unit. These values are 0–23 for hours and 0–59 for minutes and seconds. You also can specify relative times for each argument using a numeric expression representing the number of hours, minutes, or seconds before or after a certain time. The serial number returned is a double-precision fractional number between 0 and 0.99999 that represents times between 0:00:00 and 23:59:59, or 12:00:00 A.M. and 11:59:59 P.M., inclusive. If the time specified by the three arguments, either directly or by expression, falls outside the acceptable range of times, Visual Basic generates an error.

TimeValue

Type

Function

Syntax

`TimeValue(time$)`

Description

The TimeValue function returns a serial number that represents the time of the string argument. The argument *time$* is a time between 0:00:00 (12:00:00 A.M.) and 23:59:59 (11:59:59 P.M.), inclusive. Time can be entered as "2:24PM" or "14:24." Any date information used in *time$* is ignored. The serial number returned is a double-precision fractional number between 0 and 0.99999 that represents times between 0:00:00 and 23:59:59, or 12:00:00 A.M. and 11:59:59 P.M., inclusive.

Top

See *Left*…

Type...End Type

Type

Statement

Syntax

```
Type usertype
     elementname As typename
     [elementname As typename]
     .
     .
     .
End Type
```

Description

The Type...End Type statement is used in the global module to define a data type containing one or more elements. It is valid only in the global module. A user-defined type must be declared in a type declaration before it can be used in the program. Although a user-defined type can only be declared in the global module, you can declare a variable to be of a user-defined type in any of your Sub or Function procedures or in the declarations section of any module. Use Dim, Global, or Static to declare a variable to be of a user-defined type. You may use variable-length strings in user-defined types. However, you must use fixed-length strings in user-defined types used in random-access files. Line numbers and line labels are not allowed in Type...End Type blocks. In some contexts, the terms *user-defined type* and *data record* are used interchangeably. While data records can consist of a single variable, more often they consist of a number of related elements of different data types. This capability is made possible by user-defined types.

UBound

Type

Function

Syntax

```
UBound(array[, dimension%])
```

Description

The UBound function returns the largest available subscript for the indicated dimension of an array. The UBound function is used with the LBound function to determine the size of an array. Use the LBound function to find the lower limit of an array dimension.

UCase$

Type

Function

Syntax

```
UCase$(stringexpression$)
```

Description

The UCase$ function returns a string in which all letters have been converted to uppercase. The UCase$ function takes a string variable, string constant, or string expression as its single argument. Only lowercase letters are converted to uppercase; all uppercase letters and nonletter characters remain unchanged. UCase$ works with both variable- and fixed-length strings. UCase$ and LCase$ are helpful when comparing strings without regard to capitalization.

Unload

Type

Event

Syntax

```
Sub Form_Unload (Cancel As Integer)
```

Description

The Unload event applies to a form. It occurs when a form is about to be removed from the screen. When that form is reloaded, the contents of all its controls are reinitialized. This event is triggered by user action (closing the form using the control box) or by an Unload statement. Use an Unload event procedure to verify that the unloading of the form should proceed or to specify actions that should take place when the form is unloaded. You can also include any form-level validation code you might need for closing the form or saving data in it.

Unload

Type
Statement

Syntax
Unload *object*

Description
The Unload statement unloads a form or control from memory. The argument *object* is the form or control array element to unload. Unloading a form or control may be necessary or expedient in some cases where the memory used is needed for something else or when you need to reset properties to their original values. When a form is unloaded, all controls placed on the form at runtime are no longer accessible. Controls placed on the form at design time remain intact, although any runtime changes to those controls and their properties are lost when the form is reloaded. All changes to form properties are also lost. Note that when a form is unloaded, only the displayed component is unloaded. The code associated with the form module remains in memory. Only control array elements added to a form at runtime can be unloaded with the Unload statement. The properties of unloaded controls are reinitialized when the controls are reloaded.

Val

Type
Function

Syntax
Val(*stringexpression$*)

Description

The Val function returns the numeric value of a string of characters. Use the Val function to convert strings to numbers. The argument *stringexpression$* is a sequence of characters that can be interpreted as a numeric value. The Val function stops reading the string at the first character that it cannot recognize as part of a number. The Val function also strips blanks, tabs, and line feeds from the argument. Symbols and characters often thought of as being part of a numeric value, such as the dollar sign and commas, are not recognized by Val as numeric. The Val function does recognize the radix prefixes &O (for octal) and &H (for hexadecimal). The Val function always returns a double-precision value. If the result of the Val function is assigned to a variable, the double-precision value returned by Val is forced into the data type of the variable. The Str$ function converts a numeric value to a string.

Value

Type

Property

Syntax

`[form.][control.]Value[= setting%]`

Description

The Value property applies to a check box, command button, horizontal scroll bar, option button, and vertical scroll bar. The check box and option button determine the state of the control. The command button determines whether the button is pressed; it's not available at design time. The horizontal and vertical scroll bars determine the current position of the scroll bar, whose return value is always between the values for the Max and Min properties, inclusive.

Vertical Scroll Bar

See *Horizontal and Vertical Scroll Bars*

Visible

Type

Property

Syntax

[*form.*][*control.*]Visible[= *boolean%*]

Description

The Visible property applies to a form, check box, combo box, command button, directory list box, drive list box, file list box, frame, horizontal scroll bar, label, list box, menu, option button, picture box, text box, and vertical scroll bar. It sets or returns the visual state of an object. To hide a control at startup, you can set the Visible property to False at design time. Setting the Visible property in code allows you to hide and later redisplay a control at runtime in response to a particular event—for example, in response to a Click or KeyPress event in one control, you might redisplay another control. Using the Show and Hide methods on a form is the same as setting the form's Visible property in code to True (−1) and False (0), respectively.

Weekday

Type

Function

Syntax

Weekday(*serial#*)

Description

The Weekday function returns an integer between 1 (Sunday) and 7 (Saturday) that represents the day of the week corresponding to the serial argument. The argument *serial#* is a serial number that represents a date and/or time between 1 January 1753 and 31 December 2078, inclusive, where 1 January 1900 equals 2. Numbers to the left of the decimal point in *serial#* represent the date; numbers to the right represent the time. Negative numbers represent dates prior to 30 December 1899.

While...Wend

Type
Statement

Syntax

```
While condition
  .
  .
  .
Wend
```

Description

The While...Wend statement executes a series of statements in a loop, as long as a given condition is true. (Note that the Do...Loop statement provides a more powerful and flexible loop-control structure.) The argument *condition* is a numeric expression that Visual Basic evaluates as True (–1) or False (0). If condition is True, any intervening statements are executed until the Wend statement is encountered. Visual Basic then returns to the While statement and checks condition. If it is still True, the process is repeated. If it is not True, execution resumes with the statement following the Wend statement. While...Wend loops can be nested to any level.

Width

See *Height*...

Width

Type
Statement

Syntax

```
Width #filenumber%, width%
```

Description

The Width # statement assigns an output line width to a file. The Width statement permits altering the width of output lines in files that are already open.

WindowState

Type

Property

Syntax

[*form.*]WindowState[= *state%*]

Description

The WindowState property applies to a form. It sets or returns the visual state of a form window at runtime. Before a form is shown (for example, by a Load event procedure), WindowState is always set to Normal (0), regardless of its initial setting. This is reflected in the Height, Left, ScaleHeight, ScaleWidth, Top, and Width settings. If a form is hidden after it's been shown, these properties reflect the previous state until the form is shown again, regardless to any changes made to WindowState in the meantime.

Write

Type

Statement

Syntax

Write # filenumber%[, *expressionlist*]

Description

The Write # statement writes data to a sequential file. The argument *filenumber%* is the number used in the Open statement to open the file to write to. The file must be opened in output or append mode. The expressions in the argument *expressionlist* are comma-delimited string and/or numeric expressions. If you omit *expressionlist*, the Write # statement writes a blank line to the file. The Write # statement, unlike the Print # statement, inserts commas between items and quotation marks around strings as they are written to the file. You do not have to put explicit delimiters in the list. A newline character is inserted once the last item in the list has been written to the file. If you use Write # in an attempt to write data to a sequential file restricted by a Lock statement, Visual Basic generates an error message.

Year

Type

Function

Syntax

Year(*serial#*)

Description

The Year function returns an integer between 1753 and 2078, inclusive, that represents the year corresponding to the serial argument. The argument *serial#* is a serial number that represents a date and/or time between 1 January 1753 and 31 December 2078, inclusive, where 1 January 1900 equals 2. Numbers to the left of the decimal point in *serial#* represent the date; numbers to the right represent the time. Negative numbers represent dates prior to 30 December 1899.

INDEX

E

N

O

Selections from The SYBEX Library

LANGUAGES

The ABC's of GW-BASIC
William R. Orvis
320pp. Ref. 663-4
Featuring two parts: Part I is an easy-to-follow tutorial for beginners, while Part II is a complete, concise reference guide to GW-BASIC commands and functions. Covers everything from the basics of programming in the GW-BASIC environment, to debugging a major program. Includes special treatment of graphics and sound.

BASIC Programs for Scientists and Engineers
Alan R. Miller
318pp. Ref. 073-3
The algorithms presented in this book are programmed in standard BASIC code which should be usable with almost any implementation of BASIC. Includes statistical calculations, matrix algebra, curve fitting, integration, and more.

Encyclopedia C
Robert A. Radcliffe
1333pp. Ref. 655-3
This is the complete reference for standard ANSI/ISO programmers using any Microsoft C compiler with DOS. It blends comprehensive treatment of C syntax, functions, utilities, and services with practical examples and proven techniques for optimizing productivity and performance in C programming.

FORTRAN Programs for Scientists and Engineers (Second Edition)
Alan R. Miller
280pp. Ref. 571-9
In this collection of widely used scientific algorithms—for statistics, vector and matrix operations, curve fitting, and more—the author stresses effective use of little-known and powerful features of FORTRAN.

Introduction to Pascal: Including Turbo Pascal (Second Edition)
Rodnay Zaks
464pp. Ref. 533-6
This best-selling tutorial builds complete mastery of Pascal—from basic structured programming concepts, to advanced I/O, data structures, file operations, sets, pointers and lists, and more. Both ISO Standard and Turbo Pascal.

Mastering C
Craig Bolon
437pp. Ref. 326-0
This in-depth guide stresses planning, testing, efficiency and portability in C applications. Topics include data types, storage classes, arrays, pointers, data structures, control statements, I/O and the C function library.

Mastering QuickBASIC
Rita Belserene
450pp. Ref. 589-1
Readers build professional programs with this extensive language tutorial. Fundamental commands are mixed with the author's tips and tricks so that users can create their own applications. Program templates are included for video displays, computer games, and working with databases and printers. For Version 4.5.

Mastering Turbo C (Second Edition)
Stan Kelly-Bootle
609pp. Ref. 595-6
With a foreword by Borland International

President Philippe Kahn, this new edition has been expanded to include full details on Version 2.0. Learn theory and practical programming, with tutorials on data types, real numbers and characters, controlling program flow, file I/O, and producing color charts and graphs. Through Version 2.

Mastering Turbo Pascal 6
Scott D. Palmer
650pp, Ref. 675-8
This step-by-step guide to the newest Turbo Pascal release takes readers from programming basics to advanced techniques such as graphics, recursion, object-oriented programming, efficient debugging, and programming for other environments such as Vax/VMS. Includes dozens of useful exercises and examples, and tips for effective programming.

Systems Programming in Microsoft C
Michael J. Young
604pp. Ref. 570-0
This sourcebook of advanced C programming techniques is for anyone who wants to make the most of their C compiler or Microsoft QuickC. It includes a comprehensive, annotated library of systems functions, ready to compile and call.

Systems Programming in Microsoft C (Second Edition)
Michael J. Young
600pp; Ref. 1026-6
This book offers detailed information on advanced programming techniques for Microsoft C, as well as a comprehensive library of ready-to-use functions. It covers both the Microsoft C optimizing C compiler through version 6.0, and Microsoft QuickC (versions 1.0 and later). With complete code for converting a Microsoft Cprogram into a memory-resident utility.

Turbo Pascal Toolbox (Second Edition)
Frank Dutton
425pp. Ref. 602-2
This collection of tested, efficient Turbo

Pascal building blocks gives a boost to intermediate-level programmers, while teaching effective programming by example. Topics include accessing DOS, menus, bit maps, screen handling, and much more.

APPLICATION DEVELOPMENT

The ABC's of ToolBook for Windows
Kenyon Brown
300pp. Ref. 795-9
Gain the skill and confidence you need to create sophisticated applications for Windows. This hands-on introduction teaches you how to build custom graphical applications, without the need for traditional computer language. Learn to use the Script Recorder to create scripts and add animation to presentation applications.

The Elements of Friendly Software Design
Paul Heckel
319pp. Ref. 768-1
Here's what you *didn't* learn in engineering school! This entertaining, practical text shows how the same communication techniques used by artists and filmmakers can make software more appealing to users. Topics include visual thinking; design principles to follow—and mistakes to avoid; and examples of excellence.

Up & Running with ToolBook for Windows
Michael Tischer
138pp. Ref. 816-5
In just 20 time-coded steps (each taking no more than 15 minutes to an hour), you can begin designing your own Windows applications. Learn to add visual interest with lines, colors, and patterns; create a customized database form; navigate the user interface; draw and paint with ToolBook, and more.

ASSEMBLY LANGUAGES

Programming the 6809
Rodnay Zaks
William Labiak
362pp. Ref. 078-4

A step-by-step course in assembly-language programming for 6809-based home computers. Covers hardware organization, the instruction set, addressing, I/O, data structures, program development and complete sample applications.

Programming the 68000
Steve Williams
539pp. Ref. 133-0

This tutorial introduction to assembly-language programming covers the complete 68000 architecture and instruction set, as well as advanced topics such as interrupts, I/O programming, and interfacing with high-level languages.

Programming the 8086/8088
James W. Coffron
311pp. Ref. 120-9

A concise introduction to assembly-language programming for 8086/8088-based systems, including the IBM PC. Topics include architecture, memory organization, the complete instruction set, interrupts, I/O, and IBM PC BIOS routines.

Programming the 80386
John H. Crawford
Patrick P. Gelsinger
775pp. Ref. 381-3

A detailed tour of the 80386 for assembly-language programmers. Topics include registers, data types and instruction classes, memory management, protection models, multitasking, interrupts, the numerics coprocessor, and more.

Programming the Z80
(Third Edition)
Rodnay Zaks
624pp. Ref. 069-5

A self-teaching guide to assembly-language programming for the wide range of Z80-based microcomputers. Includes the Z80 architecture and instruction set, addressing, I/O techniques and devices, data structures and sample programs.

Z80 Applications
James W. Coffron
295pp. Ref. 094-6

A handbook for assembly-language programmers on the principles of Z80 hardware operations. Topics include using ROM, static and dynamic RAM, I/O, interrupts, serial communication and several specific LSI peripheral devices.

OPERATING SYSTEMS

The ABC's of DOS 4
Alan R. Miller
275pp. Ref. 583-2

This step-by-step introduction to using DOS 4 is written especially for beginners. Filled with simple examples, *The ABC's of DOS 4* covers the basics of hardware, software, disks, the system editor EDLIN, DOS commands, and more.

The ABC's of DOS 5
Alan Miller
267pp. Ref. 770-3

This straightforward guide will haven even first-time computer users working comfortably with DOS 5 in no time. Step-by-step lessons lead users from switching on the PC, through exploring the DOS Shell, working with directories and files, using essential commands, customizing the system, and trouble shooting. Includes a tear-out quick reference card and function key template.

ABC's of MS-DOS
(Second Edition)
Alan R. Miller
233pp. Ref. 493-3

This handy guide to MS-DOS is all many PC users need to manage their computer files, organize floppy and hard disks, use EDLIN, and keep their computers organized. Additional information is given about utilities like Sidekick, and there is a DOS command and program summary.

The second edition is fully updated for Version 3.3.

The ABC's of SCO UNIX
Tom Cuthbertson
263pp. Re. 715-0

A guide especially for beginners who want to get to work fast. Includes hands-on tutorials on logging in and out; creating and editing files; using electronic mail; organizing files into directories; printing; text formatting; and more.

The ABC's of Windows 3.0
Kris Jamsa
327pp. Ref. 760-6

A user-friendly introduction to the essentials of Windows 3.0. Presented in 64 short lessons. Beginners start with lesson one, while more advanced readers can skip ahead. Learn to use File Manager, the accessory programs, customization features, Program Manager, and more.

DESQview Instant Reference
Paul J. Perry
175pp. Ref. 809-2

This complete quick-reference command guide covers version 2.3 and DESQview 386, as well as QEMM (for managing expanded memory) and Manifest Memory Analyzer. Concise, alphabetized entries provide exact syntax, options, usage, and brief examples for every command. A handy source for on-the-job reminders and tips.

DOS 3.3 On-Line Advisor Version 1.1
SYBAR, Software Division of SYBEX, Inc.
Ref. 933-1

The answer to all your DOS problems. The DOS On-Line Advisor is an on-screen reference that explains over 200 DOS error messages. 2300 other citations cover all you ever needed to know about DOS. The DOS On-Line Advisor pops up on top of your working program to give you quick, easy help when you need it, and disappears when you don't. Covers thru version 3.3. Software package comes with 3½″ and 5¼″ disks. **System Requirements:** IBM compatible with DOS

2.0 or higher, runs with Windows 3.0, uses 90K of RAM.

DOS Instant Reference SYBEX Prompter Series
Greg Harvey
Kay Yarborough Nelson
220pp. Ref. 477-1

A complete fingertip reference for fast, easy on-line help:command summaries, syntax, usage and error messages. Organized by function—system commands, file commands, disk management, directories, batch files, I/O, networking, programming, and more. Through Version 3.3.

DOS 5: A to Z
Gary Masters
900pp; Ref. 805-X

A personal guru for every DOS 5 user! This comprehensive, "all you need to know" guide to DOS 5 provides detailed, A-to-Z coverage of DOS 5 commands, options, error messages, and dialog boxes—with syntax, usage, and plenty of examples and tips. It also includes hundreds of informative, in-depth articles on DOS 5 terminology and concepts.

DOS 5 Instant Reference
Robert M. Thomas
200pp. Ref. 804-1

The comprehensive quick guide to DOS—all its features, commands, options, and versions—now including DOS 5, with the new graphical interface. Concise, alphabetized command entries provide exact syntax, options, usage, brief examples, and applicable version numbers. Fully cross-referenced; ideal for quick review or on-the-job reference.

The DOS 5 User's Handbook
Gary Masters
Richard Allen King
400pp. Ref. 777-0

This is the DOS 5 book for users who are already familiar with an earlier version of DOS. Part I is a quick, friendly guide to new features; topics include the graphical interface, new and enhanced commands, and much more. Part II is a complete DOS 5 quick reference, with command summaries, in-depth explanations, and examples.

Essential OS/2
(Second Edition)
Judd Robbins

445pp. Ref. 609-X

Written by an OS/2 expert, this is the guide to the powerful new resources of the OS/2 operating system standard edition 1.1 with presentation manager. Robbins introduces the standard edition, and details multitasking under OS/2, and the range of commands for installing, starting up, configuring, and running applications. For Version 1.1 Standard Edition.

Essential PC-DOS
(Second Edition)
Myril Clement Shaw
Susan Soltis Shaw

332pp. Ref. 413-5

An authoritative guide to PC-DOS, including version 3.2. Designed to make experts out of beginners, it explores everything from disk management to batch file programming. Includes an 85-page command summary. Through Version 3.2.

Graphics Programming
Under Windows
Brian Myers
Chris Doner

646pp. Ref. 448-8

Straightforward discussion, abundant examples, and a concise reference guide to graphics commands make this book a must for Windows programmers. Topics range from how Windows works to programming for business, animation, CAD, and desktop publishing. For Version 2.

Inside DOS: A Programmer's Guide
Michael J. Young

490pp. Ref. 710-X

A collection of practical techniques (with source code listings) designed to help you take advantage of the rich resources Intrinsic to MS-DOS machines. Designed for the experienced programmer with a basic understanding of C and 8086 assembly language, and DOS fundamentals.

Mastering DOS
(Second Edition)
Judd Robbins

722pp. Ref. 555-7

"The most useful DOS book." This seven-part, in-depth tutorial addresses the needs of users at all levels. Topics range from running applications, to managing files and directories, configuring the system, batch file programming, and techniques for system developers. Through Version 4.

Mastering DOS 5
Judd Robbins

800pp. Ref.767-3

"The DOS reference to keep next to your computer," according to PC Week, this highly acclaimed text is now revised and expanded for DOS 5. Comprehensive tutorials cover everything from first steps for beginners, to advanced tools for systems developers—with emphasis on the new graphics interface. Includes tips, tricks, and a tear-out quick reference card and function key template.

Mastering SunOS
Brent D. Heslop
David Angell

588pp. Ref. 683-9

Learn to configure and manage your system; use essential commands; manage files; perform editing, formatting, and printing tasks; master E-mail and external communication; and use the SunView and new Open Window graphic interfaces.

Mastering Windows 3.0
Robert Cowart

592pp. Ref.458-5

Every Windows user will find valuable how-to and reference information here. With full details on the desktop utilities; manipulating files; running applications (including non-Windows programs); sharing data between DOS, OS/2, and Windows; hardware and software efficiency tips; and more.

Understanding DESQview
Rick Altman

300pp; Ref. 665-0

An in-depth, practical introduction to multitasking and memory management with DESQview, including DESQview 386 and QEMM. Learn to swap programs in and out of memory, transfer data between windows, use scripts to automate essential tasks, run programs in the background, and more.

Understanding DOS 3.3
Judd Robbins

678pp. Ref. 648-0

This best selling, in-depth tutorial addresses the needs of users at all levels with many examples and hands-on exercises. Robbins discusses the fundamentals of DOS, then covers manipulating files and directories, using the DOS editor, printing, communicating, and finishes with a full section on batch files.

Understanding Hard Disk Management on the PC
Jonathan Kamin

500pp. Ref. 561-1

This title is a key productivity tool for all hard disk users who want efficient, error-free file management and organization. Includes details on the best ways to conserve hard disk space when using several memory-guzzling programs. Through DOS 4.

Up & Running with DR DOS 5.0
Joerg Schieb

130pp. Ref. 815-7

Enjoy a fast-paced, but thorough introduction to DR DOS 5.0. In only 20 steps, you can begin to obtain practical results: copy and delete files, password protect your data, use batch files to save time, and more.

Up & Running with DOS 3.3
Michael-Alexander Beisecker

126pp. Ref. 750-9

Learn the fundamentals of DOS 3.3 in just 20 basic steps. Each "step" is a self-contained, time-coded lesson, taking 15 minutes to an hour to complete. You learn the essentials in record time.

Up & Running with DOS 5
Alan Simpson

150pp. Ref. 774-6

A 20-step guide to the essentials of DOS 5—for busy users seeking a fast-paced overview. Steps take only minutes to complete, and each is marked with a timer clock, so you know how long each one will take. Topics include installation, the DOS Shell, Program Manager, disks, directories, utilities, customization, batch files, ports and devices, DOSKEY, memory, Windows, and BASIC.

Up & Running with Windows 3.0
Gabriele Wentges

117pp. Ref. 711-8

All the essentials of Windows 3.0 in just twenty "steps"—self-contained lessons that take minutes to complete. Perfect for evaluating the software or getting a quick start with the new environment. Topics include installation, managing windows, using keyboard and mouse, using desktop utilities, and built-in programs.

Windows 3.0 Instant Reference
Marshall Moseley

195pp. Ref. 757-6

This concise, comprehensive pocket reference provides quick access to instructions on all Windows 3.0 mouse and keyboard commands. It features step-by-step instructions on using Windows, the applications that come bundled with it, and Windows' unique help facilities. Great for all levels of expertise.

NETWORKS

The ABC's of Local Area Networks
Michael Dortch

212pp. Ref. 664-2

This jargon-free introduction to LANs is for current and prospective users who see general information, comparative options, a look at the future, and tips for effective LANs use today. With comparisons of Token-Ring, PC Network, Novell, and others.

Mastering Novell NetWare
Cheryl C. Currid
Craig A. Gillett
500pp. Ref. 630-8

This book is a thorough guide for System Administrators to installing and operating a microcomputer network using Novell Netware. Mastering covers actually setting up a network from start to finish, design, administration, maintenance, and troubleshooting.

COMMUNICATIONS

Mastering Serial Communications
Peter W. Gofton
289pp. Ref. 180-2

The software side of communications, with details on the IBM PC's serial programming, the XMODEM and Kermit protocols, non-ASCII data transfer, interrupt-level programming, and more. Sample programs in C, assembly language and BASIC.

Mastering UNIX Serial Communications
Peter W. Gofton
307pp. Ref. 708-8

The complete guide to serial communications under UNIX. Part I introduces essential concepts and techniques, while Part II explores UNIX ports, drivers, and utilities, including MAIL, UUCP, and others. Part III is for C programmers, with six in-depth chapters on communications programming under UNIX.

Understanding PROCOMM PLUS 2.0 (Second Edition)
Bob Campbell
393pp; Ref. 861-0

This in-depth tutorial on communications with PROCOMM PLUS is now updated and expanded for version 2.0. It's still the best guide to PROCOMM PLUS, showing

how to choose and install hardware; connect with on-line services and other computers; send and receive files; create and use MetaKeys and scripts; and more.

Up & Running with PROCOMM PLUS
Bob Campbell
134pp. Ref. 794-0

Get a fast-paced overview of telecommunications with PROCOMM PLUS, in just 20 steps. Each step takes only 15 minutes to an hour to complete, covering the essentials of installing and running the software, setting parameters, dialing, connecting with and using an online service, sending and receiving files, using macros and scripts, and operating a bulletin board.

Up & Running with PROCOMM PLUS 2.0
Bob Campbell
140pp; Ref. 879-3

Learn PROCOMM PLUS 2.0 (and 2.01), and gain a basic understanding of telecommunications—all in just 20 steps. Each step takes only 15 minutes to an hour to complete, covering such topics as program installation and navigation; creating and using a bulletin board; using script files to save time; using Compu-Serve; more.

UTILITIES

The Computer Virus Protection Handbook
Colin Haynes
192pp. Ref. 696-0

This book is the equivalent of an intensive emergency preparedness seminar on computer viruses. Readers learn what viruses are, how they are created, and how they infect systems. Step-by-step procedures help computer users to identify vulnerabilities, and to assess the consequences of a virus infection. Strategies on coping with viruses, as well as methods of data recovery, make this book well worth the investment.

Mastering the Norton Utilities 5
Peter Dyson
400pp, Ref. 725-8

This complete guide to installing and using the Norton Utilities 5 is a must for beginning and experienced users alike. It offers a clear, detailed description of each utility, with options, uses and examples—so users can quickly identify the programs they need and put Norton right to work. Includes valuable coverage of the newest Norton enhancements.

Mastering PC Tools Deluxe 6
For Versions 5.5 and 6.0
425pp, Ref. 700-2

An up-to-date guide to the lifesaving utilities in PC Tools Deluxe version 6.0 from installation, to high-speed back-ups, data recovery, file encryption, desktop applications, and more. Includes detailed background on DOS and hardware such as floppies, hard disks, modems and fax cards.

Norton Desktop for Windows Instant Reference
Sharon Crawford
Charlie Russell
200pp; Ref. 894-7

For anyone using Norton's version of the Windows desktop, here's a compact, fast-access guide to every feature of the package—from file management functions, to disaster prevention tools, configuration commands, batch language extensions, and more. Concise, quick-reference entries are alphabetized by topic, and include practical tips and examples.

Norton Utilities 5 Instant Reference
Michael Gross
162pp. Ref. 737-1

Organized alphabetically by program name, this pocket-sized reference offers complete information on each utility in the Norton 5 package—including a descriptive summary, exact syntax, command line options, brief explanation, and examples. Gives proficient users a quick reminder, and helps with unfamiliar options.

Norton Utilities 6 Instant Reference
Michael Gross
175pp; Ref. 865-3

This pocket-size guide to Norton Utilities 6 provides fast answers when and where they're needed. Reference entries are organized alphabetically by program name, and provide a descriptive summary, exact syntax, command line options, brief explanations, and examples. For a quick reminder, or help with unfamiliar options.

PC Tools Deluxe 6 Instant Reference
Gordon McComb
194pp. Ref. 728-2

Keep this one handy for fast access to quick reminders and essential information on the latest PC Tools Utilities. Alphabetical entries cover all the Tools of Version 6—from data recovery to desktop applications—with concise summaries, syntax, options, brief explanations, and examples.

SYBEX

FREE BROCHURE!

Complete this form today, and we'll send you a full-color brochure of Sybex bestsellers.

Please supply the name of the Sybex book purchased.

_____

How would you rate it?

_____ Excellent   _____ Very Good   _____ Average   _____ Poor

Why did you select this particular book?

_____ Recommended to me by a friend
_____ Recommended to me by store personnel
_____ Saw an advertisement in _____
_____ Author's reputation
_____ Saw in Sybex catalog
_____ Required textbook
_____ Sybex reputation
_____ Read book review in _____
_____ In-store display
_____ Other _____

Where did you buy it?

_____ Bookstore
_____ Computer Store or Software Store
_____ Catalog (name: _____)
_____ Direct from Sybex
_____ Other: _____

Did you buy this book with your personal funds?

_____ Yes   _____ No

About how many computer books do you buy each year?

_____ 1-3   _____ 3-5   _____ 5-7   _____ 7-9   _____ 10+

About how many Sybex books do you own?

_____ 1-3   _____ 3-5   _____ 5-7   _____ 7-9   _____ 10+

Please indicate your level of experience with the software covered in this book:

_____ Beginner   _____ Intermediate   _____ Advanced

Which types of software packages do you use regularly?

_____ Accounting   _____ Databases   _____ Networks

_____ Amiga   _____ Desktop Publishing   _____ Operating Systems

_____ Apple/Mac   _____ File Utilities   _____ Spreadsheets

_____ CAD   _____ Money Management   _____ Word Processing

_____ Communications   _____ Languages   _____ Other _____
                                                             (please specify)

Which of the following best describes your job title?

_____ Administrative/Secretarial   _____ President/CEO

_____ Director   _____ Manager/Supervisor

_____ Engineer/Technician   _____ Other _____
                                              (please specify)

Comments on the weaknesses/strengths of this book: _____

_____

_____

_____

_____

Name _____

Street _____

City/State/Zip _____

Phone _____

PLEASE FOLD, SEAL, AND MAIL TO SYBEX

SYBEX, INC.
Department M
2021 CHALLENGER DR.
ALAMEDA, CALIFORNIA USA
94501

SYBEX

Name	Type	Name	Type
LinkExecute	Event	LinkExecute	Method
LinkItem	Property	LinkMode	Property
LinkOpen	Event	LinkPoke	Method
LinkRequest	Method	LinkSend	Method
LinkTimeout	Property	LinkTopic	Property
List	Property	List Box	Control
ListCount	Property	ListIndex	Property
Load	Event	Load	Statement
LoadPicture	Function	Loc	Function
Lock...Unlock	Statement	LOF	Function
Log	Function	LostFocus	Event
LSet	Statement	LTrim$	Function
Max	Property	MaxButton	Property
Menu	Control	Mid$	Function
Mid$	Statement	Min	Property
MinButton	Property	Minute	Function
MkDir	Statement	Month	Function
MouseDown	Event	MouseMove	Event
MousePointer	Property	MouseUp	Event
Move	Method	MsgBox	Function
MsgBox	Statement	MultiLine	Property
Name	Statement	NewPage	Method
Normal	Property	Now	Function
Oct$	Function	On Error	Statement
On...GoSub	Statement	On...GoTo	Statement
Open	Statement	Option Base	Statement
Option Button	Control	Page	Property
Paint	Event	Parent	Property
Path	Property	PathChange	Event
Pattern	Property	PatternChange	Event
Picture Box	Control	Picture	Property
Point	Method	Pointer	Property
Print	Method	Print #	Statement
Printer Object	Control	PrintForm	Method
PSet	Method	Put	Statement
QBColor	Function	Randomize	Statement
ReadOnly	Property	ReDim	Statement
Refresh	Method	Rem	Statement
RemoveItem	Method	Rset	Statement